S0-ASM-660

When should I travel to get the best [illegible]
Where do I go for answers to my travel questions?
What's the best and easiest way to plan and book my trip?

frommers.travelocity.com

Frommer's, the travel guide leader, has teamed up with **Travelocity.com**, the leader in online travel, to bring you an in-depth, easy-to-use resource designed to help you plan and book your trip online.

At **frommers.travelocity.com**, you'll find free online updates about your destination from the experts at Frommer's plus the outstanding travel planning and purchasing features of Travelocity.com. Travelocity.com provides reservations capabilities for 95 percent of all airline seats sold, more than 47,000 hotels, and over 50 car rental companies. In addition, Travelocity.com offers more than 2,000 exciting vacation and cruise packages. Travelocity.com puts you in complete control of your travel planning with these and other great features:

Expert travel guidance from Frommer's—over 150 writers reporting from around the world!

Best Fare Finder—an interactive calendar tells you when to travel to get the best airfare

Fare Watcher—we'll track airfare changes to your favorite destinations

Dream Maps—a mapping feature that suggests travel opportunities based on your budget

Shop Safe Guarantee—24 hours a day / 7 days a week live customer service, and more!

Whether traveling on a tight budget, looking for a quick weekend getaway, or planning the trip of a lifetime, Frommer's guides and Travelocity.com will make your travel dreams a reality. You've bought the book, now book the trip!

other titles in the

irreverent guide

series

Irreverent Amsterdam

Irreverent Boston

Irreverent Chicago

Irreverent Las Vegas

Irreverent Los Angeles

Irreverent London

Irreverent Manhattan

Irreverent New Orleans

Irreverent Paris

Irreverent San Francisco

Irreverent Vancouver

Irreverent Walt Disney World

Irreverent Washington, D.C.

Frommer's

irreverent guide to Seattle & Portland

2nd Edition

By
Jim Gullo

HUNGRY MINDS, INC.

a disclaimer

Please note that prices fluctuate in the course of time, and travel information changes under the impact of the many factors that influence the travel industry. We therefore suggest that you write or call ahead for confirmation when making your travel plans. Every effort has been made to ensure the accuracy of information throughout this book and the contents of this publication are believed correct at the time of printing. Nevertheless, the publishers cannot accept responsibility for errors or omissions or for changes in details given in this guide or for the consequences of any reliance on the information provided by the same. Assessments of attractions and so forth are based upon the author's own experience and therefore, descriptions given in this guide necessarily contain an element of subjective opinion, which may not reflect the publisher's opinion or dictate a reader's own experience on another occasion. Readers are invited to write to the publisher with ideas, comments, and suggestions for future editions.

Your safety is important to us, however, so we encourage you to stay alert and be aware of your surroundings. Keep a close eye on cameras, purses, and wallets, all favorite targets of thieves and pickpockets.

about the author

Besides writing mesmerizing guidebooks to the Pacific Northwest, **Jim Gullo** writes plays and travels the world on assignment for *Islands, Sunset,* and *Diversion* magazines. He lives in Seattle with his wife Kris and sons Michael and Joe, to whom this book is dedicated.

Published by HUNGRY MINDS, INC.

909 Third Avenue
New York, NY 10022

Copyright © 2001 by Hungry Minds, Inc.

All rights reserved. No part of this book may be reproduced or transmitted in any form or by an means, electronic or mechanical, including photocopying, recording, or by any information storage and retrieval system, without permission in writing from the Publisher.

ISBN 0-76456-6499-4
ISSN 1525-1454

Interior design contributed to by Tsang Seymour Design Studio

special sales

For general information on Hungry Minds' products and services please contact our Customer Care Department within the U.S. at 800-762-2974, outside the U.S. at 317-572-3993 or fax 317-572-4002.

For sales inquiries and reseller information, including discounts, premium and bulk quantity sales, and foreign-language translations, please contact our Customer Care Department at 800-434-3422 or fax 317-572-4002.

Manufactured in the United States of America

Trademarks: Frommer's is a registered trademark or trademark of Arthur Frommer. Used under license. All other trademarks are property of their respective owners.

what's so irreverent?

It's up to you.

You can buy a traditional guidebook with its fluff, its promotional hype, its let's-find-something-nice-to-say-about-everything point of view. Or you can buy an Irreverent guide.

What the Irreverents give you is the lowdown, the inside story. They have nothing to sell but the truth, which includes a balance of good and bad. They praise, they trash, they weigh, and they leave the final decisions up to you. No tourist board, no chamber of commerce will ever recommend them.

Our writers are insiders, who feel passionate about the cities they live in, and have strong opinions they want to share with you. They take a special pleasure leading you where other guides fear to tread.

How irreverent are they? One of our authors insisted on writing under a pseudonym. "I couldn't show my face in town again if I used my own name," she told me. "My friends would never speak to me." Such is the price of honesty. She, like you, should know she'll always have a friend at Frommer's.

Warm regards,

Michael Spring

Michael Spring
Publisher

contents

IRREVERENT GUIDE TO SEATTLE XV

INTRODUCTION 1

GREATER SEATTLE NEIGHBORHOODS MAP 4

YOU PROBABLY DIDN'T KNOW 5

ACCOMMODATIONS 8

Winning the Reservations Game (10)
Is There a Right Address? (10)

THE LOWDOWN 12

Big-city elegance (12)
The boudoir alternative (13)
At water's edge (14)
The inn thing to do (14)
For the tragically hip (15)
Who needs a suite when you can get an apartment? (16)
Hanging out in Huskyville (17)
Shoppers' specials (17)
For the embraceable you (18)
With children in tow (18)
The bottom end (19)

THE INDEX 20

An A to Z list of places to stay, with vital statistics

Seattle Downtown Accommodations Map 26

Seattle–North & Northeast Accommodations Map 28
DINING 30
Only in Seattle (32)
Getting the Right Table (33)
Tipping (33)
How to Dress (34)
Where the Chefs Are (34)
THE LOWDOWN 35
The ultimate Market graze (35)
Four Market restaurants worth searching for (36)
Where great views equal great seafood (37)
If you're more interested in the seafood than the view (38)
When only exquisite will do (38)
Say "Olé!" to international flavors (40)
On the cutting edge (thou art truly groovy) (41)
Room service never had it so good (42)
Fun and cheap, and your kids will love it (43)
Ciao, bambino! (43)
Coffee shops to fall in love with (44)
THE INDEX 45
An A to Z list of restaurants, with vital statistics
Seattle Downtown Dining Map 52
Seattle–North & Northeast Dining Map 54

DIVERSIONS 56
Getting Your Bearings (58)
THE LOWDOWN 59
The Big Three Festivals (59)
When the mountain is out (60)
When the mountain is in (61)
The newest and coolest (62)
Museums the whole family can explore (62)
More grown-up museums (63)
Animal magnetism (64)
Truly cheesy attractions (65)
The eye of the Needle (65)
Visualizing Ballard and other neighborhoods (66)
Homes of the rich and famous (67)
The duck stops here, and other tours (68)
Ferry-tale ride (69)

THE INDEX 70

An A to Z list of diversions, with vital statistics

GETTING OUTSIDE 76

THE LOWDOWN 78

One if by land (78)
And two if by sea (79)
Calling all Ahabs (80)
Paradise is at Mt. Rainier (80)
Hitting the slopes (81)
Take a dip (81)
Golf where the greens are really green (82)
The tennis racket (83)
A day at the races (83)
Pick-up hoops (83)

SHOPPING 84

Target Zones (86)
Bargain-Hunting (87)
Trading With the Natives (88)
Hours of Business (88)
Sales Tax (88)

THE LOWDOWN 89

Seafood that is literally fresh off the boat (89)
Deep inside the Market (89)
Market musts (90)
Going retro with antique clothes (90)
Hip threads for now people (91)
Why we love Nordstrom (91)
Buy the book (92)
Gearing up for the great outdoors (93)
For those who choose to dress like professional jocks (94)
Specialty food markets to die for (94)
Ultimate kitsch (95)
Music to soothe the savage beast (96)
Toy havens (97)
A gift for your home (97)

THE INDEX 98

An A to Z list of shops, with vital statistics

Seattle Downtown Shopping Map 102

Seattle–North & Northeast Shopping Map 104

NIGHTLIFE & ENTERTAINMENT 106
Sources (108)
Liquor Laws and Drinking Hours (109)
Getting Tickets (109)
THE LOWDOWN 109
One price fits all in Pioneer Square (109)
Unlike a good man, a good martini is easy to find (110)
The world is your brewpub (111)
Bars with attitude (112)
Live rockin' and jammin' (113)
Where the music swings (114)
Dispatches from the gay front (114)
Superstar athlete needs your support (115)
A thriving theater scene (116)
The culture club: ballet, opera, and the Seattle Symphony (116)
Where the big acts play (117
THE INDEX 118
An A to Z list of nightspots, with vital statistics

HOTLINES & OTHER BASICS 124
Airports (125)
Airport transport into the city (125)
Baby-sitters (126)
Buses and other public transit (126)
Car rentals (126)
Convention centers (126)
Dentists, doctors, and emergencies (127)
Events Hotline (127)
Ferries (127)
Festivals and special events (127)
Gay & lesbian hotlines & info (128)
Newspapers (128)
Parking (128)
Restrooms (128)
Smoking (129)
Taxes (129)
Taxis & limos (129)
Time (129)
Tipping (129)
Travelers with disabilities (129)
Visitor information (130)

IRREVERENT GUIDE TO PORTLAND 131

INTRODUCTION 133

PORTLAND NEIGHBORHOODS MAP 136

YOU PROBABLY DIDN'T KNOW 137

ACCOMMODATIONS 140

Winning the Reservations Game (142)

Is There a Right Address? (143)

THE LOWDOWN 143

Your doorman awaits (143)

For quick convention access (144)

Rooms with a view (146)

The best for business (147)

Boutique hotels with big-hotel service (148)

If you're bringing the kids (149)

Make mine romance (149)

For fitness buffs (150)

Moveable feasts (151)

Bang for the buck (151)

THE INDEX 153

An A to Z list of places to stay, with vital statistics

Portland Accommodations Map 156

DINING 158

How to Dress (160)

Getting the Right Table (161)

THE LOWDOWN 161

Scene-makers where the food is as good as the look (161)

When you need to close the deal (163)

Serious seafood (163)

Satisfying your meat tooth (165)

The view crew (166)

Where the pizza is as good as the beer (166)

Grand finales (167)

THE INDEX 168

An A to Z list of restaurants, with vital statistics

Portland Dining Map 172

DIVERSIONS 174

Getting Your Bearings (176)

The Portland Rose Festival (177)

THE LOWDOWN 177

Best depiction of a kneeling giantess in bronze (and other civic art) (177)

Come Saturday morning (Sunday, too) (178)

Gawking and walking downtown (179)

Gardens so grand you'll throw in the trowel (179)

Come see-um museums (180)

Elvis has left the building, and other cheesy attractions (181)

Where kids get their kicks (181)

Second-run movies, first-rate setting (182)

Paddlewheel or jetboat? The Willamette cruise (182)

And they're off (182)

THE INDEX 183

An A to Z list of diversions, with vital statistics

Portland Diversions Map 188

GETTING OUTSIDE 190

THE LOWDOWN 192

Climb every mountain (192)

Happy trails to you (193)

Up the river (preferably with a paddle) (194)

Great public golf (195)

Hooking the big one (196)

Skating with the ice queen (196)

SHOPPING 198

Target Zones (200)

Bargain-Hunting (201)

Trading With the Natives (201)

Hours of Business (201)

Sales Tax (201)

THE LOWDOWN 201

How many books fit into an acre? (201)

For that rugged, active person lurking inside you (202)

All the tunes all the time (203)

For that uniquely Portland look (204)

Artful and interesting (204)
Where shopping equals noshing (205)
Zones of antiquities (206)
Home decor (206)

THE INDEX 207

An A to Z list of shops, with vital statistics

NIGHTLIFE & ENTERTAINMENT 212

Sources (214)
Liquor Laws and Drinking Hours (214)
Getting Tickets (214)

THE LOWDOWN 215

Where beer is king (215)
Watering holes with style (216)
For vintage sipping (216)
Where to go to rock 'n' roll (217)
Just for dancing (218)
Cool and jazzy (218)
Gay gatherings (218)
The pro sports scene (219)
The play's the thing (219)
Culture nights at the Civic and the Shnitz (220)
Second-run movies, first-rate setting (220)

THE INDEX 221

An A to Z list of nightspots, with vital statistics

HOTLINES & OTHER BASICS 226

Airports (227)
Airport transport into the city (227)
Baby-sitters (227)
Buses (227)
Car rentals (228)
Convention centers (228)
Dentists, doctors, and emergencies (228)
Festivals and special events (229)
Gay & lesbian hotlines & info (229)
Newspapers (229)
Parking (229)
Restrooms (230)
Smoking (230)
Taxes (230)
Taxis & limos (230)

Time (230)
Tipping (230)
Travelers with disabilities (230)
Visitor information (231)

INDEX 233

i r r e v e r e n t
g u i d e t o
S e a t t l e

introduction

This is what I love about Seattle. My friend Sam Gladstein, a high-school teacher and father of three rambunctious boys, was on a boat ride on Lake Washington, the enormous body of water that separates Seattle from its eastern suburbs. As everyone does who cruises the lake, Sam slowed down to admire Bill Gates's house, a compound of big natural-wood buildings sprawling up a hillside from water's edge. Sam saw a person in the front yard standing partly hidden by a tree, and, being a friendly Northwesterner, Sam threw him a wave. He was rewarded by Bill Gates stepping into sight and waving back.

Seattle really is a town where the richest guy in the world can be seen puttering around his front yard on the lake, and he'll stop to wave back at you. There is a reason why Gates and his pal, Paul Allen—the other Microsoft cofounder who is richer than most Third World nations—continue to live and work in Seattle, and in these pages I'll try to show you why. It's a town where the guy sitting next to you at a Mariners game might be the creator of your favorite website, or the mayor, or a plumber, and they'll all be wearing the same flannel shirt and jeans. Almost effortlessly, Seattle mixes a big-business, big-city atmosphere with a let's-get-along-together quality that smaller towns always boast but rarely achieve. There is very little crime, and few places you should avoid at night. The absence of racial tension here would make an East Coast city blush with envy (though some argue that that's because Seattle is an overwhelmingly white city, with fewer and fewer places that minorities can afford anymore). Restaurants are great; so are the parks. Seattle has a tangible sense of community that I never felt when I lived in New York, L.A., or even Honolulu.

Personally, I love the place. I came here in the early '90s in search of a mid-sized city where I could settle and raise a family. And baseball. Seattle has the Mariners, without Ken Griffey Jr. or A-Rod, alas, but still fun, not to mention the NBA Sonics in the winter, and the frequently hapless Seahawks for fall football. It also has the world-class University of Washington (which I soon learned to call U-Dub just like a local). The city offers an international airport, good bookstores and art, Tom Robbins living nearby for moral support, and coffee. Lots of good coffee.

In our first days here, we couldn't get over the vistas of hillsides packed with single-family houses. Maps don't show you those San Francisco–like inclines all around town, slopes that are hell to walk but great for stunning views. Most of the distinctive neighborhoods around town are made so by being at the top or bottom of a hill: Queen Anne, Capitol Hill, First Hill, Magnolia, Wallingford, Phinney Ridge, Fremont, and Ballard. Maps show that the place is surrounded by water, but I hadn't really realized that crossing water, looking at it, and being stuck at a drawbridge over it would become such a daily pleasure. The defining image of Seattle is a drawbridge opening over a shimmering waterway with snowcapped mountains in the distance in every direction.

Don't get me wrong, the place isn't Nirvana, and wasn't even before Kurt Cobain of the eponymous grunge band got famous and then killed himself here. (I refuse to tell you where it happened, because so many tourists went gawking at his house that poor Courtney Love had to sell it.) The traffic is awful, among the worst in the country. Do yourself a huge favor by avoiding I-5, the major north-south artery, like the plague that it is. In a civic aberration for forward-thinking Seattle, there has been a great failure to build adequate public transportation, and the plans for a light-rail system won't reach fruition for at least another 10 years. There is the occasional earthquake, and dot.coms have been crashing with alarming regularity lately. Parking downtown sucks.

And it rains. Sometimes it rains a lot; usually it just rains a little but *threatens* to rain all day. In summer it almost never rains—but summer doesn't start until July 5. Low, overcast skies with scudding gray clouds are the standard around here, and it can be quite maddening to go out the front door in May and be greeted by the same damp, 52-degree weather that you had in February. So if you choose your travel destinations based on whether it might rain or not, Seattle isn't the place for you. On the other hand, I hear that Fresno is nice and dry—but good luck getting a decent cup of coffee there.

That said, you'll be enchanted by how pretty and green the place is, and how well it works. You might notice it in any number of ways: how drivers will let you into their lane and wave thanks when you do the same for them. How the neighborhood parks are free of graffiti and bands of skulking teens (we do have teens who skulk, but they mostly do it around their computers or at technoraves). How the coffee bars always seem to have exactly the right cookie that you're craving. There have been attempts to glamorize the place in popular culture, and Seattle has produced a modest body of celebrities—from Jimi Hendrix, who grew up here, to Ray Charles, who gigged in Pioneer Square clubs—but it's hardly a glam hotspot. Californians who move up here expecting to find the next trendy city get quickly discouraged by the weather and the absence of celebrity sightings.

Remember that the predominant employers in Seattle are Boeing and Microsoft; this is a town of engineers and technicians, not movie stars. A century ago, when Seattle was the last staging area for gold-mining forays into Alaska, the predominant spirit was one of hard work combined with a giddy optimism, and that hasn't changed (as witnessed by the meteoric rise of local companies like Amazon.com).

What I hope to point out is why Seattle is well worth a visit—and why you really, really don't want to move here. Honest, you wouldn't like the wet winters. Your black, urban clothes would mildew. The place is crowded enough with polite, considerate people, and your well-deserved city "edge" wouldn't play here. You'd get bored with eating fresh salmon, fish and chips make you fat, and too much coffee gives you hives. Don't move here! Don't move here!! Fresno would love to have you, but for God's sake, don't even think about moving here!

Have a nice visit, and don't forget to confirm your return ticket. And if Bill Gates or anyone else waves at you, by all means wave back.

Greater Seattle Neighborhoods

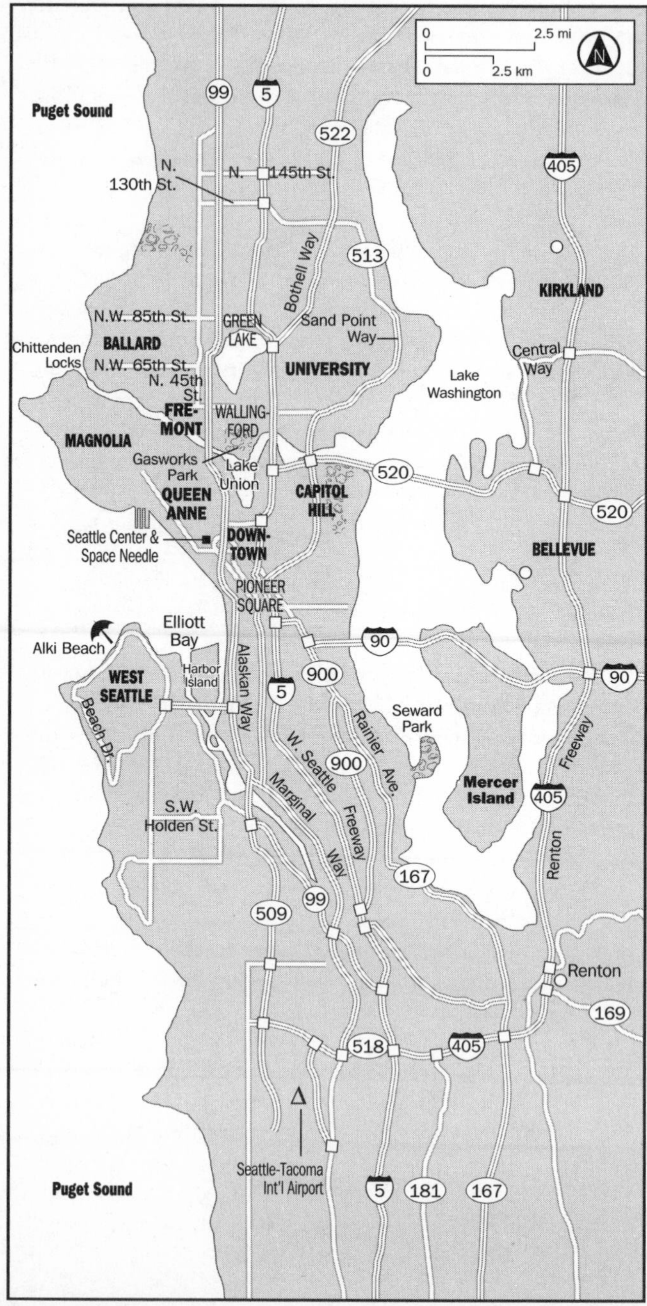

you probably didn't know

How can you tell the tourists in Seattle?... They're the ones carrying the umbrellas. Most locals don't bother with "brellies," but we always keep a baseball cap handy. Remember that it rarely pours here, but it frequently drizzles. They're also the ones who don't look like their websites just went bankrupt.

How else can you tell the tourists in Seattle?... They're the ones standing in a clump at the Pike Place Market staring at the fish as if it might spring to life and dance the *Macarena* at any moment. They ogle the fish, take pictures of the fish, have their pictures taken with the fish. Then they move on to do the same with the meats, cheeses, and produce. People who come to actually buy stuff get stuck behind the gawkers, which frustrates the whole purpose of the market. Do us all a favor and keep it moving, don't clog the aisles, and buy a few things to separate yourself from the mobs. The locals and the vendors will appreciate it.

Where can I rub elbows with Bill Gates?... Bill doesn't rub; from what we've heard, he positively shies away from physical contact. But he can be seen at Sonics games and around town at charity benefits and openings. And of course, he goes to work at Microsoft every day.

What does $517 million buy these days?... Safeco Field, the new stadium for the Seattle Mariners baseball team, opened in July 1999 as the most lavishly expensive ballpark in the country (due in large part to its retractable roof). Although original Mariners stars Ken Griffey Jr. and Alex Rodriguez are long gone, the M's are still a local favorite and draw big crowds, especially when they play the loathsome Yankees. The park itself is a superb place to watch a ballgame, and that oh-so-corporate name refers to a local insurance company with deep pockets, not the field's reputation for security.

Where does Frasier live?... Get real—Dr. Frasier Crane, everybody's favorite radio shrink, lives in Los Angeles. His supposed favorite restaurant, however, Chez Shea, is in Seattle's Pike Place Market. We have no idea how he manages that one.

Pray tell, what's a short skinny shot of hazelnut? A tall Americano, room for cream?... Those are both cheerleaders on the Sonics dance team. Just kidding—they're how we'd order a couple of espresso drinks, the first being a caffe latte in an eight-ounce (short) cup with nonfat milk (skinny) and a slug of hazelnut syrup added for flavoring. The latter is a regular cup of black coffee (Americano) with room in the cup to add milk. As a rude Starbucks counterperson once said to my visiting friend Ed, who didn't know the lingo, "Speak to me in my language, and you'll get what you want." By the way, most locals only go to Starbucks as a last resort. Why take coffee from a chain, when there are so many wonderful private coffee shops, espresso carts on the sidewalk, and drive-through espresso stands in Seattle? That is, unless you need to use a restroom or get change for the bus and you really like blackened (okay, some will say *burned*) coffee from ultra-dark-roasted beans.

Where would I go to meet someone at the pig?... The life-sized bronze piggy bank (her name is Rachel) is in the Pike Place Market, at the crook of the street as it bends right, a half-block from First Avenue. It's a popular place to rendezvous.

How can I drive to the Market?... For goodness sake, don't try to drive into the market on Pike Place, the continuation of Pike Street as it crosses First Avenue. You'll get into the world's worst traffic jam, and there's absolutely no parking if you're not a certified vendor. Park somewhere else and walk into the market.

Where the hell am I?... Your guess is as good as mine. Seattle is divided into sections in a system that the pioneers apparently made while drunk. Downtown streets have no directional designation, until you cross Yesler Way in Pioneer Square, at which place the streets all begin to be designated South. Cross Denny Way and you're in the North zone, unless you're west of First Avenue, at which point you're West. Driving around madly because you've confused Third Avenue North and Third Avenue West is a unique Seattle experience that we hope will leave you chuckling for hours. East streets are mostly on Capitol Hill, West are Queen Anne and Magnolia, Northeast the University district, Northwest is Ballard, and North can mean anything from the backside of Queen Anne Hill to the Fremont and Wallingford neighborhoods. And don't ever, EVER assume that if you drive in the correct direction on, say, North 49th Street, you'll eventually wind up on Northeast 49th Street. Get thee instead to an "arterial," local parlance for a main thoroughfare, and use it to get to the right part of town.

What kind of car should I rent?... A model that has variable windshield wiper controls. It makes an enormous difference when you're driving around here if you don't always have to turn the wipers on and off by hand.

What is "aggressively plain"?... It's my description of the local fashion sense, which allows people, entirely without shame, to gather together in business suits alongside scruffy jeans, cocktail dresses next to shorts. Roughly defined, it might be, "Why dress up, fix my hair, and wear heels when I can brush it straight down and wear comfy flannels and jeans and my old sneakers to dinner? God gave me this face and I'm not going to alter His will by applying makeup or trimming my scruffy beard." A Seattle fashion dilemma: For an evening out that starts with drinks at the Four Seasons and continues on to dinner in Belltown, the ballet at Seattle Center, and cocktails in Queen Anne, should I wear the black leggings and tent dress with my hiking boots, or match my hiking boots with shorts and an Eddie Bauer shirt?

What will I hate in Seattle?... You'll hate that you didn't buy a condo with a sound view in Belltown 20 years ago when they were dirt-cheap. You'll hate the traffic on I-5, I-90, or SR-520 during rush hours or practically anytime on weekends. You'll hate that you have to leave town before eating at every new restaurant downtown.

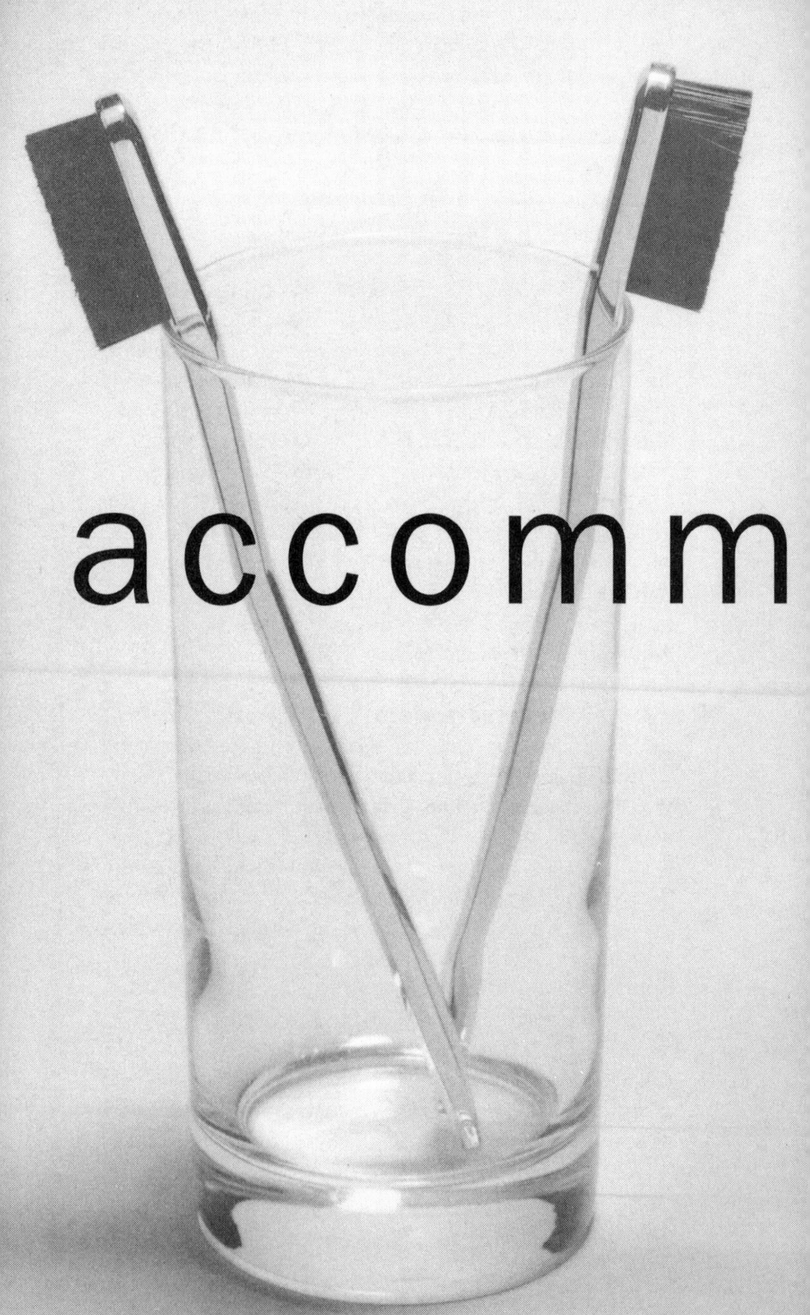
accomm

1

odations

To use a well-worn phrase, there's no need to go sleepless in Seattle. This is a city with an eclectic hotel scene, ranging from big-city downtown hotels that have hosted sultans and presidents to a floating home that looks just like the one Tom Hanks lived on in the movie (in large part because it *is* the one he used in the movie). The good news is the superb selection of small, intimate boutique hotels with great service and decor, many of which are attached to excellent restaurants. To escape the convention bustle, we'd head directly to the **Hotel Monaco Seattle**, **W Hotel**, or **Sorrento Hotel** and relax in style while our colleagues were battling the crowds.

In a city that is surrounded by water, the biggest surprise is the almost complete lack of waterfront hotels. Although condo development on the water is booming, the **Hotel Edgewater** is really the only full-service lodging in the city that can boast a water's-edge location. If you want to make a pile of money, develop a fancy waterfront hotel here with a totally happening restaurant, and the world, Sir or Madam, will beat a path to your watery door.

Winning the Reservations Game

The hottest time for tourism is summer, when the weather finally allows it to come in mid-July—and hotel choices can narrow considerably. Thanks to new cruise-ship traffic that is calling in Seattle, the ferries to Victoria, and the general perception that summer is the time to come to the Northwest, the city can get jammed, especially when the convention center heats up, too. The solution is to book as early as you can or replan your trip for another season.

Every winter, a group of some 30 hotels lowers its rates considerably in the **Seattle Super Saver** promotion, which runs from October 1 through the end of March. The savings off posted rates can be as much as 50 percent; don't even think about paying rack rate during this time. You have to specifically request the Super Saver rate if you book directly with the hotel, or use the **Seattle Convention & Visitors Bureau**'s hotel hotline (tel 800/535-7071) to find out which hotels are participating and make reservations. At other times of the year, the hotline will quote rates and find you the best deal; use your savings to buy even more Space Needle souvenirs.

Is There a Right Address?

Downtown is where most of the action takes place, but within that hilly wedge of the city there is a lot of variety. The **Shopping District** is centered around Nordstrom on Fifth

Avenue and Pine Street and spreads out in several blocks in either direction, with several hotels that are within a block or two of Nordie's, the Bon Marché, Pacific Place, and Westlake Center. **Belltown** is only a few blocks away on First and Second avenues and Bell Street, but the mood changes considerably to hip and stylish. This is where most of the great new restaurants are based, as well as the most fashionable boutiques. Hotels are just starting to catch up. Just down the street, a few blocks from Belltown, is the **Pike Place Market**, known to all simply as the market, with its flower sellers, fishmongers and produce merchants, and as much browsing as you could possibly handle.

There are few lodgings near **Pioneer Square**, Seattle's oldest neighborhood and a considerable tourist magnet. The buildings around here are elegant and old, the nightlife howls, and Elliott Bay Books and massive Safeco Field are within easy walking distance. **Queen Anne**, an urban neighborhood of private and public buildings and older apartment houses just north of downtown, has plenty of restaurants, espresso bars, and entertainment. Add to the mix Seattle Center, home to the city's opera, ballet, important theaters, and museums, and it may remind some of Manhattan's Upper West Side. Then there's the **U-District**, the crowded University of Washington (a.k.a. "U-Dub," the local shorthand for U.W.) neighborhood off the 45th Street exit on I-5. The shady, hilly campus has stately brick buildings commanding long views of Lake Washington and Mount Rainier; the neighborhood, with

A Note about Crime

Street crime in Seattle is very, very rare, and there are few places where you'll feel any sort of street menace. Maybe it's the rain, or the city's frowning attitude towards loitering, but even the panhandlers and sidewalk drunks have that self-effacing Pacific Northwest non-attitude. We don't recommend strolling alone through the Pioneer Square area late at night—particularly the Square itself—but if you stick to the main streets around First Avenue and Yesler Way you'll be trouble-free. There are some seedy bars (with the requisite seedy patrons) on lower Third Avenue near James Street (coincidentally or not, where the courthouse is), and the streets near the Greyhound Bus terminal on Eighth Avenue and Stewart Street have been hangouts for junkies in past years. Aurora Avenue, north of the ship canal through Fremont Avenue, and then again north of 80th Street, is pretty crummy, thanks to hookers and cheap motels, but there's nothing of interest to strollers there anyway.

University Avenue NE (a.k.a. "The Ave") as the main drag, has a little bit of everything, from cheap restaurants to boat rentals on Boat Street and sprawling Ravenna Park to explore. It also has some of Seattle's most aggressive panhandlers, a crew of teens and grungers who hang out there day and night. Husky Stadium—named for the team mascot of the University, a dominant force in PAC-10 sports (*the* major West Coast athletic conference, which includes schools like Stanford, UCLA, and Arizona)—is so close to Lake Washington that many football fans travel to big games by boat.

The Lowdown

Big-city elegance... When only a grand urban hotel will do—the kind of place with a sweeping entrance patrolled by uniformed doormen and a bustling lobby that reeks of business deals in progress—you have three options. The **Four Seasons Olympic** delivers that feeling when you ascend escalators into its towering lobby, with wide staircases on either side that lead to ballrooms and restaurants and a balconied mezzanine. Michael Jordan and the Bulls stayed here when they beat the pants off the Sonics in the NBA finals a few years ago (surely they gained a competitive edge from that classy Four Seasons treatment), and the Rolling Stones and U2 have bunked here. Rooms are large and tasteful, the Garden Court is a wonderful place to bring your mom for afternoon tea, and chef Gavin Stephenson turns out classic continental fare in the Georgian Room (bring small parties to his new chef's table in the kitchen). Two cylindrical towers near Westlake Center that look like a 1960s urban renewal scheme announce **The Westin, Seattle**, where Bill Clinton stayed during the APEC conference with other world leaders (he ordered burgers and fries from the McDonald's across the street). The corporate headquarters of this prestigious hotel chain, recently acquired by Starwood Resorts, is right across the street, making this hotel something of a flagship for the chain. Upper floors yield great views of the Space Needle and the sound, and the location on the northern edge of the shopping district makes it closer to Nordstrom and Bon Marché than the Four Seasons, but the Westin is a little too big and convention-friendly to feel cozy. Another convention center hotel teeming with the nametag–afflicted is the downtown high-rise **Seattle Sheraton Hotel & Towers,** which is anything but intimate and cozy. But there are pockets of blissful serenity here, most notably Fullers, a tasteful, hushed restaurant that serves exquisite gourmet fare, and the Pike Street Cafe, with its calorie-laden (but oh-so-soothing) dessert bar. Concierge-level floors at the top have their own reception and lounge. There's also a good sports bar (Schooners). The lobby bustles day and night and has a lounge with a piano player who will break into everything from "It Had to Be You" to Led Zeppelin. Snag a north-facing room for the best views of Lake Union and the Space Needle; western rooms give you a great look at an enormous, view-blocking skyscraper.

The boudoir alternative... The intimate, European-style boutique hotel is almost a perfect match for Seattle's laid-back atmosphere. The best are the **W Hotel, Hotel Monaco,** and **Hotel Vintage Park,** all of which are located within a couple of blocks of each other at the south end of the downtown shopping district. **The Hotel Monaco** is extravagantly decorated—a true boudoir—with striped walls and canopy beds draped in bright fabrics. The lobby is charming, with its blue, leaping dolphins on the walls, wrought-iron chandeliers hanging low from the high ceilings, and a front desk that looks like a giant steamer trunk. The guest rooms are the most daring in town, with striped walls, clashing colors, and fabrics draped everywhere, and if you miss your pets back home, they'll bring you a goldfish bowl with a couple of stunners to keep you company. Its sister, the **Hotel Vintage Park,** is considerably more sedate, with burgundy accents on hunter-green walls, and rooms named after local wineries. The **W Hotel** is cool in a kind of New York/L.A. way, with muted gray rooms, comfortable sofas set in window alcoves, and an array of high-tech goodies that include in-room CD players and fax machines. Wonderful (make that "heavenly," in W parlance) beds too, with thick, feathery comforters. On First Hill (also called Pill Hill for its hospitals), the **Sorrento Hotel,** although a bit out of the way and a difficult walk from downtown, looks like an Italian villa, with its lovely courtyard and fountain at the entrance. Its mellow interior offers a quiet, comfortable lobby with a fireplace and the darkly paneled Hunt Club, a restaurant and bar for fine Northwest dining and some of the best martinis in town.

At water's edge... The coolest thing about the **Hotel Edgewater,** at the north end of the waterfront, is not that it's Seattle's only true hotel on the water, but that the Beatles once stayed here (you can buy posters of them fishing from the windows into Elliott Bay, a practice that is no longer allowed). Although it struggles to overcome a kind of motor-inn atmosphere and the reception area is usually jammed with people coming and going from the nearby ferry to Victoria, the Edgewater is roomy and comfortable, with rough-hewn pine furniture and unbeatable views at night of the ferries crossing to Bainbridge Island. And the location is pure gold; don't miss Myrtle Edwards Park to the north for strolling and biking and the marvelous Seattle Aquarium to the south. Water views of a different kind are offered at the **Silver Cloud Inn - Lake Union**, which is just across the street from Seattle's downtown lake. Here you'll see floatplanes taking off and landing from the middle of the lake and sailboats and paddlers plying the waters. The location is central to many neighborhoods, and the rooms are spacious, if totally chain-a-fied. They have microwaves and refrigerators, and the hotel boasts a pair of pools (indoor and outdoor), which sure beats swimming in the chilly lake. All the way across Lake Washington in the eastside suburb of Kirkland (convenient to Microsoft and Bellevue), the **Woodmark Hotel** is a gem of a lakeside place with attentive service and quiet, elegant rooms. Rooms look out over the broad lake, with muscle boats docked at the adjacent marina alongside sailboats; a downstairs sitting room, reached by a sweeping staircase, has a grand piano and quiet bar. If you want to go into the city from here, however, you'll be at the mercy of the Evergreen Point Floating Bridge, which produces the worst daily traffic snarls in town.

The inn thing to do... A cluster of downtown inns lets you walk out your door right into the middle of the Pike Place Market, with its cafes, fresh flowers, and hidden restaurants. The most central of these is the **Inn at the Market**, a very European little nook on Pine Street with superb views of the water. Practically a guesthouse, with only 65 rooms, this has been the getaway of choice for years for those who want a small, intimate hotel experience in Seattle. Set in the thick of the Market, the inn has large, tastefully decorated rooms with bay windows overlooking the waterfront, a rooftop patio above the Market, and room service coming from one of the best French restaurants in town, Campagne, with an accompanying bistro. Two blocks south on First Avenue, the **Inn at Harbor Steps** occupies the bottom floors of a condominium building. You may feel a bit like the creature in the basement, but the rooms are large and have high ceilings, fireplaces, wet bars, and balconies that open onto a garden courtyard. There's also a lovely paneled library and a dining room for large breakfast spreads, which are included in the room rate.

Even further south on First Avenue, and now a good four-block walk to either the Market or Pioneer Square, the **Alexis Hotel** is a very stylish small property, big on service (it has its own concierge, a nice surprise in a hotel of this size). The Sultan of Brunei set up home and harem here during the APEC conference. If hip and trendy Belltown is your kind of neighborhood, **The Wall Street Inn**, above the El Gaucho restaurant, is awfully civilized. Yes, it has a lousy entrance, a doorway beside the restaurant that looks like a come-on for time-share sales. But then you see fresh flowers in a vase, and a bright, white staircase leads upstairs; the lobby sitting area is comforting, with leather furniture and a fireplace, and its large guest rooms have trestle beds and wonderful views of Elliott Bay. Breakfasts are custom-made spreads including quiches and fresh baked goods.

For the tragically hip... Trendy magazines and the fashion elite have been gushing about the **Ace Hotel**, a 15-room boutique hotel that opened in 1999 on the second floor of a Belltown walk-up above the Cyclops bar on First Avenue. A bare white reception area, low beds on simple platforms, stainless-steel sinks and counters—its minimalist attitude is far more SoHo than Space Needle, the kind of spartan chic New York travel writers adore. The **Paramount Hotel**, just behind Pacific Place in the downtown shopping district, is often the headquarters for acts that play at the Paramount Theater (including Marilyn Manson, who, one bellman told us, demanded a cab for a trip around the corner to a doughnut shop). Its lobby makes a bid for coolness, with a polished marble fireplace and plump sofas, but the rooms are surprisingly mundane—think beige decor and old prints. An Executive King room on an upper floor makes up for it with a jetted bathtub and view of downtown. On Ninth Avenue downtown, the **Camlin Hotel** is a faded old place with a big empty lobby; the elevators are ancient and the carpets dingy, but guest rooms are big and clean, and many command views of the Space Needle. All in all, it's a good deal for the price. A terrific bar-restaurant on the top floor, the Cloud Room, is a hangout for visiting musicians and actors. The **Commodore Motor Hotel**, on Second Avenue between the Market and Belltown, is an absolute dive that can be recommended only to those in search of extreme slumming. The lobby is dingy and smells of cigarette smoke, rooms are small and dank, and even the chambermaid was dangling a cigarette the day we visited. Nevertheless, the Commodore attracts a crowd that ranges from Los Angelenos in town for a rock concert (the Moore Theater is across the street) to sailors on leave from the Bremerton Naval Station. If Pioneer Square pub-crawling tops your agenda, the **Pioneer Square Hotel**, a run-of-the-mill Best Western property on a quiet corner of Yesler Way under the viaduct, is an easy stumble from the clubs.

Who needs a suite when you can get an apartment?... Renting two fairly large rooms and a kitchenette in a cool neighborhood is a viable option in Queen Anne. On Queen Anne Avenue North, the main commercial strip, the **MarQueen Hotel** is a converted brown-brick apartment building with a handsome mahogany-and-leaded-glass entryway with a uniformed doorman, room service from the Figaro Bistro, and a direct entrance to Caffe Ladro for breakfast and coffee. Its apartments are now spacious suites with small sitting areas and kitchenettes. Two blocks away, on the Key Arena side of Seattle Center, another converted apartment house, the **Inn at Queen Anne**, also has kitchenette units and suite-like layouts. It's a little more rundown and funky than the MarQueen—the beds were rather creaky when we visited—but it's clean and safe and a good value.

Hanging out in Huskyville... Whether you're planning to crash a frat party or watch a PAC-10 football or basketball game, staying in the heart of Huskyville is a decent option. Right off the freeway and a bit of a hike to campus, the **University Tower Hotel** is an older, Art Deco–inspired place that provides the only true hotel facilities in the U-District. It looks better on the outside than it does on the inside, but the location is handy and the price is right. Get a room away from 45th Street if you want a little peace and quiet, and don't expect much more than corner-room digs with decent campus views and a bar-restaurant that's outclassed six times over by any hash-house on the Ave. Closer to the heart of things is the motel-like **University Inn**, which has a pool; rooms are nothing special, but it's within quick striking distance of Lake Union restaurants, Gasworks Park, and the Wallingford shopping and commercial district. Bring your bike, and you can hook up easily to the Burke-Gilman Trail for long rides north to Lake Washington. On University Ave itself is the **College Inn**, a low-rate hostel good for youthful budget travelers. It doesn't give you much more than a small room (sans TV) with a rickety bed and shared bath, but the exterior is a handsome Tudor edifice that dates back to 1909. The **Silver Cloud Inn - Lake Union** is a bland, modern cookie-cutter property in University Village, a huge shopping center at the base of a wicked hill (if you're hoofing it from campus).

Shoppers' specials... If shopping is your thang, you'll conserve energy by staying at a place in the midst of the downtown retailing scene (the better to tote your overflowing bags back quickly). Right in the heart of things, the **Mayflower Park Hotel** is actually attached via walkway to Westlake Center, which is itself connected by monorail to Seattle Center (great for shopping on rainy days, of which we have plenty). This grand old property in a 1927 building has so much going for it—the lobby is elegant and expansive, and the lively wood-paneled bar, Oliver's, with its floor-to-ceiling windows overlooking Fourth Avenue, makes what are indisputably the best martinis in Seattle. Yet the Mayflower Park's smallish rooms, blandly decorated, may well disappoint style-conscious guests. The wannabe-hip **Paramount Hotel** is just across the street from brand-new Pacific Place, and the trio of downtown convention palaces—the **Four Seasons Olympic, The Westin, Seattle,**

and **Seattle Sheraton Hotel & Towers**—are all within an easy (meaning flat) walk from the stores, perfect for idle convention spouses who want to pick up a little something (like a Tiffany bracelet) to remember Seattle by. Those fabulous Kimpton twins, the **Hotel Vintage Park** and **Hotel Monaco** boutique hotels, are also handy to shopping, though the Vintage Park is set at the farthest end of the downtown retail corridor, and a little too close to the freeway for our tastes. In the middle of Fifth Avenue with a lobby below the street level is the **West Coast Grand on Fifth Avenue**, a chain place with blandly predictable rooms but an undeniably good location. Some upper-floor rooms have nice views of downtown buildings and the sound, and the first-rate pub, the Elephant & Castle, never fails to be lively.

For the embraceable you... And then there are those stolen weekends (ah, we remember zem well) when you haven't the slightest desire to leave your cozy little love nest. The **Alexis Hotel** has rooms with big jacuzzi tubs and wood-burning fireplaces, massage therapists who will come to your suite, and a private steam room that you can reserve. Have in-house chef Tim Kelley whip up a five-course room-service meal from The Painted Table while you're at it. Likewise with the **Hotel Monaco,** where the fluffy beds with exotic print bedding have a definite come-hither quality and room service is delivered from the spicy, Cajun-inspired Sazerac restaurant. Your stock options having vested, perhaps you'd like to spring for the $1,000-a-night penthouse suite at the aristocratic **Sorrento Hotel,** with grand piano, jacuzzi, and a patio offering sweeping views of the city. Who cares about the steep walk downtown from here, if you're not planning to leave your room? You could also renew your vows, or even make up a few new ones, on the "heavenly" beds at the **W Hotel,** where the extra-large TVs are ideal for watching old movies or catching up on the ones you just missed at the theaters (as if you need extra entertainment on a heavenly bed).

With children in tow... The kiddies want Nintendo, you want room to stretch out without tripping over Pokémon cards. The kids want a pool, you want a free breakfast. What to do, what to do? For sheer space and familiar surroundings, try the **Hampton Inn and Suites**, which occupy adjoining buildings side-by-side behind Tower Records on the Space Needle side of Seattle Center. Expect the expected: inoffensive decor in the double rooms and big antiseptic suites, with a continental breakfast buffet included and a jacuzzi on the property. We found the front desk to be a bit brusque and service nonexistent, but hey, it's on the quiet side of the Queen Anne neighborhood and only a short walk to the Seattle Center amusement park. Also in Queen Anne, the dowdy **Inn at Queen Anne** and the somewhat spiffier **MarQueen Hotel** are both converted apartment houses with small kitchenettes and lots of different room configurations for mixing and matching sleeping arrangements. The **Residence Inn by Marriott** is across a traffic-crazy thoroughfare from Lake Union, but it does have suites with kitchens, as well as a pool, as does the nearby **Silver Cloud Inn - Lake Union.** For more of that chain-hotel charm, the **West Coast Grand on Fifth Avenue** downtown and the **University Tower Hotel** near the university campus will satisfy the Nintendo jones (additional points awarded for driving the children by Nintendo's American headquarters off Route 520 in Redmond). At the luxury end of the spectrum, the **Four Seasons Olympic** is the friendliest to very young guests, with large rooms and welcome kits (at those prices, they can afford to give away a few crayons and balloons). The under-six set will swoon over the Teddy Bear Suite that goes up every holiday season, a room decorated for and occupied by bears, with free cookies for visitors.

The bottom end... The **American Youth Hostel (AYH)** in Seattle has one of the best hostel setups in the country: It's tucked into a quiet side street under the Pike Place Market and is close to the waterfront. A true backpacker's refuge, it always has lots of international languages and accents mingling on its sidewalk, and its proximity to the waterfront, Market, and Pioneer Square is extraordinary. A similar place, the **American Backpackers Hostel** is in the thick of the Capitol Hill scene on Broadway; you may pass it three or four times before you find the small sign hanging from a storefront that announces it. Remember hippie buses? The **Green Tortoise Backpackers Hostel** will evoke memories of long road trips, with its clientele of footloose pioneers and Aussie backpackers. The place has a terrific location, near Belltown on Second

Avenue near the Market. If you really need ultra-cheap digs, of course, and don't mind the truckers and hourly rentals going on nearby, the strip of Aurora Avenue North just beyond the Ship Canal is studded with cheap fleabag motels.

The Index

$$$$	over $200
$$$	$150–$200
$$	$100–$150
$	under $100

Price applies to a standard double room for one night.

Ace Hotel. This trendy Belltown hotel's spare decor reminds many of the sleekest hotels in New York or San Francisco; to the rest of us, it looks like Alcatraz, but at least at Alcatraz you had your own toilet. Of course, you'll pay a premium for such discomfort.... *Tel 206/448-4721. www.TheAceHotel.com. 2423 1st Ave., 98121. 15 rooms. $–$$* **(see p. 15)**

Alexis Hotel. A small hotel with a big-hotel feel, occupying a handsome older building on 1st Avenue between the Market and Pioneer Square. Amenities include evening wine tastings in the lobby, an in-house Aveda spa, the Book Store bar, and The Painted Table for fine dining.... *Tel 206/624-4844 and 800/426-7033. www.alexishotel.com. 1007 1st Ave., 98104. 109 rooms. $$$* **(see pp. 15, 18)**

American Backpackers Hostel. A tiny place in the heart of the Broadway action on Capitol Hill, it's less crowded than some hostels—if you're lucky enough to get a bed here. The staff will even drop you or pick you up downtown or at the airport (for groups of four or more).... *Tel 206/720-2965 or 800/600-2965. 126 Broadway E., 98102. 35 beds, 1 private room with shared bath. $* **(see p. 19)**

American Youth Hostel (AYH). A lounge, library, and self-service kitchen and laundry give you some space to stretch out in this popular hostel underneath the Pike Place Market.... *Tel 206/622-5443. www.hiseattle.org. 84 Union St., 98101. 193 beds with shared baths. $* **(see p. 19)**

Camlin Hotel. This 1926 dowager in a fairly dreary part of downtown needs sprucing up; at least it has a small pool for those infrequent days when Seattle gets hot enough for a dip. The Cloud Room on the eleventh floor is a favorite hipster piano bar.... *Tel 206/682-0100 or 800/426-0670. 1619 9th Ave., 98101. 100 rooms. $$* **(see p. 16)**

College Inn. A hostel-style property on the quieter, south end of University Avenue NE, with a nice coffee shop on the street and a bar in the basement. The U-Dub campus is right across the street and the included continental breakfasts are plentiful.... *Tel 206/633-4441. www.speakeasy.org/collegeinn. 4000 University Way NE, 98105. 25 rooms. $* **(see p. 17)**

Commodore Motor Hotel. This seedy joint draws both scenesters and scum, mostly due to its location, which is great for excursions into Belltown and the Market. You can't beat the price.... *Tel 206/448-8868. 2013 2nd Ave., 98121. 100 rooms. $* **(see p. 16)**

Four Seasons Olympic. The lodging of choice for high-end customers (not to mention their offspring).... *Tel 206/621-1700 or 800/223-8772. www.fourseasons.com. 411 University St., 98101. 450 rooms. $$$$* **(see pp. 12, 17, 19)**

Green Tortoise Backpackers Hostel. A friendly hostel with a large common area, communal kitchen, and free breakfast.... *Tel 206/340-1222. www.greentortoise.net. 1525 2nd Ave., 98101. 37 rooms, 98 bunk beds. $* **(see p. 19)**

Hampton Inn and Suites. Close to Seattle Center, these two hotels have been combined into one big one with either double rooms or kitchenette suites. Rooms are large, comfortable, and predictable; there's a continental breakfast buffet.... *Tel 206/282-7700 or 800/426-7866. www.hampton-inn.com. 700 5th Ave. N., 98109. 198 rooms. $$* **(see p. 18)**

Hotel Edgewater. From a rustically decorated waterfront room sitting on pilings over Elliott Bay you can see Bainbridge Island, the Olympic Mountains, and ferries crisscrossing Puget Sound. And yes, the Beatles slept here. How totally gear and fab is that?... *Tel 206/728-7000 or 800/624-0670. www.noblehousehotels.com. 2411 Alaskan Way, 98121. 236 rooms. $$$* **(see p. 14)**

Hotel Monaco, Seattle. Though this is a chain property—owned by the San Francisco–based Kimpton Group, which has Monacos in Denver, Chicago, and San Francisco, too—it's truly a chain with a difference. With daring decor and a big-city sense of fun, it's as close to a chic San Francisco hotel as you'll find in Seattle, and well worth the price.... *Tel 206/621-1770 or 800/945-2240. www.monaco-seattle.com. 1101 4th Ave., 98101. 189 rooms. $$$* **(see pp. 10, 13, 18)**

Hotel Vintage Park. A businessman's hotel that tries mightily to deliver a comfortable, friendly experience modeled after European hotels. And it succeeds: You feel it in the warm lobby, with a fireplace roaring, books on the shelves, and wine served every afternoon. Spring for a junior suite—they're definitely the way to go.... *Tel 206/624-8000 or 800/624-4433. www.hotelvintagepark.com. 1100 5th Ave., 98101. 126 rooms. $$$* **(see pp. 13, 18)**

Inn at Harbor Steps. Set on the bottom floors of a high-rise condo building, this tasteful urban inn is a real find in the heart of the city, at the south end of the Pike Place Market. Guests share expansive health-club facilities, including pool and spa, with the condo residents.... *Tel 206/748-0973 or 888/728-8910. www.foursisters.com. 1221 1st Ave., 98101. 20 rooms. $$$* **(see p. 15)**

Inn at Queen Anne. Just across the street from Seattle Center and Key Arena sits this somewhat faded apartment building, converted into a variety of studios and suites—many with kitchenettes—that offer bed-and-breakfast digs.... *Tel 206/282-7357 or 800/952-5043. www.innatqueen anne.com. 505 1st Ave. N., 98109. 68 rooms. $* **(see pp. 16, 19)**

Inn at the Market. This small, French-inspired inn combines a Pike Place Market location with big water-view guest rooms. The adjoining restaurant, Campagne, is excellent, and for a fee, you can use the Seattle Club, one of the better health clubs in town, a few blocks away at the north end of the Market.... *Tel 206/443-3600 or 800/446-4484. www.innatthemarket.com. 86 Pine St., 98101. 70 rooms. $$$* **(see p. 14)**

MarQueen Hotel. In gentrified Queen Anne, a renovated apartment building offers suites with full kitchenettes and small sitting areas. Outside the door are all the restaurants and coffee bars of lower Queen Anne, with Seattle Center only two blocks away.... *Tel 206/282-7407 or 888/445-3076. www.marqueen.com. 600 Queen Anne Ave. N., 98109. 56 rooms. $$* **(see pp. 16, 19)**

Mayflower Park Hotel. A grand lobby and excellent downtown location, but ho-hum rooms and a faded air make the Mayflower Park come up a bit short; it's the kind of faded businessman's lodging that makes you understand why they started building Embassy Suites and Doubletrees.... *Tel 206/623-8700 or 800/426-5100. www.mayflower park.com. 405 Olive Way, 98101. 171 rooms. $$* **(see p. 17)**

Paramount Hotel. Touted as a hipper, newer vision of the old Camlin, it has a sleek lobby but ordinary rooms. Pacific Place's shopping and restaurants are right across the street.... *Tel 206/292-9500 or 800/426-0670. www.west coasthotels.com. 724 Pine St., 98101. 146 rooms. $$$$* **(see pp. 15, 17)**

Pioneer Square Hotel. Tucked away in a turn-of-the-century building near the waterfront, this modest Best Western property is the only decent option for staying in raucous Pioneer Square. The rooms are simple and undistinguished, and breakfast is included.... *Tel 206/340-1234 or 800/800-5514. www.pioneersquare.com. 77 Yesler Way, 98104. 75 rooms. $$* **(see p. 16)**

Residence Inn by Marriott. The location isn't great, across busy Fairview Ave. from Lake Union, but fully equipped kitchens, an indoor pool, and free breakfasts make it a good choice for families and long-term guests.... *Tel 206/624-6000 or 800/331-3131. www.residence inn.com. 800 Fairview Ave. N., 98109. 234 rooms. $$$* **(see p. 19)**

Seattle Sheraton Hotel & Towers. Everything you desire in a towering convention hotel, with a lobby that never ceases to resemble Grand Central Station at rush hour. Fullers restaurant serves exquisite gourmet fare; there's also the Pike Street Cafe. The health club on the 35th floor is among the best in town.... *Tel 206/621-9000 or 800/325-3535. www.sheraton.com. 1400 6th Ave., 98101. 840 rooms. $$* **(see pp. 13, 18)**

Silver Cloud Inn - Lake Union. Two up-to-date chain properties—one downtown near Lake Union and one adjacent to the University Village shopping area in the U-District—worth a try for family travelers who want little more than a pool, breakfast, and a clean bed for the troops.... *Lake Union: Tel 206/447-9500 or 800/330-5812. 1150 Fairview Ave. N, 98109. University Village: Tel 206/526-5200 or 800/206-694. www.scinns.com. 5036 25th Ave. NE, 98105. Each 180 rooms. $$* **(see pp. 14, 17, 19)**

Sorrento Hotel. This Italianate mansion, with a lovely courtyard entrance, would be one of the finest lodgings in town...if it were *in* town, instead of perched on a hillside on busy Madison Street. Still, it's an elegant getaway, with its woody charm, attentive service, and the Hunt Club restaurant.... *Tel 206/622-6400 or 800/426-1265. www.hotel sorrento.com. 900 Madison St., 98104. 76 rooms. $$$$* **(see pp. 10, 13, 18)**

University Inn. Not a bad choice for U-District camping out. It has a pool, is adjacent to a lively cafe, and is in a quiet, residential part of the U-District.... *Tel 206/632-5055 or 800/733-3855. www.universityinnseattle.com. 4140 Roosevelt Way NE, 98105. 102 rooms. $* **(see p. 17)**

University Tower Hotel. Also known as the Meany Tower, this high-rise with the Art Deco lettering holds more promise than it actually delivers. Proximity to campus is the attraction here, not to mention quick access to I-5 and some basic amenities, such as room service, in-room movies, and Nintendo.... *Tel 206/634-2000 or 800/899-0251. www.meany.com. 4507 Brooklyn Ave. NE, 98105. 155 rooms. $$*

(see pp. 17, 19)

W Hotel. Trying to appease all of those hip L.A. and New York wheelers and dealers with a fashionably gray boutique approach, this business hotel is loaded with amenities, including in-room fax machines and fast Internet service.... *Tel 206/264-6000 or 877-W-HOTELS. 1112 4th Ave. at Seneca St., 98101. 426 rooms. $$$$* **(see pp. 13, 18)**

The Wall Street Inn. A find in the heart of Belltown, with large bedrooms, a homey living room, and dazzling views of Elliott Bay. A big breakfast spread is included in the room rate.... *Tel 206/448-0125 or 800/624-1117. www.wallstreet inn.com. 2507 1st Ave., 98121. 20 rooms. $$$* **(see p. 15)**

West Coast Grand on Fifth Avenue. Part of a small West Coast chain set up for business travelers on a budget, the Seattle property is a cut above, with a central location on Fifth Avenue. The Elephant & Castle pub keeps things hopping, and in-room movies and Nintendo amuse guests.... *Tel 206/971-8000 or 800/325-4000. www.coasthotels.com. 1415 5th Ave., 98101. 300 rooms. $$$* **(see pp. 18, 19)**

The Westin, Seattle. Though it bustles with a big-city vibrancy, the twin-towered Westin is overwhelming and cold. There is an excellent pool and fitness center. Check out Roy's, a seafood and fusion restaurant owned by Roy Yamaguchi from Honolulu.... *Tel 206/728-1000 or 800/WESTIN-1. www.westin.com. 1900 5th Ave., 98101. 865 rooms. $$$$* **(see pp. 12, 17)**

Woodmark Hotel. Set on Lake Washington in the east-side neighborhood of Kirkland, this peaceful, tasteful property is the retreat of choice for visiting business dignitaries and Microsoft executives.... *Tel 425/822-3700 or 800/822-3700. www.thewoodmark.com. 1200 Carillon Point, Kirkland, 98033. 100 rooms. $$$$* **(see p. 14)**

Seattle Downtown Accommodations

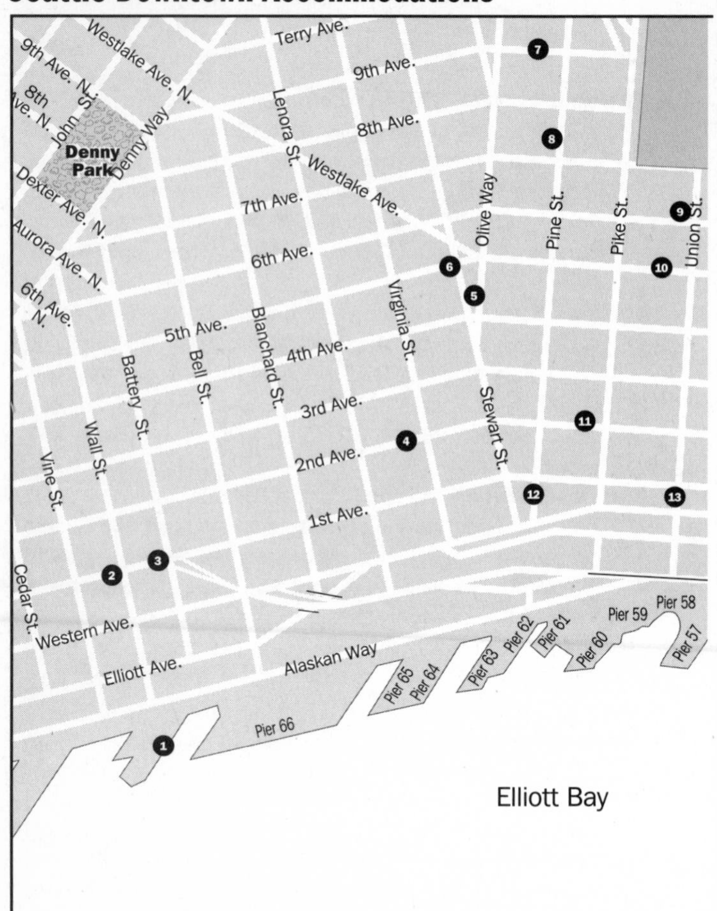

Ace Hotel **3**
Alexis Hotel **15**
AYH **13**
Camlin Hotel **7**
Commodore Motor Hotel **4**
Four Seasons Olympic **19**
Green Tortoise Backpackers Hostel **11**
Hotel Edgewater **1**
Hotel Monaco **18**
Hotel Vintage Park **20**
Inn at Harbor Steps **14**
Inn at the Market **12**

Mayflower Park Hotel **5**
Paramount Hotel **8**
Pioneer Square Hotel **16**
Seattle Sheraton Hotel & Towers **9**
Sorrento Hotel **21**
W Hotel **17**
The Wall Street Inn **2**
West Coast Grandon Fifth Avenue **10**
Westin Seattle **6**

Seattle–North & Northeast Accommodations

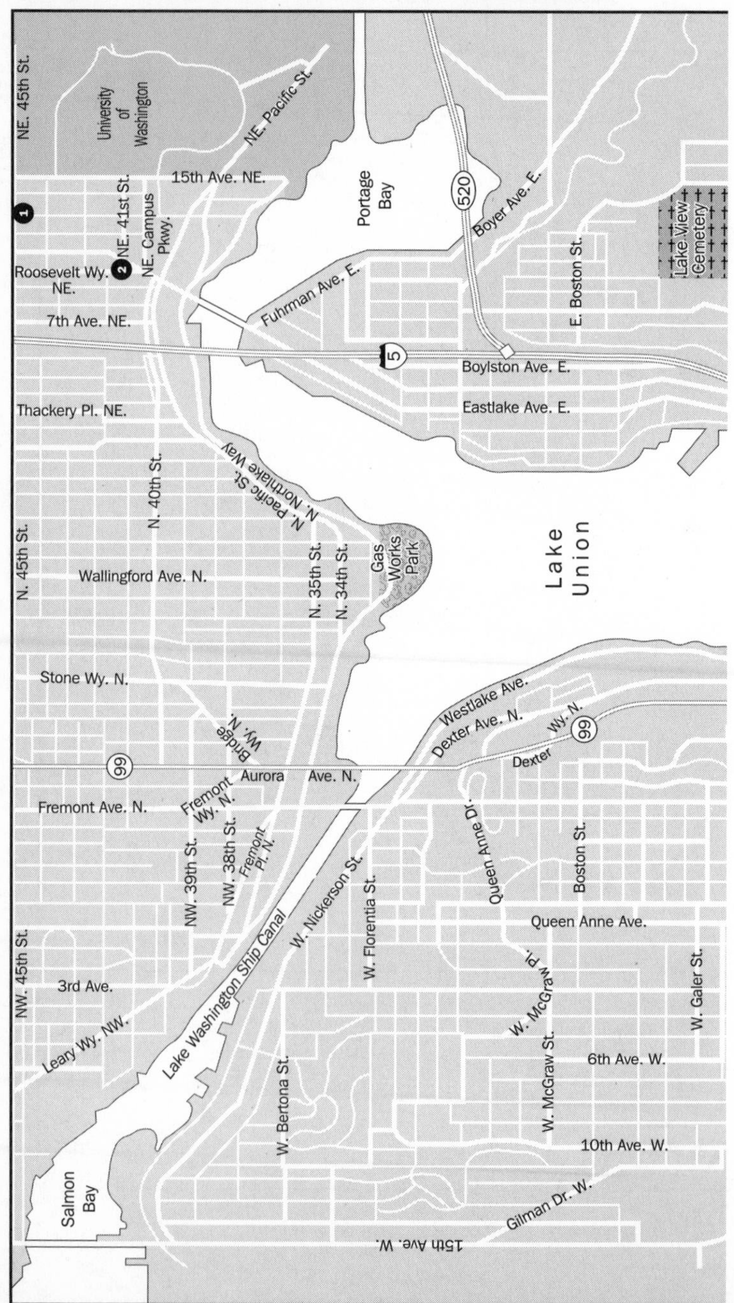

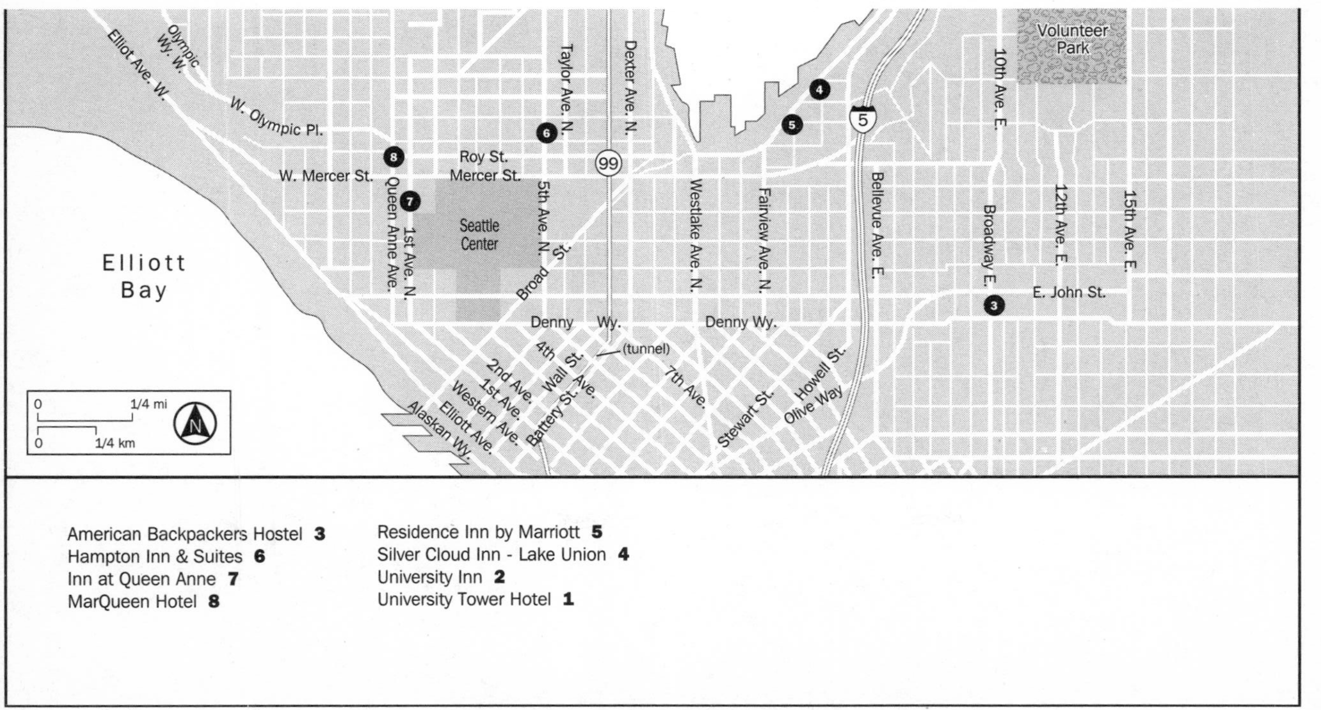
Volunteer Park
10th Ave. E.
12th Ave. E.
15th Ave. E.
Broadway E.
E. John St.
Bellevue Ave. E.
Fairview Ave. N.
Westlake Ave. N.
Dexter Ave. N.
Taylor Ave. N.
5th Ave. N.
Broad St.
Roy St.
Mercer St.
W. Mercer St.
Seattle Center
1st Ave. N.
Queen Anne Ave.
W. Olympic Pl.
Olympic Wy. W.
Elliot Ave. W.
Elliott Bay
Denny Wy.
Denny Wy.
(tunnel)
Howell St.
Olive Way
Stewart St.
7th Ave.
4th Ave.
Wall St.
Battery St.
2nd Ave.
1st Ave.
Western Ave.
Elliott Ave.
Alaskan Wy.
5
99
0
1/4 mi
0
1/4 km
N
American Backpackers Hostel 3
Hampton Inn & Suites 6
Inn at Queen Anne 7
MarQueen Hotel 8
Residence Inn by Marriott 5
Silver Cloud Inn - Lake Union 4
University Inn 2
University Tower Hotel 1

din

ing 2

Tuck your napkin under your chin, sharpen your steak knife, and grasp your fork firmly in hand. We've come to the part of our story where Seattle blossoms into a world-class city that rivals San Francisco and New York (and I don't mention those places lightly). Fresh local ingredients are a key part of Seattle's culinary stardom: seafood in wild abundance, salmon and halibut flown directly in from Alaska, and oysters from local estuaries; gorgeous apples, peaches, and berries from Washington farms; local growers who compete to offer the freshest herbs and heirloom fruits and vegetables; Ellensburg lamb; fresh bread and pastry from bakeries around the city; and ripe goat cheeses from farmhouse producers. We owe much of this wealth to the **Pike Place Market,** which resisted the T-shirt sellers and trinket salesmen and insisted on being a true farmer's market, thus spurring citywide culinary awareness. Add a burgeoning, competitive restaurant community and chefs who are achieving national reputations, and you'll find yourself in gustatory heaven.

You won't find many of those grand, high-ceilinged, profusely decorated spaces that seem to exist on every corner in San Francisco, nor will you encounter many of L.A.'s trendy (read "chi-chi") watering holes, where the food is secondary to the atmosphere. The emphasis in Seattle restaurants is on food, and you'll be hard-pressed to get a bad meal here. So don't you dare toddle off with the other tourists to the Space Needle Restaurant or the waterfront chain places like Ye Olde Spaghetti Factory, which packs them in every night for some of the worst Italian food in town. Enjoy the view from the Space Needle and the waterfront and then head into town for some decent food. You won't be sorry you did.

Only in Seattle

There was a time, many years ago, when Seattle was at the forefront of fusion cooking, when Asian influences and things like lemongrass, sashimi, and star anise were being combined with traditional continental cooking. That craze gave way (thankfully, in my opinion) to a Northwest regional cuisine that emphasized the freshest local ingredients. Northwest cooking has lately lost its hard, doctrinaire edge, and chefs are now integrating all sorts of cooking styles and dishes, with the emphasis still on fresh ingredients and imaginative preparations. While you're here, you shouldn't miss the fresh salmon, especially when it's plank-grilled over an alderwood fire; other seafood specialties include Dungeness crab, melt-in-your-mouth black cod (known as sablefish on the East Coast), delicate and hard-to-find razor clams, big, meaty geoduck clams (pronounced gooey-duck), and the full variety of oysters from different growers around the Puget Sound. Local fruits are another distinctive touch, including salalberry, which coastal Indians ate and modern chefs use for a tart vinegar, and golden raspberries and marionberries, tasty summer dessert toppers and delicious treats all by themselves.

How to Eat a Crab

Dungeness crabs, the sweet, oval crustaceans that are harvested in the estuarial waters around Puget Sound, are one of the great delicacies of Seattle. Boiled at the point of harvest, you'll find them on ice at the fishmongers in the Market or in most local grocery stores. We eat them cold or reheated, with fresh asparagus and crusty bread. If you buy your own, ask the seller to clean it, which he'll do by ripping off the disc-shaped back and washing out the viscera.

You don't want to miss a morsel of meat inside that cantankerous shell. First pull the legs off one at a time. Crack the big claw with a nutcracker, and scrape out the meat, using either a pick or one of the crab's own pointy feet. Then use a fork tine to tear the smaller legs open and extract the meat. Don't forget also to break the main body into pieces and pick all of the sweet, white flesh from between the membranes. You can dip each mouthful of meat either in cocktail sauce (our local fish merchants make some great ones) or simply in melted butter, with maybe a dollop of fiery Caribbean hot sauce stirred in. Dip judiciously.

Getting the Right Table

The newest place in town will always be a tough reservation for about the first two weeks it's open, but the competition is so fierce among downtown restaurants that you'll rarely get shut out of your top three picks. Since locals eat anywhere between 6 and 10 pm, there are plenty of tables being turned. If you want to eat in a Belltown hot spot like **El Gaucho** or **Cascadia** at prime time (8 to 9 pm), try to call two weeks in advance, or have your concierge pull a few strings.

Tipping

This is not a town of super-professional waiters who come from the French school of snobbery-laced service; nor are they graybeards who have been slinging hash for 40 years. Waitpersons in Seattle generally manage to be friendly, knowledgeable, and efficient while exuding the air of being just a week away from completing their sculpted artwork or embarking on a monthlong climb in the mountains. Fifteen percent of the entire tab is the standard tip, 20 percent is truly appreciated, and if you leave your last two bucks they'll probably inquire with genuine concern if you have enough cash for busfare home.

How to Dress

Conversation with my friend Jeff Alexander, a Boston transplant and local executive who prides himself on his sartorial elegance:

> "Jeff, can you think of any restaurants in town that require a jacket?"
> (Audible gasp) "Oh, wow. I can't really think of any...how about **El Gaucho** or the **Hunt Club**?"
> "Nope, I checked with both of them. No jackets, no ties required."
> "**The Georgian Room** at the Four Seasons? **Canlis**?"
> "**The Georgian Room** for sure. **Canlis** just *suggests* that men wear a jacket."
> "One place."
> "One place."
> (Short pause) "That's really pathetic."

Where the Chefs Are

Tom Douglas really looks like he belongs in Seattle. Tall and curly-haired, with about as much temperamental-chef pretension to him as a fry cook at Denny's, he has helped define the downtown dining experience for the last 12 years. In 1989, he opened the **Dahlia Lounge** on Fourth Avenue as one of the first upscale, fine-dining restaurants in Seattle with a bit of edge. The Dahlia still packs them in for Asian-influenced dishes and Douglas's sublime crab cakes; I can't get out of there without at least one helping of the best coconut-cream pie in history. A few years later, Douglas added the sublime **Etta's Seafood** at the Market, and followed it in 1996 with **Palace Kitchen**, a big, open restaurant on Fifth Avenue with a long, curving bar and bistro menu. All three places are thriving. Douglas has picked up accolades like "Best Chef in the Pacific Northwest" from the James Beard Foundation, and recently began selling spice rubs in a foray into packaged foods, but his success is firmly grounded in the food that comes out of his three kitchens. "Now they eat what they like, rather than what they should eat, or because the food is considered cool and sophisticated," he says about his downtown clientele. "They're sophisticated enough to trust their own palates. We've gone beyond having to impress the neighbors."

Douglas has plenty of company in the crowded city dining scene. The most recent honoree from the Beard Foundation is Christine Keff, whose **Flying Fish** and **Fandango** restaurants in Belltown get raves for their innovative, international seafood preparations. Thierry Rautureau, who began a culinary career at the tender age of 13 in his native France, now finds himself at the top of his game with **Rover's** restaurant packing in high-end diners for exquisite French fare. Tamara Murphy and Kerry Sears have both moved on from seminal restaurants (**Campagne** for Murphy, and **The Georgian Room** for Sears) to create new masterpieces in **Brasa** and **Cascadia**, respectively. Tim Kelley has refined classic Asian-fusion cooking with great success at **The Painted Table**.

The Lowdown

The ultimate Market graze... Munching one's way through the Pike Place Market is one of the truly great ways to spend an afternoon. Anyone who does invariably winds up heading home with sacks of groceries and treats. Start with beers served in frosty mugs at **Lowell's Restaurant**, a working-class place with windows looking out onto Puget Sound. Lowell's serves sandwiches and basic meat-and-potatoes plates to the fishmongers and vendors who work the tourist crowd; come here for the beers, the view, and the down-to-earth atmosphere, but save your appetite. Head across Pike Place to the stainless-steel lunch counters at **Jack's Fish Spot** for crab cocktails that are all celery, Dungeness crab, and tangy sauce. Now duck into the market behind Jack's for a tasty Philly cheese steak at **Philadelphia's Deli**, or a mixed-vegetable-and-noodle dish at **Rasa Malaysia**. Head north past the Seattle Garden Center to **Cucina Fresca**, a superb Italian deli, for Arancini rice balls and sauce or exquisite mozzarella and tomatoes, but you absolutely must save room for the unbelievable cabbage-and-onion or salmon pierogies two doors north at **Piroshky, Piroshky**. Now it's time for a crucial decision: Dessert can be the Moscow rolls of sweet farina or apple tarts at Piroshky, Piroshky, or double back on Post Alley and ask for the thick slices of apple or marionberry pie at **Biringer Farms**. Intersperse these noshings with shots of Irish whiskey at **Kells Irish Restaurant and Pub**, more beers at **Lowell's Restaurant,** and finally, steaming cups of coffee at **Seattle's Best Coffee,** on the corner of Post Alley and Pine Street. Stagger home and sleep until you're hungry again. What a day.

Four Market restaurants worth searching for... The Market also has several fine-dining restaurants, most of which are tucked away in little crannies deep inside. The newest and best is **Le Pichet** (you Francophiles know that it means "the pitcher"), a sweet little bistro with tables crammed together that does the Parisian cheap eats thing just right. Grab an *assiette* of cheese or charcuterie, a crunchy pork confit, or a perfectly roasted chicken. You wash it all down with a variety of imported wines served in (naturally) ceramic pitchers. It can be a tough reservation, so book early. The same goes for **Chez Shea**, favorite Seattle restaurant of TV's Frasier—an elegant little nook with a view of Elliott Bay from the uppermost floor of the Corner Market building on First Avenue and Pike Street. Enter on First Avenue and keep going upstairs until you're at the top floor. The French/continental fare here might include rosemary butternut bisque, pan-roasted oysters with a pumpkin-seed crust, or a caramelized onion phyllo tart. **Campagne**, attached to the Inn at the Market, takes its culinary cues from Provence and has long been regarded as one of the great French bistros in town. Its courtyard location, views of the water, and linen tablecloths aim for a homey setting in the heart of the city. Try the tarte *Lyonnaise*, or three-course family dinners that might be poulet rôti one night, steak-frites another. The adjoining **Café Campagne** packs them in for Sunday brunches of *croque-madame* (ham and Gruyère on a thick slice of fresh bread with a fried egg on top) and big bowls of coffee. Fans of **Wild Ginger,** Seattle's most popular Asian restaurant, will be happy to hear that it's moved to spacious new digs near Benaroya Hall, but is still serving up terrific

Thai satays, Vietnamese spring rolls, and elegant little Chinese and Japanese nibbles. Despite the expansive quarters, it's still one of the toughest places in town to get a table, so book well in advance and be prepared to wait.

Where great views equal great seafood... Not so coincidentally, the great waterfront restaurants of Seattle double as the top seafood places. Huge **Palisade** is extremely popular, despite its out-of-the-way location adjoining the Smith Cove Marina between Queen Anne and Magnolia. You walk in on gray slate, past a pond with swimming fish and clinging starfish, to view an enormous dining room packed with everyone from grandparents on dates to prom kids in their finery. Palisade specializes in fish and does an annual promotion featuring seafood from around the world (at which time we head straight for the Moreton Bay Bugs—langoustines from Australia). It's anything but intimate, but the food is consistently good and you'll feel like you just ate well, albeit with the entire city sitting nearby. **Ray's Boathouse**, on Shilshole Bay in Ballard, is the local favorite for views and seafood. The decor is all polished wood and padded banquettes, but it's eclipsed by the floor-to-ceiling windows looking out onto Shilshole Bay and the bluffs of Discovery Park. We've had exquisite feeds of steamed clams, black cod, and smoked-salmon pasta here, but we've also had disappointments when the service was slow and the food spotty, thanks to the sheer volume of meals they turn out. The upstairs bistro, with a lively outdoor deck, provides lighter fare and a better chance for a drop-in seat than the downstairs dining room. **Anthony's Pier 66 & Bell Street Diner**, on the downtown waterfront a few doors down from the Edgewater Hotel, has a bit of a chain-restaurant feel, too, but we've eaten quite well there. The loftlike upstairs dining room has exposed steel beams counterpointed by dark Hawaiian koa wood accents. You can get first-rate salmon preparations or a Northwest "potlatch" of fresh shellfish. A family favorite is **Ivar's Salmon House**, on a quiet stretch of lakefront near Gasworks Park. While there are several fish-and-chips spots around town under the Ivar's name, this is the true experience, an authentic Seattle throwback. Built as an Indian longhouse, with totem poles and hand-carved canoes for decoration, Ivar's grills salmon the old way, butterflied and roasted over an alderwood fire. Families also flock to **Chinook's at Salmon Bay**, a sunlit industrial-type space overlooking the Alaskan fishing fleet in Magnolia. Its kitchen does a marvelous job with chowders and oyster stews, pan roasts and scallops, and a merely serviceable job with fresh salmon and halibut that come on a plate piled with roasted potatoes and vegetables. For a really unique view, **Salty's on Alki Beach,** in the bedroom community of West Seattle, has a magnificent city panorama, particularly from its outdoor deck on a warm summer night. It's big and noisy and serves seafood standards like alder-smoked salmon (try it stuffed with crab), fish and chips, and steamed clams.

If you're more interested in the seafood than the view... To avoid the crowds that flock to the waterfront places, head directly, while containing your unsightly drool, to Belltown's **Flying Fish** and **Etta's Seafood** in the Pike Place Market, both of which apply the highest culinary standards to seafood dishes. Chef/owner Christine Keff brings Asian influences to bear at Flying Fish; Thai crab cakes are a good bet, lobster risotto is a *really* good bet, or simply put yourself in the kitchen's capable hands with a fish dish you've never tried before. Expect a buzzing young urban crowd and a bustling, open kitchen. Tom Douglas, the presiding genius at Etta's Seafood, introduces you to marvels such as katzu black cod in a Japanese-style marinade, grilled prawns, or a whole tilapia with a crispy skin. The atmosphere is hip and informal, and you can eat your fish at a counter or one of two lively (okay, noisy) dining rooms.

When only exquisite will do... Although belts have been somewhat tightened thanks to the high-tech shakeout, you can still eat like you're on top of the wave. The "Best French" sobriquet has passed to **Rover's,** a favorite among Microsoft millionaires, which achieves a real French country-restaurant atmosphere, set in a frame house in Madison Park, away from the bustle of downtown. Warm and intimate, it makes you half expect to see a family watching TV in the next room. Chef Thierry Rautureau dazzles with his stocks and sauces; his lobster sauce is pure velvet, and he'll pinch pieces of foie gras and white truffle into the most unlikely places. The eight-course chef's choice menu accompanied by Northwest and French wines is the single most lavish meal in town. The old guard cling to their memories of **Canlis,** perched atop Queen Anne hill with a view of Lake Union and the Cascade Mountains, as the dress-up place of choice since 1950. Dark and atmospheric, it's dressed in Asian antiques (the waitresses only recently stopped wearing kimonos). It still has superb service and one of the best wine lists in town, though the traditional chophouse menu—prime rib, steaks, and broiled mahimahi—is a bit dated. It's the kind of fare your grandpa might get misty-eyed over. Considerably more hip (yet every bit as expensive) is Tamara Murphy's **Brasa,** which competes with **Cascadia** for the bragging rights to high-end cooking and clientele in Belltown. It's named after the wood-stoked oven that dominates the kitchen, but don't kid yourself that this place is a roast house. Murphy puts together wonderful combinations of ingredients, and the menu changes every few days. A lovely piece of slippery foie gras comes out alongside honey polenta and a dab of roasted acorn squash, for example, or suckling pig is nestled among clams, chorizo, and a laurel-scented potato. An eclectic wine list and sensational desserts put it over the top. **Fullers,** at the Sheraton, has slipped a bit since chefs like Caprial Pence and Monique Barbeau catapulted it to national attention, leading diners on dizzying journeys of artfully prepared and conceived continental food and memorable nights of plates dotted with three dazzling sauces, a perfect piece of grilled Alaskan char, a puff of blue potatoes, a drizzle of truffle oil. Newer Belltown restaurants threaten to make Fullers seem old and fusty, but that doesn't mean you shouldn't give it a try for a three-hour, multi-course meal that can still wow on occasion. The room is somewhat stiff and stuffy, with soft lighting and European oils on the walls—the kind of decor that would make Grandma nod appreciatively and whisper, "Fancy." A private dining room is a bit brighter and has a wonderful collection of pieces by renowned Northwest glass artist Dale Chihuly. And bet on **Cascadia**, the fine-dining restaurant in Belltown by Aussie Kerry Sears, who put The Georgian Room at the Four Seasons onto the local culinary map. He's trying to pull all of his ingredients from the Pacific Northwest and Cascade Range region: Oregon white truffle potato soup, or an herb-baked partridge with blackberry reduction. This boy can flat-out cook, and his wife, Heidi Grathwol, ably runs the cool, modern dining room with a fireplace accented in cherry woods and etched glass—look for the etching of Mount Rainier that is washed in perpetual rain. Sears' former restaurant **The Georgian Room**, now presided over by chef Gavin Stephenson, delivers that big-hotel dining feeling with white tablecloths, soaring ceilings, hushed atmosphere, and liveried waiters. The menu tends to be more conservative than in Sears's day—a grilled salmon, a rack of lamb, a beef tenderloin—but all are expertly prepared. For fun, check out the chef's table that Stephenson has created in the kitchen that gives a small group a bird's-eye view of the cooks at work.

Say "Olé!" to international flavors... Seattle's newest restaurants are reaching out toward international flavors that haven't been seen or tasted in these parts before. The prime example is Christine Keff's vibrant new **Fandango,** which brings pan-Latin flair to its big, cheerful space in Belltown. As calypso and salsa music pours out, waiters load you up with dishes that Keff discovered in her travels through Mexico and Latin America, then refined. She certainly hit a nerve, because the place is always packed. Try oxtail and chicken stew with yucca and plantains, or a rich Oaxacan green mole with chunks of pork and white beans. Eating in **Wild Ginger** is like doing a seminar on Asian food. They know their way around the cuisines of southeast Asia and allow you to mix and match styles and flavors. For French bistro fare, you can't go wrong with Seattle's two new hole-in-the-wall cafes. You could easily drive past **Cassis,** on Capitol Hill, or the Market's **Le Pichet,** and remain blissfully unaware of the fine French cooking served in both places. This is not fancy and stratospherically pricey *nouvelle cuisine* (you'll find that at **Rover's**), but simple, hearty fare with strong flavors. Try the steak-frites and a jug of red wine at either place and you'll go away a happier person. And if you love the food of northern Italy, especially from the Piedmont region, you'll have to haul yourself across Lake Washington to the suburb of Kirkland, where you'll be amply rewarded at **Café**

Juanita. There isn't a tomato in sight, but chef Holly Smith makes a stunning *fonduta* of melted fontina cheese and white truffles, and a highly satisfying spring lamb served with gnocchi.

On the cutting edge (thou art truly groovy)... At the heart of the Seattle restaurant scene is a clutch of independent restaurants that are all chasing the same upscale diners with magnificent food and ever-more-dazzling decor. Trendy Belltown is ground zero for these scene spots. Christine Keff's **Flying Fish** is a great example, a bright, vibrant place in the heart of Belltown that does impeccable seafood presentations with subtle Far Eastern flavor. Across the street, **El Gaucho** has been a huge hit ever since it opened as a retro urban steakhouse, with dark gray walls and a selection of meats unabashedly slathered in butter and rich sauces. The side dishes are called "starches" with no apologies, and salads come with Roquefort dressing. You finish off the whole thing with bananas Foster prepared at tableside, then vow to bring down your cholesterol count some other day. Behind its movie-style marquee out front, the **iCon Grill** in the shopping district is playful and fun, an airy space with lots of banquettes and a wild decor of blown-glass globes and dozens of small lamps. The not-so-serious theme carries over to the food, too, adding items like macaroni-and-cheese, fried chicken, and meatloaf to the pizzas and burgers, but you can still get a good piece of salmon, expertly broiled, and a Merlot-braised lamb shank that would be at home in any fine-dining eatery. Tom Douglas's sophisticated **Palace Kitchen**, also near the department stores and downtown malls, knows its urban clientele well, giving them a huge, horseshoe-shaped bar from which to watch each other, a view into the bustling kitchen, and a menu of flavorful, upscale bistro fare that satisfies most cravings. A few blocks away, Douglas's **Dahlia Lounge** has been revitalized by moving into larger digs uptown on Fourth Avenue. The crowd dutifully followed. It has the most Asian-fusion flavor of any of his places. The crab cakes are absolutely worth any price they ask, as is the delectable coconut-cream pie with shavings of white chocolate and coconut cascading off the plate. On the other end of the shopping district, **Sazerac**, at the Hotel Monaco, brings a New Orleans flavor to a big, loud room and a banging, open kitchen where chef Jan Bierbaum occasionally presides while splitting his duties between this and another restaurant in the Napa Valley. Two upscale eateries in Belltown, **Cascadia** and **Brasa**, showcase the respective culinary talents of Kerry Sears, late chef of the Four Seasons, and Tamara Murphy, the founding chef and wizard of Campagne. Cascadia's name refers to the nearby Cascade Mountains, source of many ingredients in Sears's inventive Northwest cooking; Brasa is named after the wood-fired oven and grill from which springs its Mediterranean menu, including delicacies like roasted shad roe or foie gras pizza. The crowd here is upscale Belltown, right down to the brass eyelets in their REI hiking boots.

Room service never had it so good... The hotel restaurant is usually the last place you want to eat, but Seattle hotels are blessed with terrific restaurants that stand on their own merits and compete with the indies. **Fullers,** at the Sheraton, **The Hunt Club**, at the Sorrento, and **The Georgian Room**, at the Four Seasons, are all fine-dining places with an air of lofty (okay, stuffy) service and standards. Fullers and The Georgian Room have lost the star chefs that first rocketed them to prominence, but their staying power has been remarkably good. The Hunt Club's chef Eric Lenard does a more-than-capable job with a fresh, lively Northwest cuisine—the Dungeness crab cakes in a lemon-butter sauce are awfully good—and the surroundings have an air of deal-making to them. The Alexis Hotel's **The Painted Table**, with its artfully presented Asian-fusion fare, and the Provençal charmer **Campagne** (Inn at the Market) are more fun and decorative but still take their food very seriously. At **Tulio Ristorante**, at the Hotel Vintage Park, chef Walter Pisano does a northern Italian turn and gets it all exactly right, from a convivial, welcoming room dressed in antique fabrics and coved ceilings to the handmade breads and pasta. The smoked-salmon ravioli is exquisite, as is the roasted chicken stuffed with garlic and sage. **Sazerac**, at the Hotel Monaco, is a scene-making room with huge portions of Creole-influenced food. It may be named after an obscure New Orleans cocktail of whiskey and Pernod, but this place is anything but obscure—it's a big, lively room with soaring ceilings and huge chandeliers, where chef Jan Birnbaum produces great slabs of beef smothered in spicy sauce, bowls of jambalaya, or spicy shrimp from an open kitchen.

Fun and cheap, and your kids will love it... Your kids will love the playful and wildly fanciful decor of **iCon Grill,** and you'll be able to get a good meal of grilled meats or fish while they knock back burgers or macaroni and cheese. The menu is broad enough to please everyone. Make sure you have them visit the restrooms, which are just as crazy as the rest of the place. The men's room has large video monitors that show continuous clips of gushing waterfalls, just in case you needed a little extra encouragement. The **Yankee Diner** is a real throwback, a traditional diner in a waterfront setting in the quiet, residential community of Ballard. It bakes its own breads and muffins, and pot roast is the specialty of the house. As you'd hope, breakfasts are enormous servings of eggs and potatoes. **Ivar's Salmon House** pleases with its Northwest-Indian longhouse-style decor and totem poles. If you can't talk the kids into trying salmon, sample the good fish and chips (tell 'em it's fish sticks) and clam chowder. **The Five Spot,** at the top of Queen Anne Hill, attracts both families and singles to its hip decor of hand-painted murals over chophouse-style booths and menus that change quarterly, but it always has a juicy burger or chicken dish available for kids. Go here for breakfasts of excellent coffee cakes, omelettes, and culinary salutes to far-flung lands (places like Brooklyn and New Orleans). If you want to try a local burger that's a cut above the fast-food chains, head to **Dick's Drive-In**, in Wallingford and Queen Anne, and accompany the cow and fries with a real, freshly made milkshake. Kids dig the *American Graffiti*–style drive-in scene; on most nights, the crowds are four-deep at the ordering windows.

Ciao, bambino!... Italian is another good bet for children and families, not to mention romantic couples who want to gaze at each other over long strands of spaghetti (it worked so well for Lady and the Tramp). The top of the line is in Kirkland at **Café Juanita,** where food critics are raving about chef Holly Smith and her northern Italian cuisine. If you've never been introduced to the pleasures of the white truffle, this is the place to try it. **Assaggio** is equally refined, an Old World restaurant with attentive service and excellent food. Occasionally, a local tenor stands up for an impromptu aria. The owner greets you in a tuxedo, and the walls are covered in Michelangelo-inspired frescoes in a downtown building that tries very hard to look like it was transported straight from Tuscany—and very nearly succeeds. **Tulio Ristorante** does a terrific job with northern Italian dishes; it's like coming home to Mama's kitchen. **Andaluca,** at the Mayflower Park Hotel downtown, broadens the menu to include pan-Mediterranean dishes, but the Italian risottos and bruschettas are first-rate.

Coffee shops to fall in love with... We'd be utterly remiss if we didn't mention coffee, Seattle's drug of choice, and the wonderful neighborhood coffee bars and espresso joints that make chain places like Starbucks seem like McCoffees. For fresh pastries, croissants, or bagels in the morning, foccacia sandwiches for lunch, or late-night desserts like exquisite pies and cakes, try some of these stops. **Café Bambino**, in Phinney Ridge, is a great example of the neighborhood coffee bar, a little shop owned and decorated by artist Andhi Spath (those are his faux bronzes decorating the counter and his cubist oils on the walls) with an outdoor patio, cookies and muffins from local bakers, and generous shots of that black espresso gold. The *barista* may play you in cribbage on the patio when she's not pulling espressos. On Capitol Hill, it's the **B&O Espresso**, which has a marvelous selection of sweets—thick slabs of gooey chocolate cake, apple pie, and cookies—that are eagerly scarfed by a mostly gay and tragically hip crowd clothed in black. On Queen Anne Avenue N., the **Uptown Espresso** and **Caffe Ladro** are just a couple of blocks away from each other. Each has fiercely loyal patrons who come for the coffee and buzzing ambience, especially late at night when the movie theaters and Seattle Center stages let out. Caffe Ladro tends to fill up at night with cineastes who love to debate movies and remember the place as "Cinema Espresso" a few years ago; patrons of the MarQueen Hotel use it as their breakfast hangout and aren't disappointed by the cinnamon rolls and croissants that go with the coffee. The Uptown is worth visiting time and again for a sensational apple pie, chocolate cake, and interesting muffins studded with delectable little things like marionberries. **Still Life in Fremont** is an old-style coffeehouse, a holdover from the hippie days, with its rickety wood tables, local art on the walls, folk musicians playing on weekends, and a kitchen that produces excellent soups, sandwiches (the Veggie Roll makes health food actually tasty), coffee cakes, and cookies. Of course, we're just scratching the coffee surface here; go around the block in any Seattle neighborhood and you'll find an espresso cart on the corner, a drive-through shack with excellent java and cookies, or a sit-down place with furniture and a fireplace.

The Index

$$$$$	over $50
$$$$	$40–$50
$$$	$30–$40
$$	$20–$30
$	under $20

Price categories reflect the cost of a three-course meal, not including drinks, taxes, and tip.

Andaluca. Mediterranean fare done just right, from paellas to risottos, with a long list of shareable appetizers to pass around.... *Tel 206/382-6999. 407 Olive Way. Reservations suggested. $$$* **(see p. 44)**

Anthony's Pier 66 & Bell Street Diner. One of the newer and more upscale places to dine on the downtown waterfront; it specializes in seafood and views, not necessarily in that order. The food is quite satisfying, however: Try the fresh shellfish "potlatch" or salmon done any way... *Tel 206/448-*

6688. 2201 Alaskan Way. Reservations advised. $$$
(see p. 37)

Assaggio. A great place for an atmospheric dinner of pasta, a lively *dolcetto*, and thou. It's a little bit of Tuscany in Seattle.... *Tel 206/441-1399. 2010 4th Ave. Reservations advised. $$$* **(see p. 44)**

B&O Espresso. Coffeehouse catering to a hip, Capitol Hill clientele.... *Tel 206/322-5028. 204 Belmont Ave. E. $* **(see p. 44)**

Biringer Farms. Pike Place Market outpost of a local grower, its berry pies and fruit tarts are fabulous.... *Tel 206/467-0383. 1530 Post Alley. $* **(see p. 36)**

Brasa. Newest venture of local star Tamara Murphy (late of Campagne).... *Tel 206/728-4220. 2107 3rd Ave. Reservations advised. $$$* **(see pp. 35, 39, 42)**

Café Bambino. A small neighborhood coffee bar with an outdoor patio.... *Tel 206/706-4934. 405 NW 65th St., Phinney Ridge. $* **(see p. 44)**

Café Juanita. Exquisite job done on strictly northern Italian high-end cuisine; the odor of white truffles permeates the place.... *Tel 425/823-1505. 9702 NE 120th Place, Kirkland. Reservations essential. $$$$* **(see pp. 40, 43)**

Caffe Ladro. One of Queen Anne's favorite coffee bars.... *Tel 206/282-1549. 600 Queen Anne Ave. N. $* **(see p. 44)**

Campagne. One of the great French restaurants in the city, situated in a lovely courtyard at the Market. The adjoining **Café Campagne** does a bistro menu.... *Tel 206/728-2800. 86 Pine St. Reservations required. $$$*
(see pp. 35, 36, 42)

Canlis. Chris and Alice Canlis continue a family tradition that began in 1950 with their classy (if somewhat dated) restaurant, perched high up on Queen Anne Hill.... *Tel 206/283-3313. 2576 Aurora Ave. N. Reservations required, jackets advised for men. $$$$* **(see pp. 34, 39)**

Cascadia. Chef Kerry Sears has upped the Belltown ante by bringing a white-tablecloth, fine-dining restaurant to the heart of trendsville.... *Tel 206/448-8884. 2328 1st Ave. Reservations advised. $$$$$* **(see pp. 33, 39, 42)**

Cassis. This little neighborhood restaurant on Capitol Hill serves French bistro fare with a flair. Good value, too, especially on the early-bird specials.... *Tel 206/329-0580. 2359 10th Ave. E. Reservations suggested. $$* **(see p. 40)**

Chez Shea. A lovely, romantic spot in a quiet, upper-floor corner of the Market. If you can't get in, try the tartly named **Shea's Lounge** next door for a bistro version of the menu.... *Tel 206/467-9990. 94 Pike St. Reservations advised. $$$* **(see p. 36)**

Chinook's at Salmon Bay. A bright, lively place with terrific oyster stew.... *Tel 206/283-HOOK. Fisherman's Terminal in Magnolia. Reservations advised. $$* **(see p. 38)**

Cucina Fresca. Wonderful Italian deli has some of the most interesting take-out in the city.... *Tel 206/448-4758. 1904 Pike Place (in Pike Place Mkt.). $* **(see p. 35)**

Dahlia Lounge. Tom Douglas's first solo restaurant is still doing bang-up business downtown (look for the neon sign of a chef carrying a fish).... *Tel 206/682-4142. 2001 4th Ave. Reservations advised. $$$* **(see pp. 34, 41)**

Dick's Drive-In. Move over, Wendy's and McDonald's: Dick's two locations rule Seattle's fast-food scene with juicy burgers and even better fresh milkshakes.... *Tel 206/632-5125. 111 NE 45th St., Wallingford; 500 Queen Anne Ave. N., Queen Anne. No reservations. $* **(see p. 43)**

El Gaucho. This hugely popular Belltown steakhouse has given Seattle diners-out divine license to eat meat again, and even dress up for a change. The Pampas Room downstairs is a lively jazz club.... *Tel 206/728-1337. 2505 1st Ave. Reservations advised. $$$* **(see pp. 33, 34, 41)**

Etta's Seafood. Tom Douglas's original seafood restaurant in the Market does some marvelous things with the abundant fresh catch of the region.... *Tel 206/443-6000. 2020 Western Ave. Reservations advised. $$$* **(see pp. 34, 38, 41)**

Fandango. Lively and bold Latin cuisine gets the fine-food approach from chef Christine Keff in this spacious Belltown space.... *Tel 206/441-1188. 2313 1st Ave. Reservations advised. $$$* **(see pp. 35, 40)**

The Five Spot. Atop Queen Anne Hill, it attracts a young, urban crowd with its rotating menus for breakfast, lunch, and dinner.... *Tel 206/285-SPOT. 1502 Queen Anne Ave. Reservations advised. $$* **(see p. 43)**

Flying Fish. One of the first defining restaurants of the Belltown dining scene, it's presided over by chef/owner Christine Keff, who brings Asian influences to the fresh seafood.... *Tel 206/728-8595. 2234 1st Ave. Reservations required. $$$* **(see pp. 35, 38, 41)**

Fullers. For many years one of the top fine-dining places in town, a big achievement for a hotel restaurant.... *Tel 206/621-9000. 1400 6th Ave. (at the Sheraton Seattle). Reservations required. $$$$* **(see pp. 39, 42)**

The Georgian Room. The fine-dining room at the Four Seasons Olympic, it delivers exactly what you'd expect.... *Tel 206/621-7889. 411 University St. Jackets required. Reservations advised. $$$$* **(see pp. 34, 35, 40, 42)**

The Hunt Club. Tally-ho, and it's off to this elegant, paneled room at the Sorrento Hotel. The Fireside Room is a delightful, dark bar that serves great big martinis.... *Tel 206/343-6156. 900 Madison St. Reservations advised. $$$* **(see pp. 34, 42)**

iCon Grill. This place exists purely for fun, with a menu that blends comfort food with fancier fare.... *Tel 206/441-6330. 1933 5th Ave. Reservations advised. $$* **(see pp. 41, 43)**

Ivar's Salmon House. Ivar's, named after a local restaurateur, is a chain of seafood restaurants around town. The real gem of the group is this quiet waterfront restaurant between the University district and Gasworks Park.... *Tel 206/632-0767. 401 NE Northlake Way. Reservations advised. $$* **(see pp. 37, 43)**

Jack's Fish Spot. It's mostly a fishmonger, but the stainless-steel counter on the side serves up terrific crab cocktails and fish and chips.... *Tel 206/467-0514. 1514 Pike Place. $* **(see p. 35)**

Kells Irish Restaurant and Pub. Handsome bar/restaurant at the Pike Place Market featuring Irish food and drink.... *Tel 206/728-1916. 1916 Post Alley at the Pike Place Market. $* **(see p. 36)**

Le Pichet. The cramped tables and dark room are straight out of Paris; fortunately, so is the food.... *Tel 206/256-1499. 1933 1st Ave. Reservations advised. $$$* **(see pp. 36, 40)**

Lowell's Restaurant. A working-class diner in the Market with unparalleled views of the sound, particularly when seen through the filter of numerous frosty beers.... *Tel 206/622-2036. 1519 Pike Place. No reservations. $* **(see pp. 35, 36)**

The Painted Table. A delightful fine-dining restaurant alongside the Alexis Hotel.... *Tel 206/624-3646. 92 Madison St. (at 1st Ave.). Reservations required. $$$$* **(see pp. 35, 42)**

Palace Kitchen. Top chef Tom Douglas uses this upscale bistro as his base of operations and serves sophisticated bistro fare.... *Tel 206/448-2001. 2030 5th Ave. Reservations advised. $$$* **(see pp. 35, 41)**

Palisade. Popular waterfront seafood restaurant, with a good array of local seafood plus fish flown in from around the world.... *Tel 206/285-1000. 2601 W. Marina Place. Reservations advised. $$$* **(see p. 37)**

Philadelphia's Deli. Little hole-in-the-wall joint at the Market satisfies those East Coast cravings.... *Tel 206/464-1899. 1514 Pike Place. $* **(see p. 35)**

Piroshky, Piroshky. The lines go out the door for to-die-for fresh pierogies and great apple tarts.... *Tel 206/441-6068. 1908 Pike Place. $* **(see p. 36)**

Rasa Malaysia. Indonesian lunch counter whips up remarkable stir-fries.... *Tel 206/624-8388. 1514 Pike Place. $* **(see p. 35)**

Ray's Boathouse. People absolutely fall in love with this big, two-story place on Shilshole Bay in Ballard, for years the undisputed champ for fresh seafood and views.... *Tel 206/789-3770. 6049 Seaview Ave. NW. Reservations advised. $$$* **(see p. 37)**

Rover's. Chef Thierry Rautureau's French restaurant has become the single best fine-dining restaurant in town, a speed-dial place for Microsoft executives and the business/gourmet elite. Take a trip to the French countryside.... *Tel 206/325-7442. 2808 E. Madison St. Reservations required. $$$$* **(see pp. 35, 38, 40)**

Salty's on Alki Beach. Seattleites cross the West Seattle bridge and go to Salty's for an unparalleled downtown skyline view from the spacious outdoor patio. It serves a standard seafood menu of salmon, crabs, and clams.... *Tel 206/937-1085. 1936 Harbor Ave. SW, West Seattle. Reservations advised. $$$* **(see p. 38)**

Sazerac. A fun restaurant where the food is good, spicy, and plentiful.... *Tel 206/624-7755. 1101 4th Ave. Reservations advised. $$$* **(see pp. 41, 42)**

Seattle's Best Coffee. Chain coffee place whose best outlet is the open-air venue at the Market.... *Tel 206/467-7700. 1530 Post Alley. $* **(see p. 36)**

Still Life in Fremont. A throwback to the hippie coffeehouse in funky Fremont. Music on weekends.... *Tel 206/547-9850. 709 N. 35th St. No reservations. $* **(see p. 45)**

Tulio Ristorante. Lively Italian place adjoining the Hotel Vintage Park.... *Tel 206/624-5500. 1100 5th Ave. Reservations advised. $$$* **(see pp. 42, 44)**

Uptown Espresso. One of the most vibrant and successful coffeehouses in town.... *Tel 206/281-8669. 525 Queen Anne Ave. N. No reservations. $* **(see p. 44)**

Wild Ginger. Last bastion of the Asian fusion craze, Wild Ginger endures with a fiercely loyal clientele. New and more spa-

cious digs have only served to raise the volume..... *Tel 206/623-4450. 1401 3rd Ave. Reservations advised. $$$*
(see pp. 36, 40)

Yankee Diner. Something for everyone in the family, and the diner food is a cut above. It's a good stop on the way to or from the Ballard Locks.... *Tel 206/783-1964. 5300 24th Ave. NW, Ballard. Reservations not required. $$* **(see p. 43)**

Seattle Downtown Dining

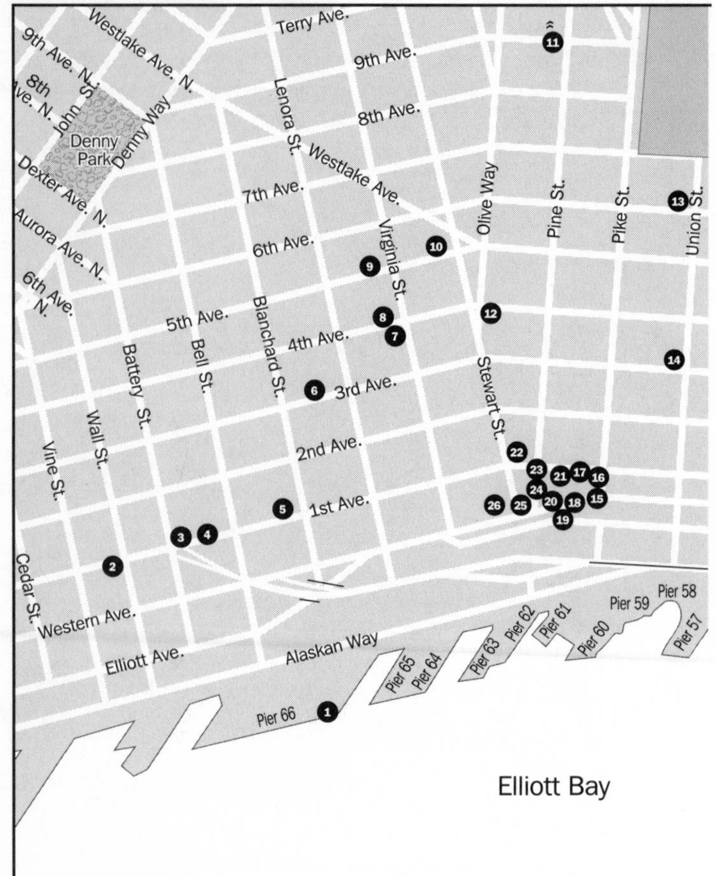

Andaluca **12**
Anthony's Pier 66
& Bell Street Diner **1**
Assaggio **8**
B&O Espresso **10**
Biringer Farms **18**
Brasa **6**
Campagne **24**
Cascadia **4**
Chez Shea **17**
Cucina Fresca **20**
Dahlia Lounge **7**
El Gaucho **2**
Etta's Seafood **26**
Fandango **3**
Flying Fish **5**
Fullers **13**
The Georgian Room **29**

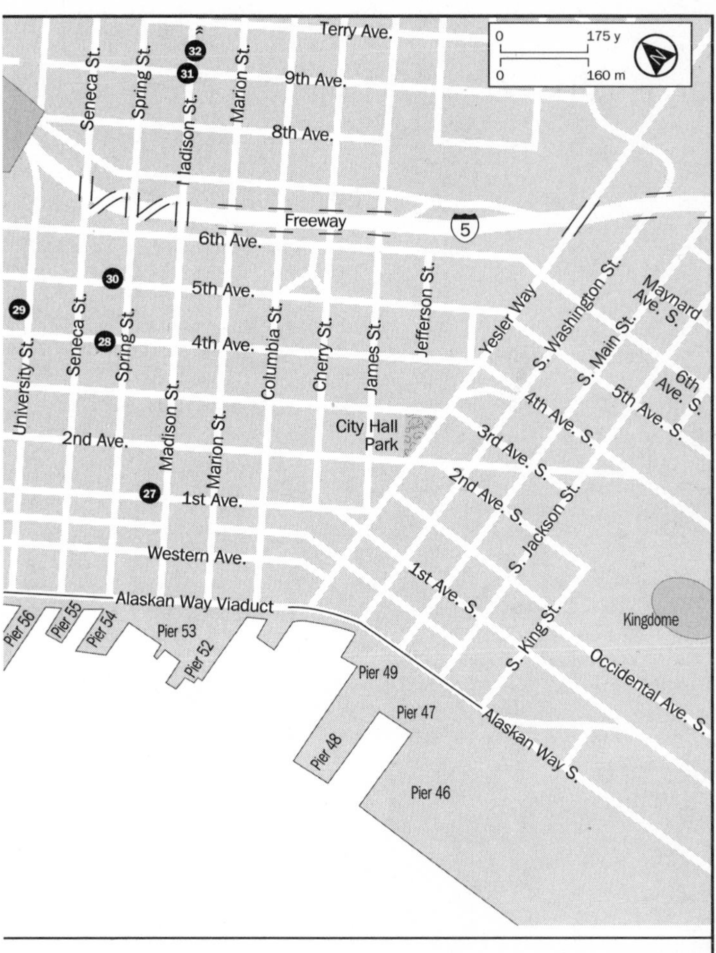

The Hunt Club **31**
iCon Grill **10**
Jack's Fish Spot **15**
Le Pichet **22**
Lowell's Restaurant **19**
The Painted Table **27**
Palace Kitchen **9**
Philadelphia's Deli **16**
Piroshky, Piroshky **25**
Rasa Malaysia **21**
Rover's **32**
Sazerac **28**
Seattle's Best Coffee **23**
Tulio Ristorante **30**
Wild Ginger **14**

Seattle–North & Northeast Dining

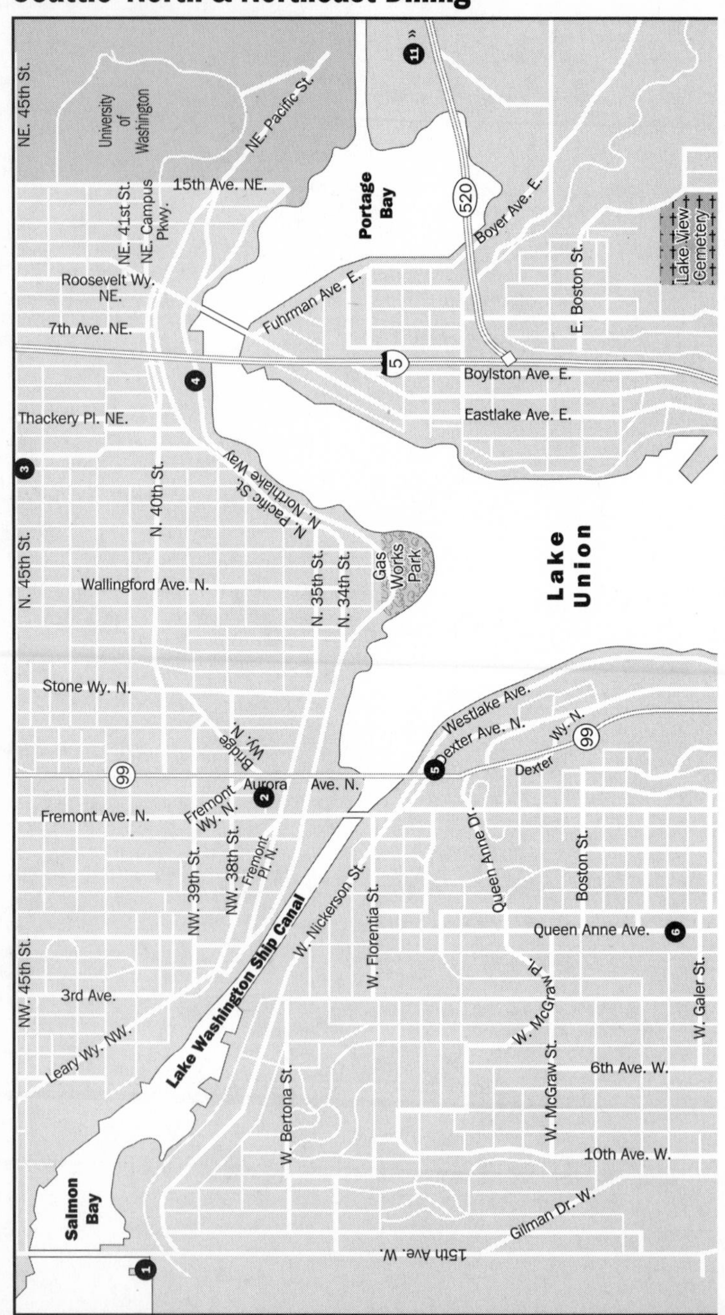

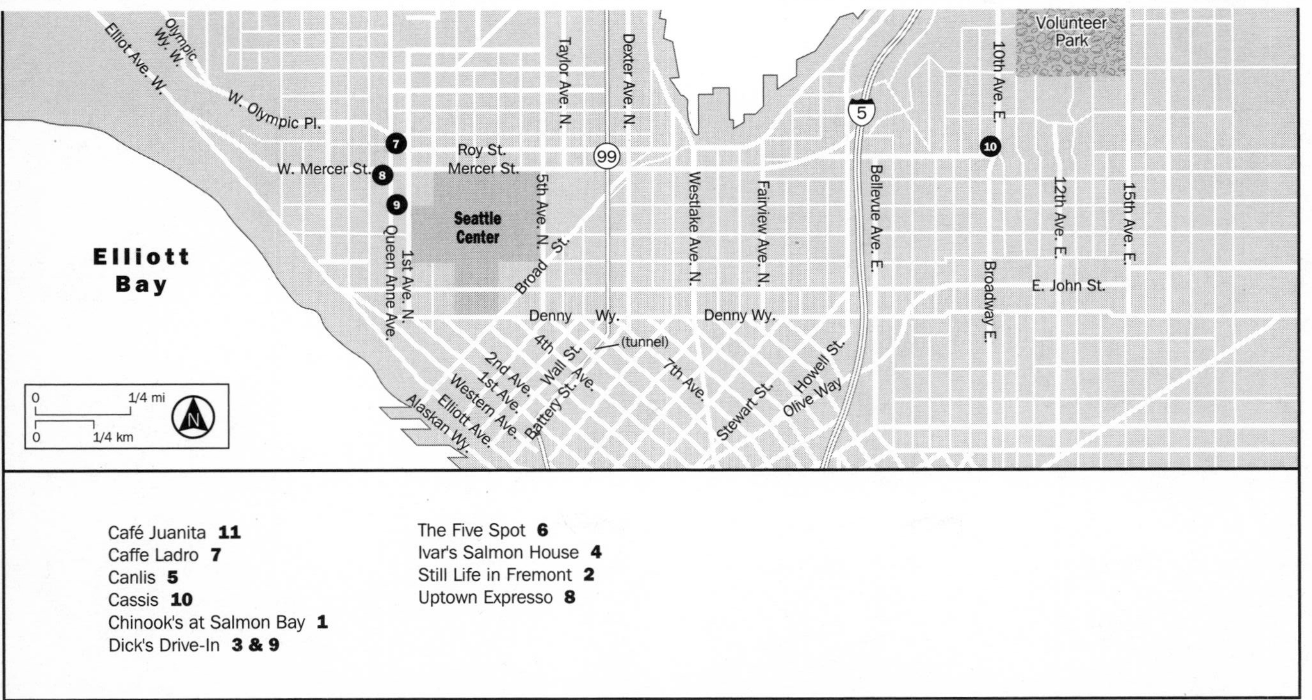

Volunteer Park
Olympic Wy. W.
Elliot Ave. W.
W. Olympic Pl.
Taylor Ave. N.
Dexter Ave. N.
99
5
10th Ave. E.
Roy St.
Mercer St.
W. Mercer St.
Seattle Center
5th Ave. N.
Broad St.
Westlake Ave. N.
Fairview Ave. N.
Bellevue Ave. E.
12th Ave. E.
15th Ave. E.
Elliott Bay
1st Ave. N.
Queen Anne Ave.
Broadway E.
E. John St.
Denny Wy.
Denny Wy.
(tunnel)
4th Ave.
Wall St.
2nd Ave.
1st Ave.
Western Ave.
Elliott Ave.
Alaskan Wy.
Battery St.
7th Ave.
Stewart St.
Howell St.
Olive Way
0
1/4 mi
0
1/4 km
Café Juanita 11
Caffe Ladro 7
Canlis 5
Cassis 10
Chinook's at Salmon Bay 1
Dick's Drive-In 3 & 9
The Five Spot 6
Ivar's Salmon House 4
Still Life in Fremont 2
Uptown Expresso 8

diver
SETH THOMAS

3

sions

Spend one winter here, and you quickly realize that if you stayed inside on every rainy day, you'd run out of food in a hurry and develop a terrible TV habit. So get over it, it's only rain. Seattle's many parks are even more lovely when viewed through the filter of a light mist that spritzes the trees and makes the grass glisten. We get outside at every opportunity for a walk or to play ball with the kids in a park, but when a storm front hovers over the city for a week at a time, there's plenty of other things to do. In other words, even when your stock options have collapsed, you can still enjoy a nice walk in a park.

A Traffic Advisory

It has been scientifically proven that the traffic here sucks. Avoid at all costs driving on I-5, the north-south artery that slices through town. Your best friend in Seattle will be ***Route 99****, also known as* ***Aurora Avenue****, a north-south thoroughfare that parallels I-5 through the center of town but has much less traffic. Use it to get from downtown to the airport (connecting with Routes 509 and 518; it's easy), or from downtown north to Green Lake. Or use* ***Westlake Avenue North*** *to shoot from downtown to Fremont, passing Lake Union and crossing the Fremont Bridge, which puts you onto Fremont Avenue North for access to Wallingford or the zoo.* ***Elliott Avenue West*** *connects to Alaskan Way at the waterfront and then becomes* ***15th Avenue West****, a main arterial that crosses the Ballard Bridge to Ballard.* ***Boren Street*** *is a shortcut from downtown to Capitol Hill and First Hill, turning left at Olive, Pike, or Madison street.*

Families with kids will love the parks with swing sets, slides, and wading pools, as well as the variety of amusements in Seattle Center. Romantics can get all snuggly over waterfront walks, ferry rides, and discovering absolutely the right restaurant. Everyone can enjoy an urban environment with plenty to do but few of the dangers of some cities. There's no single museum or attraction that you must absolutely see. Seattle itself is the main attraction, and gathering it all in will be your number-one goal.

Getting Your Bearings

Let's start at Safeco Field in **SoDo** (south of downtown), since it's the most expensive ballpark in the history of the earth. The **Downtown** area hugs the curve of Elliott Bay and Puget Sound to the west and then climbs steeply to **Capitol Hill** on the east. Within downtown are several sub-sections, all of which are close enough together to walk to. It begins with **Pioneer Square**, the oldest section of the city, which starts just north of Safeco Field. A few blocks up First Avenue is the **Pike Place Market**, centered on First and Pike streets, and beyond that starts **Belltown**, the newest trendy neighborhood in town. The center of the downtown **Shopping District** is at Fifth Avenue and Pine Street. Downtown officially ends when you cross Denny Way to the north, which puts you at the **Seattle Center** development that includes the Space Needle and the neighborhood of **Queen Anne**, which has commercial districts at both the top and bottom of Queen Anne Avenue North. **Magnolia** is the bedroom community on a hilly bluff to the north and west of Queen Anne. Beyond Queen Anne, a ship canal connects Puget Sound to **Lake Union** just north of downtown and **Lake Washington** to the east of the city. Drawbridges over the canal connect the city's northern neighborhoods, which include the Scandinavian-influenced **Ballard**, funky **Fremont**, gentrified **Wallingford**, and the **University District**, home of the University of Washington.

The Lowdown

The Big Three Festivals... If mega-crowds don't faze you (we're talking upwards of 80,000 people at a time here) and you want to experience a cherished part of the local cultural scene, attend one of the three huge civic festivals held every year at **Seattle Center**. On Memorial Day weekend every spring, the **Northwest Folklife Festival** brings three days of folk acts to a dozen different venues inside Seattle Center. For a daily admission fee, you can see Scandinavian dancers, Native American drummers, bluegrass guitar players, and polka bands, among many others, in a massive celebration of folk music and culture. Food is the sole concern of **Bite of Seattle**, held in July, again at Seattle Center, where most of the best restaurants and bistros in town set up booths and sell small portions of their specialties for a few bucks per serving. The grazing potential is unsurpassed, even if the place is absolutely mobbed—get there early on Friday for the smallest crowds and best access. I usually dart in for a surgical strike of gyros, salmon, and an enormous strawberry shortcake, and then get out of there just as fast, but there are people who spend all day wandering the stalls and communing with the throngs. Last year's top find: "miyis" (pronounced MY-wise), an Australian empanada with a superb crust and spicy fillings. The biggest and best event of the year is

Bumbershoot, held over Labor Day weekend, when Seattle Center is transformed into an enormous concert venue, this time with everyone from grunge bands to cowboy poets doing their thing on different stages, capped by national acts like Bonnie Raitt or Elvis Costello headlining in Memorial Stadium. Any festival that includes everyone from Janis Ian to Sonic Youth can't be bad. One ticket price usually covers everything but the headliner, and you can wander from dance performances to literary readings to musical events until you are completely glutted with culture. Don't even think about parking near Seattle Center for these festivals; hoof it in or take the bus, and you'll save yourself an extraordinary amount of hassle and stress.

When the mountain is out... When finally the clouds lift (as they always do eventually, if you just wait a month or two), locals head straight to their favorite lookouts to see *IT*, the guardian spirit that hovers over the city, that is, when it's not vanishing for months at a time. *IT* is **Mount Rainier** [see Great Outdoors], the 14,410-foot sentinel that starts about 100 miles south of the city but appears to be looming right up from South Seattle, just behind the downtown skyscrapers. At different times, in different lights, it looks like a great, craggy heap of snow and rock, a big mound of whipped cream with a swirl on top, or a mirage floating on a bank of clouds. Seeing it, especially after a rough period of winter weather, is an instant reminder of how dramatically beautiful this place can be and how summer weather, with its entire weeks of Rainier vistas, is never too far away. It's the locals' favorite mood enhancer. "The mountain is out!" they say with great relief to friends and neighbors. Everyone also thrills to the sight of the Cascade and Olympic Mountain ranges standing as snow-capped sentinels on either side of the city. Head to **Kerry Park**, on Highland Avenue North in Queen Anne, for an unsurpassed view of the city and Mount Rainier, and then walk west on Highland to catch a great view of the sound and the Olympics. The Alaskan Way waterfront and **Bainbridge Island Ferry** are also superb places to gaze at the snowcapped Olympics; from the northern end of Alaskan Way, near the Edgewater Hotel, you can see Mount Rainier peeking down on Safeco Field, the Mariners' hypercool new stadium.

On the University of Washington campus, find your way to Red Square, bordered by the two main libraries, and then look past the fountain for a stellar view of Mount Rainier, Lake Washington, and the Cascades.

About That Weather

Though the tourist bureau folks crow that Seattle receives less annual rainfall than New York City, that fact, while true, is seriously misleading. Our rain comes in small amounts spread out over more than 200 days a year. It's rare to get two successive days of true downpour, but from mid-October to mid-March, it rains almost continuously—which is to say that the skies remain gray and showers can fall at any time. We are compensated for this by the fact that it very rarely gets below freezing, thanks to those same Pacific breezes that bring the rain. It can get very scary around here when it freezes—roads get icy on a moment's notice, and the city's so hilly that driving becomes a real adventure. Snowy days in Seattle are rare—maybe one a year—and enjoyed by all, because the city virtually shuts down. Spring can be maddening, with temperatures rarely breaking 60. Summer doesn't start until after the 4th of July—and then it's like a magic switch has been flicked. We'll get about 80 continuous days of dazzling sunshine and 75-degree weather. In truth, we locals don't really mind all the rain, unless it brings landslides and flooding, that is.

When the mountain is in... Here's a question for you theologians: If Our Maker had intended us to stay inside on rainy days, why did he give us Gore-tex shoes and Helly-Hansen raingear? Walking in a park is a lovely way to get a big dose of Northwest trees and that addictively lovely, rainy smell. Grab a hat and your rubber shoes and head off to **Carkeek Park** to follow a winding, muddy trail all the way down a hillside to Puget Sound. **Woodland Park**, home of the zoo, lives up to its name with acres and acres of tall trees. If you stumble upon the rockery where people leave heads of lettuce and bunches of carrots, you'll know you've found the bunny hutch, residence of dozens of wild rabbits. The **Washington Park Arboretum** labels its acres of trees for quick identification, and adds a lovely Japanese garden that is perfect for misty-day contemplations. When the flowers bloom in April, the place is a wonderland (but frequently a boggy wonderland; wear appropriate footwear). **Discovery Park,** in Magnolia, is enormous and sprawling, with trails that lead through heavy woods to a rocky beach or to play areas (the one on the north side of the park has the longest slide in Seattle). The beaches are also great places to stroll (God knows we get little swimming use out of them). Go to the end of the boardwalk at **Golden Gardens** in Ballard, and you might see egrets, cormorants, dolphins, or sea lions.

The newest and coolest... That bizarre building that looks like a pile of the Space Needle's rumpled laundry is Paul Allen's **Experience Music Project,** a $100 million museum dedicated to (try to follow me here) experiencing music. Design is by architect Frank Gehry (we still can't decide if we like the building or not), and inside you'll find galleries with rock artifacts like Jimi Hendrix's guitars and Elvis's leather jacket. An enormous video wall called the Sky Church doubles as a concert venue, and a very cool, very high-tech Sound Lab allows you to play instruments and learn the opening notes to "Jumping Jack Flash," among other rock anthems. Headphone devices bludgeon you with just as much background info and sound bites as you could possibly want. Allen, who is fast becoming our favorite billionaire, also shelled out the cash to renovate the **Cinerama Theater** on Sixth Avenue downtown. It was on the brink of being torn down before he threw wads of money at it and made it the premier movie house in town with every imaginable digital bell-and-whistle and that still-impressive, curving Cinerama screen.

Museums the whole family can explore... Boeing shocked the city by moving its corporate big cheeses out of town, but it still has a considerable presence. The **Museum of Flight** showcases a spectrum of aircraft (many of them built by Boeing), including a replica of the Wright Brothers' glider, a DC3, a biplane, and an Apollo space capsule that you can look into. The adjacent Red Barn, with an exhibition on the history of flying, was Boeing's original factory dating from 1910. The hangar-sized galleries give a properly grand scope to the whole aviation theme. You can also tour the **Boeing** manufacturing facility in the northern suburb of Everett, which takes place in a building touted as the world's largest space under one roof. From catwalks, you watch as enormous pieces of fuselage and wing come together and are connected; you may be surprised to see the greenish metal skin of an unpainted airliner before the logo colors of an airline go on. At the hands-on **Pacific Science Center**, part of the Seattle Center entertainment complex, you can study dinosaur fossils and play with kinetic exhibits while younger children blow enormous bubbles or play with waterjets and older kids try a virtual basketball game played against a giant. A number of interactive stations demonstrate how your eyes, ears, and bones work; animatronic dinosaurs move and bellow: a good time is generally had by all. An IMAX Theater and a planetarium are also inside the Science Center, with separate admission. The above-mentioned **Experience Music Project** has stations where you can play instruments, as well as a motion-simulator ride that takes you into the heart of a funky concert. The **Burke Museum of Natural History and Culture**, on the University of Washington campus, has fossils, dinosaur bones, an enormous wall of bugs under glass, and a walk-through volcano in its Life and Times of Washington State exhibit. It makes a nice stop on a walk around the campus, but we wouldn't plan a whole day around it. The cloyingly sweet quotient goes up a little at the **The Children's Museum** in Seattle Center, an interactive kid-sized environment with tubes to crawl through and a simulated mountain to explore. Younger children will love it, though, and you can get a decent cup of coffee and a fresh beignet or elephant's ear from the take-out counters of the Seattle Centerhouse to ease your pain. Okay, it's not a museum, but **GameWorks**, the video-game chain created by Steven Spielberg's DreamWorks SKG Studio, might as well be. It has incredible games and simulations that represent the best of computer gaming technology, much of it created in Seattle.

More grown-up museums... When the **Seattle Art Museum** relocated downtown in 1991, it was an instant sensation, with Jonathon Borofsky's enormous, shadowy *Hammering Man* sculpture looming over the entrance courtyard. This museum tries a little too hard to please a lot of people, with widespread permanent collections of Northwest Coast Native American art, African art, and painting galleries that go from the medieval to the modern. Major exhibitions come through here, such as a collection of artifacts from ancient Egypt or Bill Gates's original Da Vinci manuscript, which he temporarily displayed here while his library was being built. For special exhibits, compact disc players are supplied so each patron can listen to adult- or kid-oriented commentaries on major exhibits, which allows everyone to tour at his or her own pace. The art museum's old home in Volunteer Park, a cool Art Deco stone building, is now the **Seattle Asian Art Museum**, home to a premier collection of art and artifacts from the Far East, with an emphasis on Chinese and Japanese collections, including rooms of Japanese screens or folk art. The setting is as tranquil as the galleries. The **Frye Art Museum**, a small private museum on First Hill, specializes in 19th-century painters like Winslow Homer, Edward Hopper, and Thomas Hart Benton, with a Picasso thrown in for good measure. Although its commitment to figurative art remains true to the dictates of the founding Frye family, the museum has become much more lively and vital since a 1997 remodeling.

Animal magnetism... There are aquariums that give you gaily colored tropical fish, and then there's the **Seattle Aquarium**. The coral-reef tank with its cruising sharks never fails to excite, but the aquarium's best may be the Puget Sound exhibits, where you can pet a starfish and see the lingcod, wolf eels, and a giant Pacific octopus named Neah, whose relatives inhabit the chilly waters of the sound. Short of donning scuba gear and jumping into the frigid sound, you won't get a better look at its inhabitants. In Ballard, the fish ladders and viewing windows of the **Hiram M. Chittenden Locks** can provide an absolutely jaw-dropping view of wild and farm-raised salmon fighting their way upstream from Puget Sound to inland lakes and rivers (and it's free). When the fish are really running, it beats the aquarium hands-down for sheer drama—these fish are literally fighting for their lives. The salmon used to run thick in local waters year-round, but dwindling salmon numbers now make it highly seasonal. We've had good luck at the viewing windows in recent summers, however, when chinook and salmon return to spawn. To watch a 15-pound fish trying to push its way upstream through the surging waters of the fish ladder is practically a religious experience, but even when they're not running, it's still fun to visit the park and locks, which raise and lower all kinds of boats (from barges to kayaks) from Puget Sound to lake levels. The sprawling **Woodland Park Zoo**, its entrance at the top of a hill in a quiet, residential neighborhood in Fremont, has a marvelous "African Savannah" of grasslands that houses lions, zebras, and giraffes (not all together, or there would be carnage). Even better is the perspective on brown bears from windows that front their bathing pond, revealing an over and underwater view of the bears at play. Don't miss the Nocturnal House of bats, the collection of snakes and spiders, and the excellent gorilla habitat. A summer concert series brings folk and acoustic musicians to the zoo for after-hours shows, while the adjacent Rose Garden is a microcosm of the renowned International Rose Test Garden in Portland.

Truly cheesy attractions... So you came all the way from Poughkeepsie to walk around Seattle's forgotten underground tunnels? Fine, great, have a swell time on the **Seattle Underground Tour**, which tourists flock to. The historical basis is that the downtown streets got so muddy and impassable after a fire that the city rebuilt itself one story higher, leaving the original storefronts behind. The tour basically consists of walking, doubled over, through subterranean passages of preserved turn-of-the-century storefronts, while a tour guide/comedian tries to break the world's record for bad jokes per minute. The waterfront on Alaskan Way has all kinds of cheap souvenir shops and faux–Native American artifacts, reaching a kind of cheesy zenith at **Ye Olde Curiosity Shop**, which puts carney-style oddities like a mummified body, Siamese-twin cows, and shrunken heads (their little lips sewn tightly shut) alongside its selection of T-shirts and Space Needle pencil sharpeners. Creepy, man!

The eye of the Needle... By all means, you must take the elevator to the top of the **Space Needle** at least once while you're in town. If you're brave, venture out onto the open-air observation deck, 520 feet high in the sky, which has nice signage pointing out what you can see in all directions (on a sunny day), and just enough space between the railings to give you a chilling look down. If you're chicken, stay inside the gift shop at the top and peek at the views over the Space Needle souvenirs. Have a drink in the revolving bar/restaurant, but we don't recommend dining there—it's usually packed and overpriced. That's just the start of a visit to **Seattle Center**, the aging but still quite entertaining complex just to the north of downtown that was originally built for the 1962 World's Fair. An amusement park has roller coasters and a log flume ride, along with the usual ball-and-dart games for stuffed-animal prizes. A big arcade has the latest video games (it doesn't hold a candle to **GameWorks**, a few blocks away, but it's a lot cheaper), and the Centerhouse is home to **The Children's Museum** (a hands-on experience for the under-six set) and numerous restaurant counters that specialize in kid-friendly fare like hot dogs and pizza. On most Saturday nights, the Centerhouse is crowded with ballroom dancers of all ages who twirl to live big-band music played by combos of little old men. Outside, the enormous Seattle Center fountain, encircled by amphitheater-style cement seats, gives a great free show on a warm night, as the waters surge in a computer-programmed musical spectacle and screaming kids run in and out of the spray. **Experience Music Project,** Paul Allen's new museum, is also part of the complex, with its eye-popping Frank Gehry architecture and interactive exhibits that explore the joys of music. Check out the awesome IMAX movies shown at the **Pacific Science Center,** where a gigantic screen and seriously raked auditorium set the stage for marvelous moviegoing, or snag tickets for shows at the **Seattle Children's Theater, Pacific Northwest Ballet, Intiman Theatre,** or **Seattle Opera** [see Nightlife and Entertainment for all four of these venues]. And though it's not the futuristic wonder it seemed to be in 1962, the monorail that runs from Seattle Center to the Westlake Center shopping mall downtown is still a fun ride, especially for kids.

Visualizing Ballard and other neighborhoods... Get past the downtown and you'll quickly discover that Seattle is really a city of neighborhoods, each with its own distinctive personality—or lack thereof, as in the case of **Ballard**, whose stubbornly bland and geriatric personality gives rise to the local joke "Visualize Ballard." Even Ballard, however, has its own flavor; settled by Scandinavians and sailors, it has old bars near the ship canal and the Swedish stores on Market Street that retain a nautical and Nordic feel. Then there's **Capitol Hill**, the gay, trendy quarter of town; a walk down Broadway will reveal more spiked blue hair and dog collars per square inch than any other place north of Portland. Stop for a beer or two at the Deluxe Bar & Grill, walk the walk on Broadway, and then repair to the B&O Espresso for cake, coffee, and contemplation of what the whole scene says about humanity in general (discuss amongst yourselves). Centrally located **Fremont**, the former hippie enclave (it's now the site of expensive condos and Adobe software), likes to call itself "the center of the universe" and prides itself on perverse public art, like an enormous bronze statue of Lenin (in front of a taco stand) and the hysterical one-eyed troll who lives under the Fremont Bridge and is about to swallow an entire Volkswagen. There are quiet, peaceful walking trails along both sides of the ship canal just west of the Fremont drawbridge, if you can tear yourself away from the antique and kitsch stores. The central suburb of **Wallingford** has a lively commercial district on NE 45th Street and expensive homes that look south to Gasworks Park and Lake Union, and **Madison Park** is a neat, orderly neighborhood alongside Lake Washington with some terrific bars and restaurants.

Homes of the rich and famous... Want to see some of Seattle's finest old homes? These walks are among the loveliest in town, and a great way to get out of the tourist areas and immerse yourself in local neighborhoods on a pleasant day. On **Capitol Hill**, walk the blocks from 11th to 15th avenues east around Volunteer Park and you'll see the huge Victorian homes of the lumber barons and old-money burghers who built the city of Seattle. Most of these old houses have been cut up into apartments, but they're still glorious to look at and daydream about (until you calculate what they might cost to heat). Newer money has set up the middle of **Queen Anne Hill** as its residence of choice. Stroll down Prospect Avenue North walking west from Queen Anne Avenue North to see some fancy million-dollar digs with even fancier views of downtown and the sound, and then continue up the hill to Highland Avenue North for terrific city panoramas and even more fancy mansions. The big brick building at the top of the hill used to be an elementary school and has been transformed into pricey condos for those wealthy people who could never quite get school out of their systems. **Wallingford** is a family neighborhood with great playgrounds and lots of those wood-framed Craftsman homes from the '20s and '30s that have wide porches and attics that get pinched into an inverted V shape. Stroll the streets from Wallingford Avenue North to Meridian Avenue North to see where Seattle's architects, doctors, and lawyers are living, with views of Lake Union and Mount Rainier as their backdrop. For a really sensational tour of the biggest and best estates, take a boat ride on **Lake Washington,** and you'll pass not only Bill Gates's woodsy five-acre estate but some magnificent lakefront mansions that look like they've been plucked straight out of Newport, Rhode Island, or Long Island by Seattle's wealthy scions of business and industry. You can paddle the lake yourself in a rented kayak [see Getting Outdoors] or go on an organized tour of the lake with **Argosy Cruises**.

Dropping by Bill's
You may enjoy simply cruising past Microsoft cofounder Bill Gates's home on a Lake Washington boat tour, or you may be one of those who simply has to know what goodies are inside. The 40,000-square-foot mansion is a high-tech wonder: It is said to contain a 24-screen video wall, two spas, an arcade, a theater, a library, and an outsized reception hall. Guests invited over for the weekend can kick back in the 1,700-square-foot guesthouse. For the athletically inclined, Bill has kindly supplied a 60-foot pool, sauna, sport court, dock for water skiing, and a room with a trampoline. Visiting anglers will be mighty pleased with the trout stream. And, if you want to be the neighbor of the richest man in the country, keep in mind that many of the homes in this neck of the woods have been assessed in the double-digit millions.

The duck stops here, and other tours... There are boat tours, and then there's **Ride the Ducks**, which offers wacky open-air tours of downtown and Fremont using renovated WWII amphibious landing craft that wind up by plopping into the water for a quick cruise around Lake Union. The duckboats (you may recognize them from the horrific first scene of *Saving Private Ryan*), which have been painted white and given a duck logo, waddle on their merry way accompanied by lively patter from the driver and quacks from the kazoo-like beaks handed to patrons. They're truly ridiculous and fun, and still draw plenty of astonished stares from passersby. **Argosy Cruises**, based on the waterfront, operates a number of boat tours of the lakes, sound, and Ballard Locks, including dinner cruises, a Seattle waterfront tour, a tour that passes through the Ballard Locks, and the ever-popular two-hour boat cruise past Bill Gates's house on Lake Washington. Train buffs love the **Spirit of Washington Dinner Train**, a restored classic train with cars and engine from the '30s that runs on private rails through the woodsy eastside suburbs of Renton, Bellevue, and Woodinville, with some handsome views of Lake Washington. The food is rather pricey, but it's generally tasty and is served on elegant white tablecloths. The tour makes a stop at the Columbia Winery for a wine tasting (and buying) visit before returning to its starting point in Renton, about half an hour out of town. When Seattle was rebuilt after a devastating 1889 fire, leaving the original storefronts and streets below the present street level, it unwittingly paved the way for the dopey, if wildly popular, **Seattle Underground Tour**, which could be a neat way to see a preserved city-beneath-the-city—except that the wisecracking guides and shuffling crowds can get old real fast.

Ferry-tale ride... If you want to see Seattle by water, you need only buy a $4 ticket for the Bainbridge, Vashon, or Bremerton **ferries** from the Colman Dock ferry terminal downtown. The **Bainbridge Island Ferry** run is especially scenic, a half-hour ride with lovely views of the downtown waterfront and islands in the sound. Take it at dusk and you'll see the whole city aglow as you cross to Bainbridge Island, where a short walk will take you into the town of Winslow for a drink or a coffee. Traveling back to Seattle is free if you've walked on—you'll have to wait in line and pay again if you drove—and the downtown skyline will be lit up from Safeco Field to the Space Needle if you return after dark. You can do this trip by car, too, but be warned that it's considerably more expensive and you can wait for hours in the holding lot. Walk-on passengers can always board the next ferry.

The Index

Argosy Cruises. This local boat-cruise operator has 12 different departures a day throughout the summer.... *Tel 206/623-4252. www.argosycruises.com. Ticket booth at Pier 55, 1101 Alaskan Way at Seneca St. Reservations essential in summer.* **(see pp. 68, 69)**

Bainbridge Island Ferry. See Washington State Ferries, below.

Bite of Seattle. Seattle Center's annual three-day homage to local food and massive crowds. It's held every July, with more than 90 food vendors (many of them local restaurants and bistros), live music, and several beer gardens where you can wash all the food down.... *Tel 206/232-2982. www.biteofseattle.com. Seattle Center. 11am–9pm. Fri–Sat; 11am–8pm Sun. Admission free.* **(see p. 59)**

Boeing Tour. A suitably impressive tour of a major manufacturing facility, where you can see airliners such as the new 777 being pieced together in massive sections. Tours are first-come, first-served.... *Tel 206/544-1264 or 800/464-1476. Boeing Tour Center on WA 526 in Everett, 30 miles north of Seattle. Tours 9am–3pm, Mon–Fri. Children must be at least 4' 2" tall to take the tour. Admission charged.* **(see p. 62)**

Bumbershoot. The best entertainment buy in town, with $10 advance tickets buying you a day of tromping around Seattle Center during Labor Day weekend and entrance to everything from fiction readings to nonstop movies, folk acts, and punkers. Extra charges for headline acts in Memorial Stadium.... *Tel 206/281-8111. www.bumbershoot.org. Seattle Center. Labor Day weekend only; multiple-day tickets available.* **(see p. 60)**

Burke Museum of Natural History and Culture. Located on the U-Dub campus, this natural-history museum appeals to families. Note: Parking and access are far easier on weekends.... *Tel 206/543-5590. www.washington.edu/burkemu seum. On the UW campus at 17th Ave. NE and NE 45th St. Daily 10am–5pm. Admission charged.* **(see p. 63)**

Carkeek Park. Wooded ravine that runs through a Ballard neighborhood with forested trails that lead from a hillside to Puget Sound, and broad, grassy areas for picnicking and playing.... *Tel 206/684-4081 to reserve picnic tables. 950 NW Carkeek Rd. & 9th Ave. NW. Free.* **(see p. 61)**

The Children's Museum. Designed for toddlers and preschool children, it's located in the Seattle Centerhouse, which has lots of take-out food counters and frequent special events.... *Tel 206/441-1768. www.thechildrensmus eum.org. Seattle Center. 10am–5pm Tue–Sun. Admission charged.* **(see pp. 63, 66)**

Cinerama Theater. A 68-foot screen and unbelievable digital sound system give you all the movie grandeur you could want, and you could fit several multiplexes inside its cavernous interior.... *Tel 206/441-3080. www.seattle.citysearch.com. 2100 4th Ave. at Lenora St. Admission.* **(see p. 62)**

Discovery Park. At 513 acres, it's the biggest park in town. Woodsy trails, a jogger's loop, a great play area for kids, and occasional sightings of bald eagles.... *Tel 206/386-4236 for guided tours on weekends. 3801 W. Government Way in Magnolia. Free.* **(see p. 62)**

Experience Music Project. The eagerly awaited museum of music put together by financier Paul Allen, with an incredible modern design, has rock 'n' roll artifacts and hands-on instruments.... *Tel 206/770-2700. www.emplive.com. 2901 3rd Ave., at Seattle Center. Open 10am–6pm Sun–Thur, 10am–1pm Fri–Sat. Admission charged.* **(see pp. 62, 63, 66)**

Frye Art Museum. Late–19th century American painting is the focus of this private collection.... *Tel 206/622-9250. www.fryeart.org. 704 Terry Ave. at Cherry St. 10am–5pm Tue–Sat., noon–5pm Sunday. Admission free.* **(see p. 64)**

GameWorks. The first of Steven Spielberg/DreamWorks' nationwide chain of video arcades; still a video game parlor for kids and teens, but with spectacular simulation and virtual-reality games. Great fries and pizza, too.... *Tel 206/521-0952. www.gameworks.com. 1511 7th Ave. at Pike St. Admission free; games $1.50–$2.50 per play.* **(see pp. 63, 66)**

Golden Gardens. Rocky, grassy area in Ballard that passes for a beach on frigid Shilshole Bay, but the wetlands with a boardwalk provide good wildlife spotting.... *Northernmost end of Seaview Ave. NW, past the Ballard Locks. Free.* **(see p. 62)**

Hiram M. Chittenden Locks. The Army Corps of Engineers operates locks that move boats between the high waters of Lake Union to the low waters of Puget Sound. To watch salmon migrate, head for the viewing windows showcasing the fish ladder on the south side of the complex.... *Tel 206/783-7059. 3015 NW 54th St., in Ballard. Admission free.* **(see p. 64)**

Kerry Park. Seattle's favorite views of downtown, the Space Needle, and Mt. Rainier on a clear day on this narrow strip of grass and pavement in Queen Anne.... *W. Highland Dr. at 3rd Ave. W. Free.* **(see p. 60)**

Museum of Flight. A big steel-and-glass aviation museum on the grounds of a Boeing manufacturing facility.... *Tel 206/764-5720. www.museumofflight.org. 9404 E. Marginal Way S. Daily 10am–5pm (until 9pm Thur). Admission charged.* **(see p. 62)**

Northwest Folklife Festival. A four-day Memorial Day weekend festival featuring terrific folk entertainment—including African dancers, bluegrass musicians, Irish cloggers, Kabuki performances, and cowboy and logger poets. Food booths, too.... *Tel 206/684-7300. www.nwfolklife.org. Seattle Center. Admission charged.* **(see p. 59)**

Pacific Science Center. A science museum that truly gets kids interested in the workings of the world, because it's so hands-on. IMAX films are shown throughout the day; advance tickets available at the ticket booth behind the Pacific Science Center on the northwest side.... *Tel*

206/433-IMAX. There's also a planetarium (separate admission).... *Tel 206/443-2001. www.pacsci.org. 200 2nd Ave. N. at Seattle Center. Daily 10am–6pm. Admission charged.* **(see pp. 63, 66)**

Ride the Ducks. WWII amphibious landing craft have been rehabilitated as tour vehicles; you'll get a good orientation to downtown followed by a quick cruise on Lake Union. Lots of fun.... *Tel 206/441-3825. www.ridetheducksofseattle.com. Ticket kiosk at Seattle Center between the Space Needle and Monorail. Multiple tours daily; reservations accepted.* Admission charged. **(see p. 68)**

Seattle Aquarium. This large waterfront aquarium showcases the marine life of the Northwest.... *Tel 206/386-4320. Pier 59 on Alaskan Way, roughly opposite the Pike Place Market. Daily 10am–7pm. Admission charged.* **(see p. 64)**

Seattle Art Museum. A little bit of everything, from Native American art and artifacts to modern paintings and a gallery of Northwest contemporary art.... *Tel 206/654-3100. www.seattleartmuseum.org. 100 University St. at 1st Ave. Open 10am–5pm (until 9 pm Thur), closed Mon. Admission charged.* **(see p. 63)**

Seattle Asian Art Museum. Japanese and Chinese art and artifacts are emphasized, but there are also items from Korea, the Himalayas, and Southeast Asia.... *Tel 206/654-3100. Volunteer Park, 14th Ave. E and E. Prospect St. Open 10am–5pm (until 9pm Thur.), closed Mon. Admission charged.* **(see p. 64)**

Seattle Center. Home of the Space Needle, this 20-square-block entertainment and arts complex also hosts the big three festivals (Bumbershoot, Northwest Folklife, and Taste of Seattle), an amusement park, a video game parlor, gallery spaces, and restaurants, as well as the Seattle Children's Museum, Seattle Children's Theater, Pacific Science Center, and Experience Music Project.... *Tel 206/684-7200 for program information. www.seattlecenter.com. 305 Harrison St. Admission free.* **(see pp. 59, 66)**

Seattle Underground Tour. This most popular of touristy tours begins in Pioneer Square and explores the subterranean passages and old storefronts under the current street level.... *Tel 206/682-4646. 610 1st Ave. Several tours daily. Call for advance reservations. Admission charged.* **(see pp. 65, 69)**

Space Needle. Still the most visible symbol of Seattle, and a cherished local landmark ever since it was built for the 1962 World's Fair. Climb up to the observation deck and take a few long ganders... *Tel 206/443-2100. www.spaceneedle.com. 219 4th Ave. N. at Seattle Center. Daily 9am–11 pm Admission charged.* **(see p. 65)**

Spirit of Washington Dinner Train. Scenic train ride that passes through the eastside suburbs, winding up at a winery in Woodinville for a shopping and wine-tasting break.... *Tel 206/227-RAIL or 800/876-RAIL. 625 S. 4th St., Renton (about a half-hour drive from downtown Seattle). Daily departures. Call for advance reservations. Admission charged.* **(see p. 69)**

Washington Park Arboretum. A 200-acre park that doubles as a botanical research station. Hundreds of trees and flowering shrubs are marked for identification in a gorgeous, peaceful setting. Don't miss the Japanese garden.... *Tel 206/543-8800. 2300 Arboretum Dr. E. at Lake Washington Blvd. Free.* **(see p. 61)**

Washington State Ferries. A marvelous way to see Puget Sound and get a real feeling for Seattle's maritime atmosphere, the ferry system connects the city to outlying outposts on Bainbridge Island, Vashon Island, and Bremerton on the Olympic Peninsula. From Edmonds, just north of Seattle, another ferry runs to the Kitsap Peninsula community of Kingston, and even farther north, in Anacortes, the ferries link up with many of the San Juan Islands. The 30-minute Bainbridge run is lovely, cheap, and offers great views of the city skyline, particularly if you return after dark.... *Tel 206/464-6400. www.wsdot.wa.gov/ferries. Numerous daily runs and returns. Car and passenger ferries leave from Pier 52 on the Alaskan Way Waterfront. Pedestrian walkway to terminal on Columbia St. Admission charged.* **(see p. 69)**

Woodland Park Zoo. More than 1,000 animals on 92 acres, but the most impressive things are the natural habitats in which they roam. Watch the brown bears playing in their pond—it's a show that you'll never forget.... *Tel 206/684-4800. www.zoo.org. 5500 Phinney Ave. N., Fremont. Daily 9:30am–6:30pm. Admission charged.* **(see pp. 61, 65)**

Ye Olde Curiosity Shop. Tacky souvenir shop. Be grossed out and pick up a little something for the kids at the same time. Have funne!... *Tel 206/682-5844. Pier 54, Alaskan Way. Daily 9:30am–6pm, weekends 9am–6pm. Admission free.* **(see p. 65)**

getting

4
outside

Just remember this as you pull on your Eddie Bauer parka and REI snowshoes (both companies of which, by the way, were started in Seattle): The city is surrounded by water and the water is surrounded by mountains, and that's an equation for outdoor entertainment of the highest order. Within an hour's drive in any direction you can be hiking in the mountains, skiing well into the spring, fishing, and doing every kind of boating imaginable. Or you can just stay in town and enjoy all the recreation afforded by the city, such as rollerblading around Green Lake, cycling the Burke-Gilman Trail, or paddling through houseboat communities. The question for you, then, is your basic surf-or-turf: Would you rather hit the water or head for the hills? So long as you can handle a little rain or wait out the cloudbursts, you can do most of the following activities any day of the year. (Some of us even play golf all winter, which is why they sell knee-high rubber boots with spiked soles in all the finer golf shops.) Dress warmly and in layers, stay dry, have fun, and watch your elbows if you meet me in a pick-up basketball game.

The Lowdown

One if by land... It only *seems* as if everybody in Seattle comes to **Green Lake**, the North Seattle recreation site 10 minutes from downtown, on a sunny day. This small, man-made lake has a paved 3-mile trail around it that is a magnet for every skater, jogger, dog-walker, and parent with a stroller. It's also something of a singles scene, and about the only place in town where health-club types parade the flesh. Rent skates or bikes from **Gregg's Green Lake Cycle** (tel 206/523-1822, 7007 Woodlawn Ave. NE.) at the north end of the lake. Bicyclists beware: The Green Lake path gets too crowded for cycling, but the loop of streets around the lake makes a better ride. Skates can also be rented at **Urban Surf** (tel 206/545-9463, 2100 N. Northlake Way), across the street from Gasworks Park. You can practically skate out of the shop onto the **Burke-Gilman Trail**, an old railroad bed that was torn up and paved, and runs over 12 miles from Ballard all the way along Lake Union and the Montlake Cut, through the University district and then north to Sandpoint and Lake Washington, with a connection for marathon riders to the Lake Sammamish trail. It's a great place to air out your legs on a long, fast skate or pedal. On the waterfront downtown, **Blazing Saddles Bike**

Rentals (tel 206/341-9994, 1230 Western Ave.) has a nifty computerized system to match you to the correct bike and put you on the streets, with maps of short rides along the waterfront or longer links to the Burke-Gilman. If you want to make a day of pedaling, take your bike on the **Vashon** or **Bainbridge ferries** (you pay the foot-passenger toll) and cruise those islands. Vashon is rural, but hilly and tough to cycle; Bainbridge is flatter, but has more car traffic. Joggers can find plenty of pavement to burn without any car traffic by taking to the paths at Green Lake, the Burke-Gilman Trail, or downtown on the waterfront at Myrtle Edwards Park (Alaskan Way at Broad St.).

And two if by sea... For my money, the quintessential Seattle outdoor experience is to paddle **Lake Union** in a kayak and tour the clusters of houseboats that dot its shores. I do it with every out-of-town guest, regardless of age or paddling experience, and nobody's been disappointed yet. You can rent big, steady kayaks (doubles and triples are great for taking kids along), with foot-controlled rudders and spray skirts that will keep the drips off your clothes, from the **Northwest Outdoor Center** (tel 206/281-9694, 2100 Westlake Ave. N.). You launch from their docks onto the lake and then head north or directly across the lake to see some idyllic floating homes, including the *Sleepless in Seattle* houseboat (movie buffs will recognize it on the west side of the lake). On the south end of the same lake, the **Center for Wooden Boats** (tel 206/382-BOAT, 1010 Valley St.) rents classic canoes and wooden sailboats (provided you can pass their proficiency test) that are perfect for touring the lake. For paddling into enormous **Lake Washington**, head to the University district and rent a canoe or kayak from the **University of Washington Waterfront Activities Center** (tel 206/543-9433, off Montlake Blvd. NE, on the waterfront behind Husky Stadium). The marshy areas under the Route 520 bridge are wonderful to explore. **Green Lake** is smaller and less scenic, but fun to paddle, too. On a warm day, kids will enjoy the paddleboats you can rent on the north end of the lake from **Green Lake Boat Rentals** (tel 206/527-0171, 7351 E. Green Lake Dr. N.). Serious paddlers head to the **Cascadia Marine Trail,** which runs hundreds of miles from Olympia to the San Juan Islands in the Puget Sound.

The Washington Water Trails Association (tel 206/545-9161), which lobbied to establish the path, has created stopping points with campgrounds and facilities along the trail; its staff can recommend day trips or multi-day excursions that explore the sound's islands and wildlife areas. We're talking serious paddling now—you'll have to pay attention to the currents and tidal changes (and watch out for crossing ferry traffic)—but it's extremely rewarding, especially if you happen upon one of the pods of killer whales that sometimes enters the sound.

Calling all Ahabs... **Lake Washington** is known as an excellent trout fishery, the **rivers that drain into Puget Sound** support runs of salmon and steelhead, and anglers off of **Lincoln Park** in West Seattle go after chinook salmon that can easily run over 30 pounds. Buy a license and check the pamphlet of fishing rules issued annually by the state **Department of Fish & Wildlife** (tel 360/902-2200) before you go. Buy gear or hire a guide and tackle from **Salmon Day Tackle, Guides & Outfitters** (tel 206/789-9335, 5701 15th Ave. NW). For a day of fishing on a roomy boat on the sound, contact **Sport Fishing of Seattle** (tel 206/623-6364, Pier 54 on Alaskan Way on the downtown waterfront).

Paradise is at Mt. Rainier... We're not kidding—Paradise is the name of a visitor center located at 5,400 feet in **Mount Rainier National Park** (tel 360/569-2211), about 110 miles south of downtown Seattle. You'll agree with the name when you see Rainier's glaciers and vistas. It's the place to go to walk in meadows that bloom with flowers in July and August, or to play in snow most other months of the year. Beyond Paradise, Sunrise (6,400 feet) is the highest point on the mountain that you can reach by car, with more networks of hiking trails. Check with the park to see which roads are open if you go anytime other than summer. The Cascade Range forms a spine through western Washington and provides hundreds of miles of hiking trails, campgrounds, scenic small lakes, and driving tours from Mount Rainier to Mount Baker in the north; call the **North Cascades National Park** (tel 360/873-4590) for information. It's about 75 miles northeast of the city on State Highway 20 just east of I-5. The craggy, snow capped mountains that rise so majestically on the west side of Puget Sound are the Olympics, capped by the heroically named Mount Olympus, at 7,965 feet. **Olympic National Park** (tel 360/452-0330) is another hiker's paradise, with the most popular launching point being Hurricane Ridge on the northeast side of the park. To reach it from Seattle, take the car ferry to Bainbridge Island and then drive northwest on Route 101 to the town of Port Angeles.

Hitting the slopes... It's an old cliché to say that here you can play golf and ski on the same day (honestly, do you know anyone who's ever actually done it?), but we'll air it out here. There are three major ski areas in the Cascades within a couple hours' drive from the city, and they stay open late into the spring. The closest is at **Snoqualmie Pass** (tel 206/232-8182), 50 miles due east of town, where one company manages four separate slopes: Alpental, the steepest and best for advanced skiers; Hyak, a Nordic center where they rent snowshoes and cross-country skis; and Snoqualmie Central and West, gentler hills that are frequently lit for night skiing. For an absolute blast with your kids, check out the **sledding hill** at Snoqualmie Pass, where you can rent inner tubes and fly down a well-groomed hill, with rope lifts to bring you back up. Farther south, on Mount Rainier, is the **Crystal Mountain Resort** (tel 360/663-2265) and to the north is **Stevens Pass** (tel 360/973-2441), which have more vertical drop than Snoqualmie and the opportunity for serious skiers to explore backcountry trails. They both also offer night skiing. All three ski areas have cross-country and snowshoeing trails, as well as full lines of rental equipment.

Take a dip... Puget Sound is cold. Way cold. Frostbite cold. Take-your-breath cold. It warms to a max of about 55 degrees, and that's late in the summer. For most Seattleites, it has to be a rare, 90-degree day in August before they'll dare to swim in the sound, but you still see kids out there determined to take a dip on an average, 75-degree summer day. The best beaches are located at **Golden Gardens Park** in Ballard and **Alki Beach** in West Seattle. Expect pebbly beaches, not sand, and more pasty-white Northwest flesh than you might reasonably be expected to tolerate. The preferred places to swim are the lakes, which are much more clement. On hot days

Seattleites crowd to the north and west sides of **Green Lake** just north of downtown off Aurora Avenue N., as well as **Matthews Beach** and **Seward Park** on **Lake Washington** on the east side of the city, where there are diving platforms and lifeguards on duty during summer months. Kiddie pools, by the way, are available at most Seattle city parks and fill up every day when the weather gets warm. If swimming laps is your goal, there are several public pools in the city that generally have open-swim and lap-swim periods available throughout the day for a nominal charge. Favorites are the centrally located **Ballard Pool** (tel 206/684-4094, 1471 NW 67th St., off the 15th Ave. NW thoroughfare), the **Queen Anne Pool** (tel 206/386-4282, on the top of the hill at 1920 1st Ave. W.) and, in summer months, the outdoor **Colman Pool** at Lincoln Park in West Seattle (tel 206/684-7494, 8603 Fauntleroy Way SW).

Golf where the greens are really green... Because it rarely freezes here, you *can* play golf year-round—if you don't mind a great deal of standing water at times, a true test for your waterproof golf shoes. Some locals play in a "rain or shine" event every year on Superbowl Sunday, which frequently features unique hazards like hailstorms, rain showers, and the occasional frozen tee box. The three municipal courses in the city worth exploring are the hilly **Jackson Park Golf Course** (tel 206/363-4747, 1000 NE 135th St. in North Seattle), the flatter **Jefferson Park Golf Course** (tel 206/762-4513, 4101 Beacon Ave. S., on the south side of town), and the **West Seattle Golf Course** (tel 206/935-5187, 4470 35th Ave. SW), which has some handsome views of the downtown skyline. The **Golf Club at Newcastle** (tel 425/793-GOLF, off Newcastle Coal Creek Rd. in South Bellevue, a half-hour from downtown Seattle; call for the complicated directions) is a fancy new course that is trying to capture a high-end market on the east side by charging the hitherto unheard-of greens fee of $125. It remains to be seen if it can live up to that ticket. If you want to see a quintessential Northwest course with solitary holes that disappear into the woods, check out the **Port Ludlow Golf Course** (tel 800/455-0272), which is located on the Olympic Peninsula between the towns of Poulsbo and Port Townsend.

The tennis racket... Frequent rain keeps tennis from being a big game locally, which is all the better if you have a racquet and want to locate an open court, particularly on a weekday. **Woodland Park**, just below Green Lake on the north side of town, is the best place to go. It has several tennis courts, some of which are lighted, adjacent to the big soccer field and baseball complex on E. Green Lake Way, and four more on the N. 50th Street side. You can call **Seattle Parks and Recreation** (tel 206/684-4077) to reserve a court, but just showing up will usually do it.

A day at the races... For an urban sport of another kind, you can play the ponies at the big, friendly **Emerald Downs** (tel 253/288-7000, 2300 Emerald Downs Dr., Auburn, about 45 minutes from downtown Seattle) racetrack in the southern suburb of Auburn. The place gets packed on warm weekends and is family-friendly, with a video game parlor for kids, flowing beer for the rest of us, and lively wagering on some of the finest nags to stumble out of a gate. The racing season runs from April to September.

Pick-up hoops... An active pickup basketball scene flourishes at schools and parks around the city, and unlike playground basketball in, say, Detroit or Philadelphia, you can play here without fear of having your head torn off by a six-foot-six guy named Otis with a mean attitude toward tourists. We'll even occasionally pass you the ball as part of our Northwest hospitality. The best game in town is indoors at the **Green Lake Community Center** (tel 206/684-0780, 7201 E. Green Lake Drive N., at the north end of the lake), where you'd better have some serious stuff if you expect to compete. The outdoor court there is a kind of B-game that is more accessible to those of us with modest vertical leaps. On summer evenings, there is usually a good, full-court pickup game underway at the **John Hay** elementary school (201 Garfield Street on the top of Queen Anne hill). Just slip into the shoot-around between games and wait for the next challenging team to be picked. Teams are usually chosen by shooting free throws, and players are pretty fair about choosing sides from those who've been waiting the longest. Winners hold the court forever.

shop

5

ping

It wasn't so long ago that the downtown department stores handled all of Seattle's (admit-tedly limited) fashion needs, and the only things you could buy in Belltown, besides illicit drugs, were woolly army-navy gear and retro furniture. But like so many other parts of Seattle, the retail environment is in a boom right now, with new shops and boutiques opening all over town—and especially in Belltown—to service a cash-rich local populace that has emerged bleary-eyed from behind its computer screens, sold some stock and realized that it had a lot of catching up to do in the consumer goods department. Some things haven't changed. Outdoor recreation and equipment are still big, and date back to the days when Seattle was the last stop to kit yourself out for an assault on the Alaskan goldfields. The food-crazy community supports a good selection of kitchenware and specialty-foods stores, and big, national retailers are finally moving into town, thanks to a revitalized downtown shopping district. On that front, Seattle had a brief scare in the '90s when the Frederick & Nelson department store chain abruptly folded up its proverbial tent, leaving downtown with a gaping retail hole in the form of a vacant five-story building. People worried that it might sink the whole downtown shopping district until Nordstrom, our favorite local retailer, rode in on a big white horse, planted its flag in the middle of the vacant space, and cried out, "Hail the conquering hero!" To the accompaniment of joyous cries from the citizenry, Nordstrom completely renovated the building and moved into it in 1998. At roughly the same time, Pacific Place was being built across the street as an upscale downtown mall, and big national retailers who had been eyeing Seattle for a number of years took the plunge and opened downtown outlets. Voilà, as they say in Parisian shopping malls, the downtown area was saved, keeping the base of Seattle shopping in town, rather than in the malls that fringe the city.

Target Zones

Let's start by breaking down the downtown area into its component retail pods, each with a slightly different brand of shopper (each wearing a slightly different brand of jeans). Out of respect and fealty, we'll start with the **Pike Place Market**, which brings so much character to the city as it clings to its hillside perch on First Avenue, offering just the right mix of crafts, goods, food, and produce. If you can tear yourself away from the food vendors and gorgeous specialty food products on the upper levels, you'll find all kinds of delightful, quirky shops in the lower corridors and inner chambers of the market.

Most of them have been there for years and have a loyal customer base—and you won't find a chain name in the place (outside of the flagship Starbucks). You can browse, pause for coffee or a beer, shop some more, eat, and generally fritter away the day quite pleasantly. A few blocks away, the **shopping district** is centered around the intersection of Fifth Avenue and Pine Street, where the big department stores have set up camp and attracted a swarm of smaller businesses. It's here that you'll find Nordstrom and The Bon Marché lying roughly between the two downtown malls, **Westlake Center** and **Pacific Place**. Westlake Center is a glassy, modern collection of luxury stores, but it got out-upscaled when Pacific Place opened in 1999 with even more expensive (read: Tiffany & Co.) national stores. In this stretch of Fifth and Sixth avenues, you'll find outposts of all of the familiar national brands, including local favorite Eddie Bauer and upstarts like the trendy Old Navy. A few blocks away on upper First Avenue, **Belltown** strives to be hip and SoHo stylish, and largely succeeds thanks to the fashionable boutiques that have moved in alongside Seattle's newest restaurants. It's where you'd go to find exactly the right nightclubbing outfit and a pair of designer shoes to match. Farther south, again on First Avenue, you enter the **Pioneer Square** district. The renovated old brick buildings, which were shaken but barely stirred by the 2001 earthquake, house an artsy collection of galleries. Before leaving downtown, you might head to the **waterfront** for souvenir items and trinkets to prove to the folks back home that there are Space Needle pencil sharpeners to be had for a song in this town.

Capitol Hill, with its own Broadway as the main drag, is the funky/gay part of town, with even wilder fashions, lots of good retro clothes stores and collectibles, and the only places in town to buy a studded leather collar and leash (for a human, I mean). **Fremont** clings to its former reputation as the hippie district with some wacky retro clothing and knick-knack shops and a thriving crafts market on Sundays from May through Christmas. The street art is among the best in the city, and there are plenty of places to linger over coffee or a microbrew.

If mall you must after all this, the city is bookended by two traditional shopping malls: **Northgate**, just off I-5 at 103rd Street, and **Southcenter**, near the airport.

Bargain-Hunting

You should see the stampedes when the thrift stores in **Ballard** and **Capitol Hill** announce a half-price Sunday sale: recycled dresses, shirts, and jeans that usually cost something like three bucks are reduced to the price of a cup of coffee. The selection is actually pretty good, thanks to the local charities that solicit donations nonstop from residents and then sell them to the thrifts. There are always lots of garage sales going on around town (they're listed in the Sunday *Seattle Times* if you're up for some neighborhood-hopping). The nearest factory outlets are hours away near the Canadian border or in North Bend and are better left for a lengthy road trip. You can sometimes find deals or a vendor willing to consider a price reduction at craft fairs like the **Fremont Sunday Market** or from the craftspeople renting space at the north end of the **Pike Place Market** who, towards the end of the day, are dying to unload their homemade jewelry, leathers, and carved wooden items.

Trading With the Natives

You'll get courteous, knowledgeable treatment from retailers for the most part, and places like Nordstrom will bend over backwards to find you exactly what you want and take it back without reservation if you change your mind a month later. Most stores will send your purchases home for you for the cost of shipping, or, at the very least, direct you to a nearby shop that is in the business of packaging and shipping things. Out-of-state checks are generally accepted, especially if you can show a credit card and/or picture ID.

Hours of Business

They vary widely, but figure on most downtown stores opening between 9 and 10am and closing between 5 and 6pm, with 11–5 being the standard on Sunday and later hours offered during the holiday-buying season. The shops in Pioneer Place and Westlake Center are open until 9pm, and some stores, such as downtown bookstores, will go as late as 11pm. The Market is up and running by 9 but becomes a ghost town by 6pm. Specialty stores frequently don't open until 11, and then will decide when to close based on traffic.

Sales Tax

No state income tax equals big state sales tax. Washington nicks you for 6.5% on purchases, and then King County boosts it up for a grand total of 8.8% on most purchases (excluding food). Think of it as a great bargain, because you're paying 15.6% on your hotel room (thanks to special levies in recent years to pay for our ballparks and such), for which we say, "Thank you" from the bottom of our hearts.

The Lowdown

Seafood that is literally fresh off the boat... I don't know how many times I've been on vacation in a strange city and gone looking right away for a fresh, whole tuna. Well, okay, I've never done that, but maybe that would change if I were a visitor to Seattle, and that's where we'll start. At Fisherman's Terminal, the marina between the Queen Anne and Magnolia neighborhoods that houses much of the Alaskan fishing fleet in the winter, you can frequently buy whole fresh salmon and tuna at terrific prices directly from the boats. Just walk the docks and look for signs on the boats. The drawback is that the fishermen aren't allowed to fillet or prepare the catch; they can only sell it to you whole. "But I'm not prepared to gut and fillet a salmon in my hotel room!" you exclaim. You might be more interested in the goods at the **Wild Salmon Seafood Market**, also at Fisherman's Terminal. Try Copper River or Yukon River salmon when they're in season in the spring and summer, respectively, or fresh Dungeness crab year-round. The crab at any market, by the way, were flash-cooked at the point of catch and are ready to eat as soon as they've been cleaned. Buy some cocktail sauce and bread and you'll have a meal that beats any room-service burger. The famous fishmonger at the Pike Place Market is **Pike Place Fish**, which makes a big show out of calling out orders and throwing whole fish to be wrapped. (A French chef once pleaded, "Please, will you not throw my fish?" They threw it anyway, and he walked out.) Their fish is top-notch, but they attract a big, annoying crowd of gawkers. We prefer **Jack's Fish Spot**, across Pike Place, which has equally good fish, crab, and smoked salmon without the crowds, and delicious crab cocktails or fish and chips that you can eat at a bare-bones, stainless-steel lunch counter.

Deep inside the Market... Wandering around the innards of the **Pike Place Market** is so much fun, especially when you get away from the milling crowds and head downstairs to the Down Under shops. You'll find lots of little stores selling antiques and collectibles, old comic books, imports, jewelry, and things you've completely forgotten that you wanted but must have once you lay eyes on them. Upstairs, at the end of the main arcade and spilling out onto the sidewalk, craftspeople set up tables with wares that include hand-carved toys and flutes, T-shirts, and woven clothes. Be sure to include Post Alley, the little alleyway between Pike Place and First Avenue, in your wanderings, as well as the South Arcade between Pike and Union streets for quilts and Native American crafts and the shops on Western Avenue for anything from exotic birds to expensive imports from Spain.

Market musts... **Sur La Table** is the everything shop for the gourmet cook. It has practically every kind of cooking utensil, wire whisk, cookie mold, and baking pan known to man, it seems, as well as an impressive array of cookbooks and gift items like dish towels and serving dishes. You can put those items to good use with the wonderful Italian gourmet items from the **DeLaurenti Specialty Food Market**—homemade pastas that are cut to order, a great selection of olive oils, excellent breads, and, in the winter, exquisite little white truffles flown in from Italy that are more expensive than a gambling habit. **Jack's Fish Spot** and **Pike Place Fish**, on opposite sides of Pike Place itself, sell terrific smoked salmon in vacuum bags or gift boxes that make unique Seattle-style gifts. For the kinetic you, **The Great Wind-up**, in the Economy Market Atrium (the building south of Rachel, the brass pig), is rife with windup toys, including some of the older tin classics, as well as retro toys like Slinkys and Gumbys.

Going retro with antique clothes... The insouciantly funky neighborhood of Fremont is the perfect place for dressing up in your best retro-wear and making a minor scene, which is perhaps why three of the best antique clothing stores in town are a block away from each other on Fremont Place North. **Deluxe Junk** is a great deal of fun, with sharp-looking bowling shirts and heavy woolen overcoats from the '50s to cover you in style as you lounge on the '50s and '60s furniture that's also for sale: Revamp your wardrobe and apartment in one fell swoop. Deluxe Junk also has rooms full of collectibles and kitschy stuff that's utterly whimsical and dated. **Fritzi Ritz** takes its vintage duds a little more seriously, with all clothes carefully labeled with the decade they belong to. It's laid out more like a boutique, with racks of dresses and shoes, and a good selection of costume jewelry. On the corner and down a steep flight of stairs to its basement location, the big, cluttered **Fremont Antique Mall** has several rooms crammed with vintage junk, but you can also find some real clothing steals among the dusty old radios, tea sets, and piles of unmatched shoes. In a rack of old overcoats there, I once found a dark blue tuxedo for my wedding that Jerry Lewis and Dean Martin might have fought over. **GlamOrama** mostly plays it for laughs with its toys and games, but you can occasionally find a drop-dead gorgeous dress in the mix. The most elegant vintage shop in town, however, is **Isadora's Antique Clothing**, a small boutique near the Market that has everything to do with beautiful clothes and absolutely no interest in kitsch—think lacy cream-colored gowns and classic tuxedos, all dating back to the early part of the century, with fine accessories to match.

Hip threads for now people... Even those of us who follow the local Aggressively Plain fashion code like to dress up once in awhile. Or when we have to go to New York on business. Either way, there are plenty of boutiques to serve the demands of fashion when you can't find what you're looking for at **Nordstrom**. In the downtown shopping district, **Betsey Johnson**'s urban whimsy and bright, tight things are practically scandalous in Seattle, which is half the fun of wearing them here. In Belltown, **Fast Forward** is the coolest store for up-to-the-minute fashions. It's where you go to meet your good friends, Helmut Lang and Vivienne Westwood. Down the street, **John Fluevog Shoes** has absolutely the coolest selection of spiky, leopard-printed, and otherwise highly noticeable things, many of them designed locally. For that ironically-hip dressed-down look, **Old Navy** is across from Pacific Place, with floppy sweatshirts and drawstring pants, all punctuated with the logo du jour, and far too many 40-somethings peeking over the shoulders of the 18-to-25 crowd. For a song, you'll be at the forefront of fashion and not even know it. And of course, there's the downtown outlet of **Eddie Bauer**, Seattle's favorite fashion son and the Godfather of the casual outdoor look that still looks plenty crisp and dressy around these parts.

Why we love Nordstrom... We love that it moved into a new space downtown on Fifth and Pine in 1998 and completely remade it into the fabulous department store that we so richly deserve. We love its Chanel boutique for when we really want to put on the dog, and we love the complimentary wardrobe consulting service that will make up our mind for us. We love the day spa, the jewelry, and the Nordstrom Grill, which is more than a cut above the usual store cafe. We love the service, which is still the best in town. We love the fact that it's a local company and that the Nordstrom family has been so active in civic issues. But most of all, we love **Nordstrom** for the shoes, thousands and thousands of shoes displayed around the store and calling our name. And finally, we love that it makes **The Bon Marché**, across the street, work a little harder to try and keep up. When we win the lottery, we'll be spending a great deal more time at Nordy's.

Buy the book... Just as Portlanders love their Powell's bookstore, Seattleites have a special feeling about the **Elliott Bay Book Company**, the privately owned and cavernous bookstore in Pioneer Square that stands as a civic symbol of independence and good taste. Even as the big-chain booksellers like **Barnes and Noble** and **Borders** open megastores in town, Elliott Bay is the store that you return to for browsing on a rainy afternoon. The restored brick building is cozy and welcoming with its wood floors and different levels, and a basement cafe is a great place to read your new purchase over coffee and a pastry. Excellent sections cover local authors, travel books, and children's books, and the staff is quick and knowledgeable. Here's hoping that it lasts for another 25 years. The **University Book Store**, which serves the University of Washington community, has nearly as large a selection as Elliott Bay, but it's crammed onto long, straight racks and doesn't have the same browsing appeal. Besides books, it also has a huge section of office supplies, gifts, and Husky sweatshirts and logowear (guaranteed to infuriate your Oregon Duck friends). Not far away, **Half-Price Books Records Magazines** has made a nice niche for itself by selling used books; the stock is now about half used and half new books. The large selection of pre-owned software here can save you a bundle. Head to Wallingford to find **Shorey's Bookstore**, an antiquarian bookseller that dates back to 1890; it boasts a million titles and the resources to find practically any out-of-print book you want. Poking around on its shelves is like wandering through a museum of publishing as you turn up old pamphlets and rare editions.

Gearing up for the great outdoors... Ah, the smell of the outdoors—doesn't it just put you in the mood to buy a whole new color-coordinated wardrobe for tramping through the woods? Before he became a chain with outlets in every mall in America, **Eddie Bauer** was just a guy who got his start here supplying heavy, reliable clothing to brave the wilds. You can still find a few backpacks and outdoor accessories at his downtown store, but they mostly serve as decoration for the comfortable vests, khaki shorts, and goose-down parkas that will allow you to look damned good when the bear finds you on his tail. **REI**, which started as a cooperative of Seattle mountaineers, is heading the way of Eddie, but it's still a pretty vital center for tough, durable outdoor goods. Its enormous new store in an industrial part of downtown under the freeway is a real trip, a kind of active Wal-Mart for yuppies. Besides shelves of kayaks, camping gear, and sleeping bags that would withstand a Siberian ice storm, there's a short indoor hiking path where you can try out your new boots, a vented area for firing up and comparing cookstoves, an art gallery and trip-planning center, a mountain bike trail, and an enormous indoor climbing wall made of fake rock that looks like something that came out of the Space Needle's nose. REI's stuff is utterly expensive and utterly good; you could kit out a weekend car camping expedition or an attempt at the summit of Everest with equal success. **Patagonia**, in Belltown, lies philosophically somewhere in between Eddie's and REI, with equally impressive price tags on fleecy stuff and natural cottons that make you look like the kind of person who *might* soon be fording dangerous rivers and climbing every mountain if you can just get your Ford Expedition washed before the weekend. With so much glamour wear available, I like the sturdy, down-home products sold by the **C.C. Filson Co.**, south of Safeco Field, which really did outfit Alaskan gold miners and sells its share of warm, water-resistant things to today's Alaskan fishermen, such as rough wool coats and trousers and oilskin hats. **Play It Again, Sports** traffics in used sporting goods, which means that you can get a baseball glove that's not only cheap, it's also broken in already. There's a good selection of skis, skateboards, and rollerblading gear, too.

For those who choose to dress like professional jocks... Seattle's professional sports teams have their own shops, of course, on the off chance that they didn't shake every nickel out of your pocket when you went to the game. **Mariners Clubhouse** has a downtown location and a big space at Safeco Field that sells outrageously expensive replica jerseys of the players (Edgar Martinez is the local favorite these days), as well as pennants, autographed baseballs, and those stunning blue-with-teal Mariners caps. The **Seattle Sonics Team Shop**, alongside Key Arena where they play, does a brisk business in Gary Payton jerseys in the bright green and gold team colors, as well as replica jerseys from other NBA teams. Now if they could just sell a decent relief pitcher and a quick point guard who can bury the trey.

Specialty food markets to die for... If you haven't gathered already that food is a consuming local passion, we'll have to start all over again. In the International District just east of the Kingdome, **Uwajimaya** is that rare Asian superstore that simply has everything. It's laid out like an American supermarket, but the shelves are crammed instead with noodles and soy sauces and huge bags of different rice varietals; the produce section has hot Thai peppers, Japanese eggplant, sweet basil, and the ultra-stinky durian fruits, in season. People come just to smell the exotic spices that linger in the air and see things like whole, raw octopus ready for slicing thin into sashimi. There are also gift items and a deli for take-out sushi and noodle dishes. In the Market, the **DeLaurenti Specialty Food Market** achieves that same kind of abundant quality with Italian food. It has gorgeous prosciuttos and dozens of cheeses, imported cookies, and panettone, and upstairs is an extensive collection of Italian wines at good prices. Expect enormous lines during the holiday season. Cheeseheads and other cheese lovers should make a beeline to the exquisite **James Cook Cheese Co.,** where the British Mr. Cook offers an astonishing selection of international cheeses that will make you drool quite copiously. He has a fine story to tell about each wedge of Shropshire cheddar, each delicate French *crottin* of goat cheese, and each moldy Stilton. He also carries terrific French butters and yogurts that are embarrassingly better than anything we can get domestically. To get a taste and smell of what Seattle's Scandinavian neighborhoods once were like, check out the goods at **Olsen's Scandinavian Foods** on Ballard's main drag. The staff pickle their own herring and have northern delicacies like lutefisk (an acquired taste) and lingonberries, and the fresh-baked cookies and cardamom rolls are fragrant and tasty. When do we eat? I'm starving here.

Ultimate kitsch... And then there are those times when you need a lava lamp, a book of card tricks, a whoopee cushion, and hand puppets of boxing nuns. Longtime favorite Ruby Montana's Pinto Pony has mosied down the proverbial trail, but don't despair. **Market Magic,** on a lower floor of the Pike Place Market, has not only highly practical things like card tricks and fake, plastic vomit, but also very cool posters of Harry Houdini and his conjuring pals. **Archie McPhee**, in Ballard, is another kitsch-meister who specializes in exotic toys and pranks. Yessir, step right up to get your whoopee cushion, and you, little lady, look like you could use a spritzing flower, those aforementioned punching nuns, or a big rubber dinosaur. Bring your kids here and within minutes you'll all start mugging like Pee Wee Herman. Fremont's **Deluxe Junk** is also crammed with fun, nostalgic stuff—principally furniture and fashions, as well as plenty of quirky little things in the corners and inside the glass case. If you fall in love with a retro loveseat and Formica dining set, they'll arrange to send it to your house. Around the corner, **GlamOrama** has stuff like board games from '60s television shows (surely you've saved your Partridge Family game from the '70s?), hysterically funny old lunchboxes, and tons of wacky things. On the waterfront, **Ye Olde Curiosity Shop** is essentially a souvenir shop of T-shirts, Space Needle pencil sharpeners, and the like. It adds oddities, however, like genuine shrunken heads from South America (yuk!) and an authentic mummy in a glass case (gross!!). Packs 'em in by the hundreds, too, which is why you should never underestimate the marketing value of a mummy. Somewhere in retail heaven, Eddie Bauer is sipping white wine with Ann Taylor, but Harry Houdini and Archie McPhee are lassoing jackalopes.

Music to soothe the savage beast... You'd think that the town that brought you Nirvana, Pearl Jam, and Alice in Chains would have a black-walled music store blaring temple-throbbing tunes on every block. Not so. The music scene is actually pretty modest for a city of Seattle's size. On Lower Queen Anne, **Tower Records** is still the king of selection, with rows and rows of everything from classical to rockabilly. Depth of stock and obscure artists are not big here, which seems to make the pierced and grumpy salespeople all the more glum. It also has a Ticketmaster outlet and is the most popular place in town to buy concert tix. If you're still into vinyl, **Bop Street Records & Tapes**, in Ballard, has an enormous selection of records and 45s that you can paw through to your heart's delight; shelves and boxes cram the space, and there's more in their warehouse if you really feel like a browsing marathon. Bop Street specializes in rock, jazz, and blues, but the undisputed jazz king is **Bud's Jazz Records**, which has been holed up in a Pioneer Square basement location since 1982. It looks like the kind of place where you'd run into Dizzy Gillespie sharing a cigarette with Duke Ellington. Owner Bud Young has some 15,000 recordings to sell, and an encyclopedic knowledge of his field that is now making its way into in-store search engines that will help you find whole subcategories of music, such as sidemen who played with both Billy Eckstine and Miles Davis.

Seattle is also the home of several craftsmen who make and repair musical instruments. In Fremont, **Dusty Strings** began as a maker of dulcimers and has now blossomed into a great store for just about any stringed acoustic folk instrument, from banjos and mandolins to Taylor guitars and, of course, the still-homemade dulcimers. Dusty Strings also has a large collection of sheet music. The jamming by customers can be breathtaking. In Ballard, craftsman Sten Olsen opened **Olsen Violins** in 1999 as a repair shop that also sells new and used instruments. He does exquisite work in restoring and repairing concert-quality violins and cellos, and has some very good deals on instruments that he lovingly brought back to life and sells from his small shop.

Toy havens... Let's face it—for a kid, it just isn't a successful trip if it doesn't involve coming home with a toy; the promise of an afternoon spent at a good toy store can make up for lots of standing around in museums. And if you came without the kids, you know you'd better not return empty-handed. Near Pioneer Square, **Magic Mouse** is an elegant shop with well-made, interesting toys that are longer on quality than on movie tie-ins and mass merchandising. They have the best stuffed animals and Scandinavian building sets in town. **Top Ten Toys**, in Greenwood, prides itself on its learning toys and activities and has a great selection of things for toddlers in a big area devoted to the under-two crowd. Blowing off energy in there and emerging with a shiny new toy can make anyone's day. For goofy, retro stuff that makes for great souvenirs, head first to **Archie McPhee**, in Ballard, for the kitschy toys like the famous punching nun puppets, and then take your show to the Pike Place Market's **The Great Wind-up** for a vast selection of windup toys and old favorites like Gumby and Pokey dolls.

A gift for your home... "That's it, goshdarnit!" you exclaim upon rising one morning to views of Seattle's green trees and forests, "I want to remake our home into a Pacific Northwest love nest." **The Best of All Worlds**, in the downtown shopping district, will bring a sophisticated touch to your decor with its elegant linens, tabletop accessories, tapestry pillows, and generally clever objets d'art drawn from all points of the globe. For the kitchen, you'll need about everything at **Sur La Table**, the top store in town for gourmet cooks. Located in the Market, it has everything from copper pot sets to just the right-sized wire whisk and souffle cups. If you always thought your Dad's old office stuff was way cool, you'll love Belltown's **Mint,** which traffics in retro office accessories from the '50s and '60s that now make Smith-Corona-esque fashion statements. If harking back to the American heartland is your design goal, you'll need to stop at the **Great Jones Home**, in Belltown, for aged and character-filled wooden cabinets, tables, and sideboards, as well as decorative things like wooden picture frames.

The Index

Archie McPhee. Dazzling collection of novelties, toys, and kitsch.... *Tel 206/297-0240. 2428 NW Market St.* **(see pp. 95, 97)**

Barnes and Noble. Granddaddy of the big chain bookstores.... Three locations: *Tel 206/264-0156. 600 Pine St. Suite 107; 206/517-4107. 2700 Union Village NE; 206/575-3965, 300 Andover Park W., Suite 200, Tukwilla 98188.* **(see p. 92)**

The Best of All Worlds. Hand-crafted and elegant items for the home.... *Tel 206/623-2525. 523 Union St.* **(see p. 97)**

Betsey Johnson. New York's exuberant designer, wildly daring for Seattle.... *Tel 206/624-2887. 1429 5th Ave.* **(see p. 91)**

The Bon Marché. A little more affordable than Nordstrom, with a huge breadth of merchandise.... *Tel 206/506-6000. 3rd Ave. & Pine St.* **(see p. 92)**

Bop Street Records & Tapes. Retro record store with gazillions of albums.... *Tel 206/783-3009. 5512 20th Ave. NW.* **(see p. 96)**

Borders. Mega-chain bookstore.... *Tel 206/622-4599. 1501 4th Ave.* **(see p. 92)**

Bud's Jazz Records. One of the great jazz stores in the country, with thousands of hard-to-find recordings and signed photos.... *Tel 206/628-0445. 102 S. Jackson St.* **(see p. 96)**

C.C. Filson Co. One of the oldest outdoor outfitters, selling traditional, natural-fabric clothes for harsh environments.... *Tel 206/622-3147. 1555 4th Ave. S.* **(see p. 93)**

DeLaurenti Specialty Food Market. The best Italian deli in the city.... *Tel 206/622-0141. 1435 1st Ave. at the Pike Place Market (make a left at the pig).* **(see pp. 90, 94)**

Deluxe Junk. Big space filled with less-than-serious collections of retro furniture, clothes, and knickknacks.... *Tel 206/634-2733. 3518 Fremont Place N.* **(see pp. 90, 95)**

Dusty Strings. A premier crafter of dulcimers and folk instruments.... *Tel 206/634-1662. 3406 Fremont Ave. N.* **(see p. 96)**

Eddie Bauer. Seattle boy makes good with his rugged, casual clothes.... *Tel 206/622-2766. 1330 5th Ave.* **(see pp. 91, 93)**

Elliott Bay Book Company. The local favorite for book browsing; frequent readings by national authors on tour.... *Tel 206/624-6600. 101 S. Main St.* **(see p. 92)**

Fast Forward. Cool fashions from top designers.... *Tel 206/728-8050. 1918 1st Ave.* **(see p. 91)**

Fremont Antique Mall. Cavernous basement shop with clothes, furniture, and oddities dredged from many attics.... *Tel 206/548-9140. 3419 Fremont Place N.* **(see p. 91)**

Fritzi Ritz. Retro and antique clothes with a great deal of style.... *Tel 206/633-0929. 3425 Fremont Place N.* **(see p. 90)**

GlamOrama. Kitschy, fun stuff; great at Halloween.... *Tel 206/632-0287. 3414 Fremont Ave. N.* **(see pp. 91, 95)**

Great Jones Home. Home furnishings and decor.... *Tel 206/448-9405. 1921 2nd Ave.* **(see p. 97)**

The Great Wind-up. Providing all the windup toys, all the time.... *Tel 206/621-9370. 93 Pike Place, in the Market.* **(see pp. 90, 97)**

Half-Price Books Records Magazines. A cut above most used-book stores.... *Tel 206/547-7859. 4709 Roosevelt Way NE.* **(see p. 92)**

Isadora's Antique Clothing. No retro cast-offs here. Great place to play dress-up.... *Tel 206/441-7711. 1915 1st Ave.* **(see p. 91)**

Jack's Fish Spot. Fresh seafood lunch spot.... *Tel 206/467-0514. 1514 Pike Place in the Market.* **(see pp. 89, 90)**

James Cook Cheese Co. The Godfather of cheese has something you've gotta try.... *Tel 206/256-0510. 2421 2nd Ave.* **(see p. 94)**

John Fluevog Shoes. Fashionable feet find their way to this atelier of style.... *Tel 206/441-1065. 1611 1st Ave.* **(see p. 91)**

Magic Mouse. Toy store for European hand-crafted toys and stuffed animals.... *Tel 206/682-8097. 603 1st Ave.* **(see p. 97)**

Mariners Clubhouse. Handy stop for Mariners logo wear and game tickets.... *Tel 206/346-4327. 1800 4th Ave.* **(see p. 94)**

Market Magic. Professional magicians mingle with amateurs like us in this shrine to illusion.... *Tel 206/624-4271. Pike Place Market.* **(see p. 95)**

Mint. Old staplers and file cabinets are worth a mint to the shoppers here.... *Tel 206/956-8270. 91 Wall St.* **(see p. 97)**

Nordstrom. Our favorite local department store and bastion of haute couture.... *Tel 206/628-2111. 500 Pine St.* **(see pp. 91, 92)**

Old Navy. Chain store for casual clothes with wit.... *Tel 206/264-9341. 601 Pine St.* **(see p. 91)**

Olsen's Scandinavian Foods. A taste of old Scandinavia.... *Tel 206/783-8288. 2248 NW Market St.* **(see p. 95)**

Olsen Violins. Repairing and restoring of old violins and cellos.... *Tel 206/783-7654. 6508 8th Ave. NW.* **(see p. 96)**

Patagonia. Sturdy, well-crafted, and pricey outdoor gear.... *Tel 206/622-9700. 2100 1st Ave.* **(see p. 93)**

Pike Place Fish. Seattle's most famous fish.... *Tel 206/682-7181. 86 Pike Place in the Market.* **(see pp. 89, 90)**

Pike Place Market. The best food and produce in the city.... *Tel 206/682-7453. Pike Place between Union and Virginia sts. Open 9am–6pm Mon–Sat, 11am–5pm Sun.* **(see pp. 86, 88, 89)**

Play It Again, Sports. Used balls and bats with plenty of play.... *Tel 206/264-9255. 1304 Stewart St.* **(see p. 93)**

REI. The L.L. Bean of the Northwest, an enormous store worth visiting even if you don't have $200 to spend on hiking boots.... *Tel 206/223-1944. 222 Yale Ave. N.* **(see p. 93)**

Seattle Sonics Team Shop. For the passionate NBA fan.... *Tel 206/269-SHOP. 312 First Ave. N.* **(see p. 94)**

Shorey's Bookstore. Antiquarian bookstore.... *Tel 206/633-2990. 1109 N. 36th St., Wallingford.* **(see p. 92)**

Sur La Table. Masterful kitchen-supply shop.... *Tel 206/448-2244. 84 Pine St. in the Market.* **(see pp. 90, 97)**

Top Ten Toys. Amiable toy store with games that teach kids on the sly.... *Tel 206/782-0098. 104 N. 85th St.* **(see p. 97)**

Tower Records. The biggest recorded music selection in town.... *Tel 206/283-4456. 500 Mercer St.* **(see p. 96)**

University Book Store. U-Dub's enormous bookstore.... *Tel 206/634-3400. 4326 University Way NE.* **(see p. 92)**

Uwajimaya. Great East Asian supermarket.... *Tel 206/624-6248. 519 6th Ave. S.* **(see p. 94)**

Wild Salmon Seafood Market. Excellent seafood market in Fisherman's Terminal.... *Tel 206/283-3366. 1900 W. Nickerson St.* **(see p. 89)**

Ye Olde Curiosity Shop. Crazy souvenir shop on the waterfront.... *Tel 206/682-5844. 1001 Alaskan Way at Pier 54.* **(see p. 95)**

Seattle Downtown Shopping

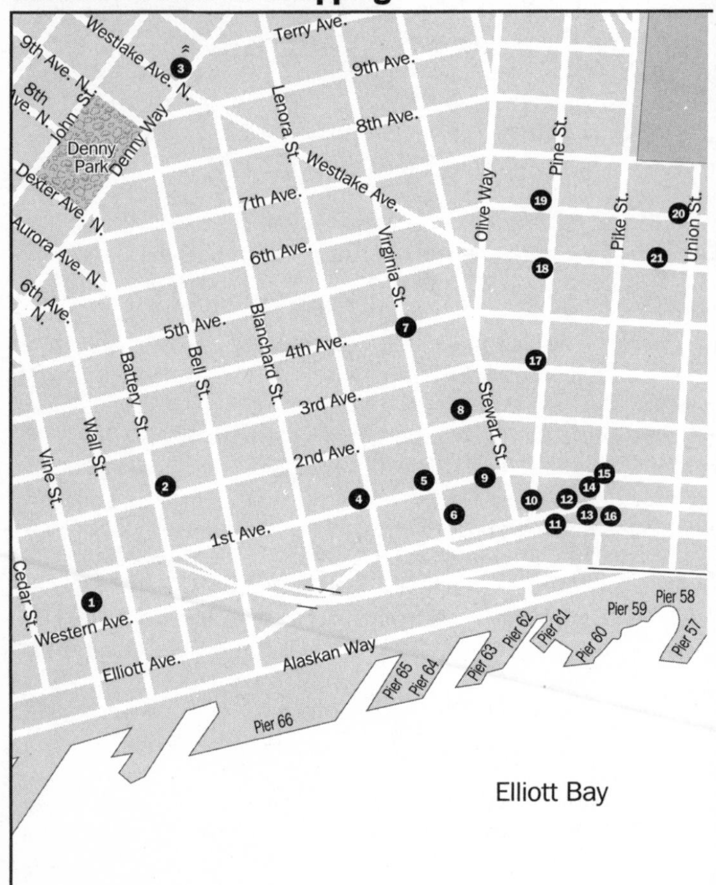

The Best of All Worlds **20**
Betsey Johnson **21**
The Bon Marché **17**
Bud's Jazz Records **26**
DeLaurenti Specialty Food Market **14**
Eddie Bauer **23**
Elliott Bay Book Company **25**
Fast Forward **5**
Great Jones Home **8**
The Great Wind-up **12**
Isadora's Antique Clothing **9**
Jack's Fish Spot **13**
James Cook Cheese Co. **2**

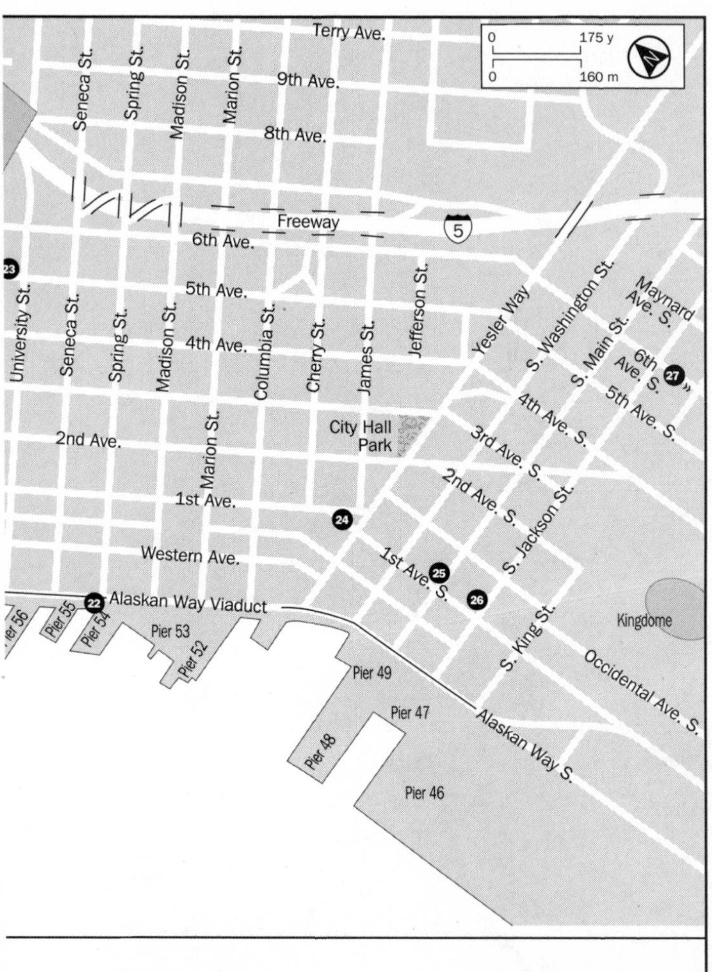

John Fluevog Shoes **6**
Magic Mouse **24**
Mariners Clubhouse **7**
Market Magic **16**
Mint **1**
Nordstrom **18**
Old Navy **19**
Patagonia **4**
Pike Place Fish **11**
Pike Place Market **15**
REI **3**
Sur La Table **10**
Uwajimaya **27**
Ye Olde Curiosity Shop **22**

Seattle–North & Northeast Shopping

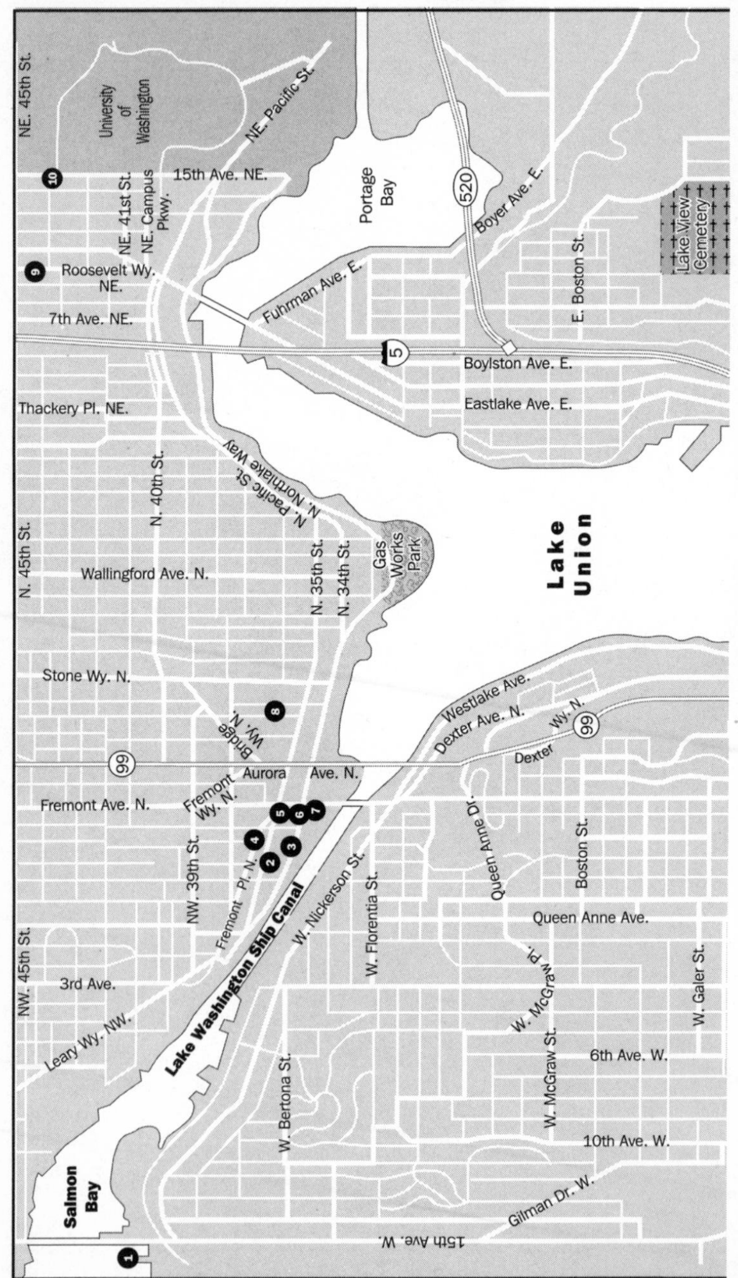

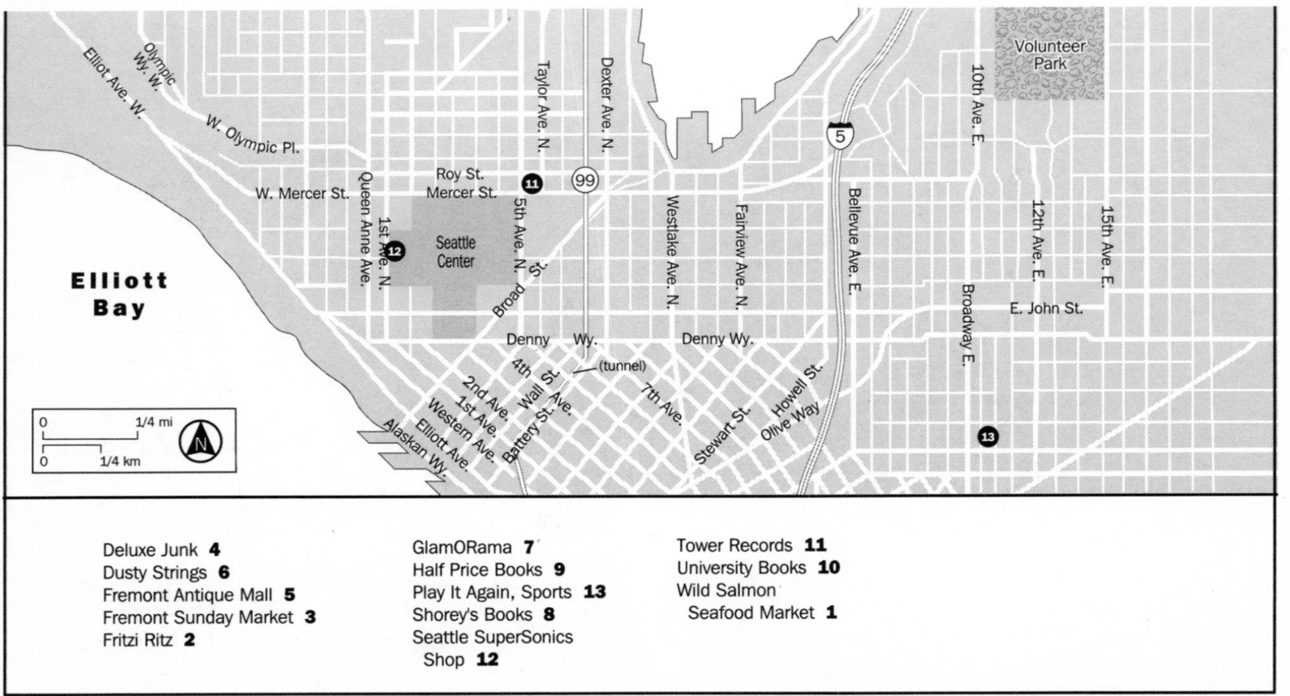

Deluxe Junk **4**
Dusty Strings **6**
Fremont Antique Mall **5**
Fremont Sunday Market **3**
Fritzi Ritz **2**
GlamORama **7**
Half Price Books **9**
Play It Again, Sports **13**
Shorey's Books **8**
Seattle SuperSonics Shop **12**
Tower Records **11**
University Books **10**
Wild Salmon Seafood Market **1**

night
enterta

6

life & inment

Sorry, grunge dude and dudette, but Courtney Love doesn't live here anymore, Kurt Cobain has quite completely left the building, and local grungers like Pearl Jam and Alice in Chains have gone on to national prominence. You can't expect to see any of the above redefining popular music in bars and parking lots anymore, and grunge, like new wave music, is referred to in the distant past tense around here.

Seattle has grown up and moved on. There's a lot more swing dancing and martini-sipping going on these days than there is alternative-rocking in torn T-shirts. Perhaps coincidentally, the high level of local heroin use, for which Seattle was also blushingly famous some years ago, is also going down.

What *is* new is that the music and cultural scene has spread out around the city. **Pioneer Square** is still the home of several long-standing bars that book rock and blues acts, as well as a raucous and slightly edgy atmosphere that hasn't changed much in the last century. But **Belltown** is trendy and chic, with new bars and jazz, folk, and rock clubs opening to cater to all of that young, urban money. **Capitol Hill**, the gay quarter of town, is home to some stubbornly gritty watering holes; people trek over the bridges to **Ballard** and **Fremont** for revival rock music and fringe theater. Local sports teams either have built or are in the process of building brand-new arenas, and the cultural scene has now spread from Seattle Center into the middle of downtown thanks to the new Benaroya Hall and ACT (A Contemporary Theater) complexes. The bottom line is that you can go about anywhere in the city and find something happening to suit your tastes. Oh, and you can smoke (if you must) at most bars and clubs, and even light up that fat stogie you smuggled in from Cuba at many places around town.

Sources

Two competing alternative news weeklies, the ***Seattle Weekly*** and ***The Stranger***, survive in large part because of their extensive entertainment listings, which are heavy on music and events but also include movie times, literary readings, theater performances, and art exhibitions. You can find them in free newspaper boxes around the city and in almost any coffee bar. The ***Seattle Gay News***, available in most bars and hangouts on Capitol Hill, has more extensive listings on gay shows, festivals, and events. The Friday editions of the two competing daily newspapers, the ***Seattle Post-Intelligencer*** and the ***Seattle Times***, have pull-out sections on entertainment that lean more heavily toward mainstream concerts and movies. Online, look to **seattle.citysearch.com.**

Liquor Laws and Drinking Hours

Washington State decrees that no liquor shall touch your lips until you reach the age of 21, and furthermore, you shall be carded until you're well into your thirties (which, if it isn't exactly the law, is the local custom). Beer and wine are available at any supermarket, bodega, or 7-Eleven in town, but you can only buy bottles of hootch (i.e., the hard stuff) at state liquor stores. Most bars and clubs stay open until 2am, at which time they have to stop selling alcohol. A few will swing on after-hours with no-alcohol policies that go to 4am.

Getting Tickets

There are three options for procuring billets, tickets, or ducats (you name the synonym, we've got it) for theatrical performances, concerts, and sporting events. The first is to go directly to the venue's ticket office and see what it has. The second is to give **Ticketmaster Northwest** a ring (tel 206/292-ARTS or 206/628-0888) and pay the requisite service charge. Ticketmaster handles all of the big concerts and Broadway-style shows that come to town, and also has tickets for all the sports teams. The third tactic is to try one of two **Ticket/Ticket** booths (tel 206/324-2744), one at the entrance to the Pike Place Market, the other inside Broadway Market shopping center on Capitol Hill. They offer half-price tickets on the day of the event to many theaters and occasionally even high-culture events like the Symphony and the Ballet, but be warned that it's usually half-price of the highest ticket price. For sports, your best bet is to go directly to the box office at the arena where the team plays; however, you can usually count on picking up scalped tickets—the price will rise in direct proportion to how bad the home team needs to win—outside of the arenas before a game begins.

The Lowdown

One price fits all in Pioneer Square... People have been drinking their brains out, falling down, and puking in Pioneer Square ever since Yesler Street was the original Skid Road, where logs were skidded down the hillside to the waterfront and loggers' paychecks were squandered. The bars and clubs these days have seen better times, but they're still a magnet for a mostly young crowd of college kids (with an emphasis on that terrifying sub-species, the frat rat) and people coming to or leaving ballgames. The place is absolutely jammed on weekends, and it's one of the few places in town where we'd warn you to keep an eye out for muggers, especially if you wander into dark streets or alleys away from the action. It also can become a dangerous mob scene during special occasions like Mardi Gras, and we don't recommend it. To keep business from taking the bus up the street to Belltown, several Pioneer Square clubs have instituted a joint cover charge ($8–10) that lets you into any of them on a given evening. They include the **New Orleans Restaurant**, a crowded, noisy space with Dixieland jazz, zydeco, or blues bands rocking alongside the platefuls of gumbo and jambalaya it serves, and **Doc Maynard's Public House**, which packs in the Tommy Hilfiger set for that antithesis of alternative music, the cover band. Also on the joint-cover ticket, the **Fenix** and its basement venue, the **Fenix Underground**, program a good alternative mix that might include Dick Dale or George Clinton upstairs and a hot reggae band or DJ belowdecks. If you can find your way to the little hole-in-the-wall **OK Hotel and Cafe** (it's under the Alaskan Way viaduct/freeway in a row of dingy storefronts), you can catch some good alternative-rock acts and a lively poetry slam that generally takes place on Wednesday nights. On the bar scene, the atmospheric **J&M Cafe and Cardroom** is a beloved old saloon that has entertained Alaskan gold diggers and merchant seamen and now packs a young, roaring crowd into its two bars. It can get noisy and congested, but there is a nice sidewalk space in summer. **Merchants Cafe** bills itself as the oldest bar in Seattle, which may explain why the bartenders and servers move as slowly as mummies, but the worn-down old joint does have character.

Unlike a good man, a good martini is easy to find... Your love affair with the juniper berry and its close personal friend, a drop of white vermouth, can continue unabated at any number of stylish drinking places around town. The best martinis in town are indisputably those poured downtown at **Oliver's,** the dark and comfortable corner bar with floor-to-ceiling windows at the Mayflower Park Hotel. We know this not only from considerable personal experience but from the Annual Martini Classic Challenge, with local celebrity judges, that Oliver's nearly always wins. Try the Glacier Blue, with a drop of curaçao added to the classic mix. On Lower Queen Anne Hill and a short walk from Belltown, **Tini Bigs Lounge** has 25 martinis on its list, and they all run double-size and cost a fortune, which the hip crowd that packs the place hardly seems to mind at all. For big-time hotel elegance and a place to buy your dear old mom a martini, check out the **Garden Court** at the Four Seasons Olympic hotel, where you can quaff your gin on comfortable furniture while surrounded by an atrium of tall trees and plants. The Olympic Gold martini is the house specialty.

The world is your brewpub... Brewpubs were all the rage around here until a couple of years ago when everybody discovered martinis and cosmopolitans. You can still drink some awfully fine beer and fill your nostrils with the heady aroma of mash and hops at several good spots around town. A block north of the ship canal in Fremont, the **Trolleyman Pub** was always a favorite, with its living room–style furniture around a fireplace and smooth pitchers of Red Hook beer, but the place was dealt a shocking blow when all of the beer production was moved across the lake to a newer facility. Still, the Trolleyman is an able neighborhood pub frequented by Fremont artist types and students from U-Dub; the ambience is warm, and the Blackhook Porter and ESB (extra special bitter) are still some of the best drafts in town. Just down the street, **Hale's Brewery and Pub**, with its leatherette couches and long polished bar, wants us all to believe that swilling beer can be sophisticated and elegant. Great pizza and sandwiches are served too, along with smooth brews like the crisp Moss Bay Extra. The **Pyramid Alehouse & Brewery,** a big, lively space in a converted warehouse that makes Thomas Kemper lagers and excellent Pyramid Ales, lucked out incredibly in 1999—it was a long three-block walk from the Kingdome, and all of those thirsty Mariners fans, but then Safeco Field opened right across the street, making this the perfect place to meet before or after a game and knock back a pitcher or three. At Pacific Place, the expansive, ultra-modern **Gordon Biersch Brewery Restaurant** has been packing them in four-deep at the bar since about two seconds after it opened. The downtown, professional crowd is young, good-looking, and very available for meeting and exchanging e-mail addresses, and the German-style beer is awfully good, too. For Portland refugees and those who fell in love with the McMenamin Brothers' brewpubs in the Rose City, there's a small outpost in lower Queen Anne: **McMenamins Pub & Brewery** offers that friendly, neighborhood feeling with polished-wood booths, a long bar, and great murals throughout. It pours the same Hammerhead Ale and Terminator Stout that we've come to love, along with good pub grub and a no-smoking policy.

Bars with attitude... You're stylin'. You're primped. You're poofed. You've wriggled into the tiny black dress and the serious pumps. Now go forth and meet your people at a bar that puts forth the same attitudinal energy you do. **Tini Bigs Lounge,** in Lower Queen Anne, is a cool, dark place with black walls, red lighting accents, and a pressed-tin ceiling where scenemakers start the night out with a good Happy Hour or end it after doing Belltown. Tini Big's specializes in enormous double martinis from a long list of specialty drinks (we like the one with a drop of smoky Scotch). **Kells Irish Restaurant and Pub,** at the Market, is all the Irish joint you could ever want, with Celtic music playing, Guinness flowing, and a lively, singing crowd that knows which side of the Jameson bottle is up. It has a polished, *Cheers*-like feel to it. Quite the opposite is the **Cloud Room,** atop the Camlin Hotel on the east side of downtown, a favorite stop for out-of-town musicians and seriously ironic hipsters in black who sink into dark banquettes and listen to a singing piano player croon standards. It's like a little bit of Holiday Inn lounge in the heart of Seattle, and the view isn't bad, either. Serious dressers show off in Belltown's **Pampas Club,** a plushly decorated downstairs lounge at the El Gaucho restaurant with a crowded little bar and cocktail tables facing a stage, where local Sinatra wannabes hold forth. You'll see more real jewelry, tuxedoes, and glittering gowns there than anywhere else in town. A few blocks away on a pier is **Waterfront**, which has a long, curving bar with stellar views of not only Elliott Bay, but also Seattle's more attractive singles. A younger dress-up crowd also packs the bars at **Jillian's Billiard Club**, just north of downtown alongside Lake Union, a very upscale two-story pool hall and video game parlor with hibachi tables for dining and an upstairs sports bar with banks of TVs. Frequent sightings of Seattle SuperSonics hoopsters up the hipness quotient of its lively bar scene. For a neighborhood place that drips bonhomie, check out **The Buckaroo**, a Fremont tavern that wouldn't look out of place in Chicago or Pittsburgh, with a long line of motorcycles out front under its neon cowboy sign.

Live rockin' and jammin'.... Don't get us wrong: Just because Nirvana isn't playing downtown anymore doesn't mean the music scene has left Seattle altogether. The king of clubs is the **Crocodile Cafe** in Belltown, whose owner is married to R.E.M. guitarist Peter Buck. On any given night in the post-grunge-apocalypse space, with bizarre papier-mâché decorations of bees and monsters hanging from the loft ceilings, you might catch former members of the Presidents of the U.S.A. jamming with Sir Mix-A-Lot or Julian Lennon; there's always something happening, whether it's national acts, cameos by famous artists, or great sets by top local bands. Across the street from the Market, the **Showbox** doesn't look like much on the outside, but this clubby industrial-chic space programs an eclectic mix of alternative and techno-pop, with national touring acts like Elvis Costello or Rickie Lee Jones bringing in crowds. On other nights it's merely crowded with trendy types who smoke a lot. You might rub your eyes in disbelief when you see the marquee outside the **Ballard Firehouse**, where acts like Styx, Al Stewart, or the Guess Who come back for one more fling. The Firehouse—which is in fact a converted red-brick firehouse with a single, brick-lined room that makes those old tunes literally bounce off the walls—brings in a lot of R&B-based rock bands from the Northwest, too, like Curtis Salgado & The Stilettos. The **Tractor Tavern**, in the same part of town, kicks butt with a very hot procession of touring acts that always has a little something different going on—maybe a zydeco-country band, rockabilly, and swing on the same ticket, or a fabled old-timer like Ramblin' Jack Elliot. It's your basic brick-walled blues bar with tractor tires hanging from the ceiling and full-sized oil paintings of horses on the wall, and it occupies a lively strip of bars that attract a T-shirt-and-jeans-wearing artsy crowd. Ravers head to the **Fenix Underground**, in Pioneer Square, when self-proclaimed "sex siren and swing diva" Candye Kane is holding forth on the turntable, and **Vogue**, on Capitol Hill, draws eclectic crowds for its world-music nights and weird crowds for fetish nights on Sundays (don't get the two mixed up or you're in for a shock). Pioneer Square's **New Orleans Restaurant** usually has a hot zydeco or Cajun band on weekends.

Where the music swings... On Capitol Hill, the **Century Ballroom** is hands-down the best place to dress up and dance like Fred and Ginger. It has textured walls, plush upholstery, and a huge dance floor for recorded and live swing. Lessons are offered, too, before the real talent shows up. You'll feel like you've died and gone to the Copa. The dressy **Pampas Club**, in Belltown, has a small dance floor for occasional sets of swing and lots of big-band and jazz standards. For serious jazz, the best club in town, and one of the best in the country, is **Dimitriou's Jazz Alley**, a little boîte hidden in a back alley downtown that brings in the top touring jazz acts week in and week out. It will book an act like T.S. Monk or the Charlie Byrd Trio for several days and let them take over the cool, comfortable space. The **Baltic Room** is another scene-making club that specializes in piano jazz most nights, attracting a hip Capitol Hill crowd in cool threads to its Deco space of gray banquettes and bent steel. Want to fox-trot with your honey on a warm Saturday night? Check out the combos of little old men who play ballroom music at the **Seattle Centerhouse** for early shows that attract everyone from blue-jeaned teens on dates to grandmas and grandpas in their Sunday finest.

Dispatches from the gay front... Seattle's large and diverse gay and lesbian community is centered around Capitol Hill. In July there's a hell of a Gay Pride parade down Broadway that never fails to shock, and therefore please. The dancing is hottest at **Neighbours** and **ARO.space**, the former relying on tried-and-true '70s disco cuts and the latter spinning industrial dance mixes with occasional breaks for funk and soul music. Crowds do turn out for ARO.space's underwear and pajama parties. Both have food service that make them popular for one-stop nights on weekends. In Capitol Hill, **Vogue** gets into the act with occasional fetish nights that bring out some of the, shall we say, more extreme segments of the community who enjoy S&M as much as (and frequently with) the next man. For drinking, **Thumpers** is a comfortable, classy place trimmed in oak with a fireplace and a nice view of downtown Seattle from its perch on the south side of Capitol Hill. Also on Capitol Hill's south side is **Linda's Tavern**, a friendly, beer-drinking joint with an outdoor patio that attracts a cross-section of the community and serves a swell weekend brunch. Great selection on the jukebox, too, and occasional spinning by guest DJs.

Superstar athlete needs your support... Please, folks, without your help we can't pay our superstar point guard and centerfielder the eight million bucks a season that they demand to stay in Seattle and not jump ship to New York. Anything you can offer will be greatly appreciated. The **Seattle Mariners** baseball team has begun to play in the splendid new Safeco Field, which you should visit just to know what it's like to be inside the most expensive baseball stadium (at $517 million) in the country. Get a seat in the upper deck on a sunny day (when the retractable roof is open) not only to see our heroes chase down fly balls in centerfield, but to snatch glimpses of Mount Rainier and the sound. Don't worry: The Mariners rarely sell out if they're not leading the league, so you can usually buy tickets on the day of the game. The **Seattle SuperSonics** have had their ups and downs in recent years, but their games at Key Arena generally attract a large, raucous crowd. If you have kids, ask about the family seats, a good bargain that you can only buy with kids in tow at the arena's box office. The **Seattle Seahawks** football team has risen considerably in local expectations since billionaire Paul Allen bought them in 1997 and promptly began to pour money into the team. Since the Kingdome was blown up in a spectacular implosion, the 'hawks have been playing at the University of Washington's rather spartan stadium, but new digs are being built just north of Safeco Field. If Allen has anything to say about it, the new stadium will likely be a great place to watch a football game. Seahawks tickets can be tough to snag, so check with Ticketmaster Northwest before you come to town, or take your chances with the scalpers on game day. For a much lower-key and cheaper sporting thrill, check out the **Seattle Thunderbirds**, a minor-league hockey team that draws a small, enthusiastic group of fans to home games at the **Key Arena.** Their hard-fought games invariably stop four or five times for fights by the young players, who are trying to make instant reputations for themselves on their way to the NHL.

A thriving theater scene... Every now and then, one raises one's nose from the proverbial grindstone and exclaims, with genuine surprise, "Damn, this is really a good theater town." Plays headed to New York, like John Irving's *The Cider House Rules* or a Broadway-bound production of *Jekyll and Hyde*, are often tried out here, and there is a lively and well-supported fringe theater scene in small spaces around town. Actors like Richard Gere, Alan Arkin, and Julie Harris have all put in time on Seattle stages, and the local talent pool is awfully good. For big, brawny productions, the **Seattle Repertory Theatre** and the **Intiman Theatre**, both located in Seattle Center, generally run neck and neck to get the most prestigious shows, such as the Seattle run of *Angels in America* (Intiman) or a terrific new production of *Hamlet* (Rep). They split their seasons so that each is open half the year. Rising up quickly, thanks to a wonderful new space in a converted old building downtown, is **A Contemporary Theater (ACT)**, which does adventurous and avant-garde works in the round like the sensuous *Goblin Market*, based on the poem by Christina Rossetti. ACT also brings in cabaret artists from time to time. In Fremont, the **Empty Space Theatre** is the setting for creative and offbeat work that befits the countercultural neighborhood—recent successes have included a satiric musical version of *Wuthering Heights* and the funny *The Complete History of America*. Children's theater is taken very seriously at the **Seattle Children's Theater**, a big, handsome space at Seattle Center, and it's not Disney fluff that they're offering but world premieres of plays like *Bunnicula* and *Mask of the Unicorn Warrior*. The productions and acting are first-rate—too bad it's only open during the school year, and performs most of its shows for school groups.

The culture club: ballet, opera, and the Seattle Symphony... Benaroya Hall is one of the great recent additions to the Seattle cultural scene—an $118-million building funded in large part by private donors (including several Microsoft millionaires) in the heart of downtown. The acoustics have been compared to those of Carnegie Hall for sheer, crystal-clear brilliance, and from this new home base the **Seattle Symphony**, under the able direction of Gerard Schwarz, has been playing up a storm of music that ranges from pops to baroque and classics. A new concert organ adds to the repertoire. Playing at Seattle Center, the **Seattle Opera** is known as one of the best in the country, with new productions of Wagner's *Ring* cycle that are eagerly awaited by the whole opera-going world. The season always balances a nice mix of opera classics and new works, and brings in some of the top singers in the world. Most shows sell out, so buy early or see if your hotel concierge has any tickets squirreled away. The **Pacific Northwest Ballet**, which also works out of Seattle Center, takes most of its cues from Balanchine during its five-show seasons. Its annual *Nutcracker* production, featuring whimsical sets by Maurice Sendak, has become a holiday ritual for Seattle families.

Where the big acts play... When those wacky *Guys & Dolls* come to town, or Penn & Teller, or Julio Iglesias, you don't put them into just any venue. *Guys & Dolls* and Julio deserve—nay, demand—a big, lavish hall to show their stuff, or at least a superior concert facility like the **Paramount Theatre**, a faded old downtown concert hall that was magically transformed and restored to the tune of some $30 million by former Microsoft exec Ida Coles. It now doubles as a concert venue for acts like Julio, Dwight Yoakam, and Chris Rock, and also brings in Broadway-style touring shows like *Ragtime*. Its sister space is the **Moore Theatre**, a dingy downtown facility that is temperamentally suited to edgier entertainment like Penn & Teller and a very successful run of *Rent*. The **5th Avenue Theatre** also goes for the musicals in a gorgeously appointed space done up to look like an Imperial Chinese throne room. The roaring lion statuary, chandeliers, and exotic trim are all marvelous and make a suitable backdrop for an ongoing series of musicals such as the aforementioned *Guys* and the aforementioned *Dolls*. In the summer, Pier 62/63 on the downtown waterfront is transformed into a lively outdoor concert facility where stars such as Nanci Griffith, Keb' Mo, and Lyle Lovett play in July and August. The series, called **AT&T**

Summer Nights at the Pier, is anxiously awaited by the locals, probably because it seems to promise that summer might actually begin once the big acts come to town. Pray for drizzle (clear skies would be too much to ask). The **Woodland Park Zoo** [see Diversions] stages an utterly pleasant concert series in the summer, where families come with picnic baskets to hear national recording artists like Marc Cohen play in an informal outdoor setting. Rilly big shews like Billy Joel and Elton John wind up at the **Key Arena**, home of the Sonics.

The Index

A Contemporary Theater (ACT). Three performance spaces in a renovated building near the Convention Center, specializing in avant-garde plays.... *Tel 206/292-7676. 700 Union St. Season runs April–Nov.* **(see p. 116)**

ARO.space. Industrial dance music for a mostly gay crowd.... *Tel 206/320-0424. 925 E. Pike St. Cover varies.* **(see p. 114)**

AT&T Summer Nights at the Pier. Outdoor summer concert series on the downtown waterfront.... *Tel 206/281-8111 for info, TicketMaster (206/628-0888) for tickets. Pier 62/63, roughly at the end of Virginia St. on the waterfront.* **(see p. 117)**

Ballard Firehouse. Big red-brick building in Ballard that often recycles the remnants of old rock-and-roll bands.... *Tel 206/784-3516. 5429 Russell Ave. NW. Cover varies.* **(see p. 113)**

Baltic Room. A cool, intimate club for piano jazz.... *Tel 206/ 625-4444. 1207 Pine St. Cover varies.* **(see p. 114)**

The Buckaroo. Neighborhood tavern hosting a mix of bikers and mellow Fremont regulars.... *Tel 206/634-3161. 4201 Fremont Ave. N.* **(see p. 113)**

Century Ballroom. The swingingest place in town and the plushest dance club.... *Tel 206/324-7263. 915 E. Pine St. Separate covers for lessons ($2), shows ($10), and dancing ($4–8).* **(see p. 114)**

Cloud Room. Hip, atmospheric old watering hole atop the Camlin Hotel.... *Tel 206/682-0100. 1619 9th Ave.* **(see p. 112)**

Crocodile Cafe. The top live music club in the city.... *Tel 206/ 441-5611. 2200 2nd Ave. Cover varies.* **(see p. 113)**

Dimitriou's Jazz Alley. Seattle's only true jazz club.... *Tel 206/ 441-9729. 2033 6th Ave. Cover varies.* **(see p. 114)**

Doc Maynard's Public House. Raucous old Pioneer Square bar that packs in a collegiate crowd.... *Tel 206/682-4646. 610 1st Ave. S. Joint cover ($8–10) with other Pioneer Square clubs.* **(see p. 110)**

Empty Space Theatre. An alternative theater company in an upstairs space in Fremont.... *Tel 206/547-7500. 3509 Fremont Ave. N. Season runs Oct–June.* **(see p.116)**

Fenix/Fenix Underground. Bringing some semblance of the cutting edge to the Pioneer Square music scene, drawing a restless young crowd.... *Tel 206/467-1111. 315 2nd Ave. S. Joint cover ($8–10) with other Pioneer Square clubs.* **(see pp. 110, 113)**

5th Avenue Theatre. Gorgeous, Chinese-influenced decor and touring musicals.... *Tel 206/625-1900. 1308 5th Ave.* **(see p. 117)**

Garden Court. Huge, light-filled atrium lounge at the Four Seasons Olympic Hotel, with some of the best martinis in town.... *Tel 206/621-1700. 411 University St.* **(see p. 111)**

Gordon Biersch Brewery Restaurant. Shiny chain brewpub attracting throngs of singles.... *Tel 206/264-9766. 600 Pine St. (top floor of Pacific Place).* **(see p. 111)**

Hale's Brewery and Pub. Elegant brewpub between Ballard and Fremont.... *Tel 206/782-0737. 4301 Leary Way NW.* **(see p. 111)**

Intiman Theatre. Top theater in Seattle, staging works from the likes of Alfred Uhry and Wendy Wasserstein.... *Tel 206/269-1900. Intiman Playhouse at Seattle Center. May–Oct.* **(see p. 116)**

J&M Cafe and Cardroom. Atmospheric old bar in the thick of the Pioneer Square action.... *Tel 206/292–0663. 201 1st Ave. S.* **(see p. 110)**

Jillian's Billiard Club. Popular yuppie poolhall.... *Tel 206/223-0300. 731 Westlake Ave. N.* **(see p. 112)**

Kells Irish Restaurant and Pub. A fun Irish pub spilling out onto the sidewalk.... *Tel 206/728-1916. 1916 Post Alley at the Pike Place Market (enter Post Alley just below the Inn at the Market).* **(see p. 112)**

Key Arena. Major venue for big rock concerts, and home to the Seattle SuperSonics and Seattle Thunderbirds.... *Tel 206/-684-7200. Seattle Center. Box office on 1st Ave. N. side.* **(see pp. 116, 118)**

Linda's Tavern. Friendly Capitol Hill bar/restaurant serves a largely gay neighborhood crowd.... *Tel 206/325-1220. 707 E. Pine St.* **(see p. 115)**

McMenamins Pub & Brewery. Seattle branch of wildly successful Portland brewpub, in Queen Anne.... *Tel 206/285-4722. 200 Roy St.* **(see p. 112)**

Merchants Cafe. Claims to be the oldest watering hole in Seattle.... *Tel 206/624-1515. 109 Yesler Way.* **(see p. 110)**

Moore Theatre. Older, funkier concert hall and theater.... *Tel 206/443-1744. 1932 2nd Ave. Box office at the Paramount Theatre (see below).* **(see p. 117)**

Neighbours. Lively, mostly gay disco on Capitol Hill.... *Tel 206/324-5358. 1509 Broadway. Cover varies.* **(see p. 114)**

New Orleans Restaurant. Pretty decent Cajun cooking, but the real attraction is the rocking southern music in the front room.... *Tel 206/622-2563. 114 1st Ave. S. Joint cover ($8–10) with other Pioneer Square clubs.* **(see pp. 110, 114)**

OK Hotel and Cafe. Pioneer Square club and diner rotates folk music, acoustic acts, and poetry slams.... *Tel 206/621-7903. 212 Alaskan Way S. (under freeway viaduct 1 block west of 1st Avenue S.) Cover varies.* **(see p. 110)**

Oliver's. Practically perfect hotel bar that serves a fabulous martini.... *Tel 206/382-6995. 4th Ave. & Olive Way at the Mayflower Park Hotel.* **(see p. 110)**

Pacific Northwest Ballet. Successful dance company that stages many of Balanchine's works.... *Tel 206/292-2787. Opera House at Seattle Center. Season runs Sept–June.* **(see p. 117)**

Pampas Club. Sophisticated after-dinner lounge for jazzy music and a see-and-be-seen atmosphere.... *Tel 206/728-1337. 2505 1st Ave. (entrance on Wall St.) Cover varies.* **(see pp. 112, 114)**

Paramount Theatre. Highly versatile performance hall for concerts, plays, and musicals.... *Tel 206/443-1744. 911 Pine St. Box office on 9th Ave. side.* **(see p. 117)**

Pyramid Alehouse & Brewery. Big, lively brewpub right across the street from Safeco Field....*Tel 206/682-3377. 1201 1st Ave. S.* **(see p. 111)**

Seattle Centerhouse. Home of the Children's Museum and connected to downtown by the monorail, it presents ballroom dancing music most Saturday nights.... *Tel 206/684-7200. Seattle Center. Usually free; small charge for dance lessons.* **(see p. 114)**

Seattle Children's Theater. Seattle Center venue for outstanding children's productions....*Tel 206/441-3322. Charlotte Martin Theatre, Seattle Center, 2nd Ave. N. at Thomas St. (between Pacific Science Center and Key*

Arena). Open Sept–June, with public shows and matinees on weekends only. **(see p. 116)**

Seattle Mariners. American League baseball team, playing in expensive digs at Safeco Field.... *Tel 206/628-9400; call 206/622-HITS for ticket information and schedules. Safeco Field at 1st Ave. S. & Royal Brougham Way. Tickets also available at the Mariners Clubhouse (tel 206/346-4327, 1800 4th Ave.).* **(see p. 115)**

Seattle Opera. Fine local company, known for acclaimed staging of Wagner's operas.... *Tel 206/389-7676. Opera House at Seattle Center. Season runs Aug–May.* **(see p. 117)**

Seattle Repertory Theatre. Prestigious theater company takes on major works and revivals, with the smaller Leo K. Theatre available for more intimate shows.... *Tel 206/443-2222. Bagley Wright Theatre, Seattle Center. Oct–May.* **(see p. 116)**

Seattle Seahawks. Only the most ass-whuppin' team on the West Coast, thanks to Paul Allen's backing.... *Tel 206/515-4760; call TicketMaster (206/628-0888) for tickets. 2001–2002 games in U-Dub's Husky Stadium, Montlake Blvd. NE on campus.* **(see p. 115)**

Seattle SuperSonics. The local NBA franchise.... *Tel 206/281-5800, or call TicketMaster (206/628-0888) for tickets. Home games at Key Arena, in Seattle Center.* **(see p. 115)**

Seattle Symphony. Classical music programs that reach a wide range of listeners.... *Tel 206/215-4747. Benaroya Hall, 200 University St. Season runs from Sept–May.* **(see p. 117)**

Seattle Thunderbirds. Minor-league hockey team with rabid local fans.... *Tel 206/448-PUCK, or call TicketMaster (206/628-0888) for tickets. Home games at Key Arena, in Seattle Center.* **(see p. 115)**

Showbox. A surprisingly lively and vital dance club that attracts many top national recording artists.... *Tel 206/628-3151. 1426 1st Ave. Cover varies.* **(see p. 113)**

Thumpers. Handsome bar that caters to a mostly gay clientele.... *Tel 206/328-3800. 1500 E. Madison St.*
(see p. 115)

Tini Bigs Lounge. A dark room with red-light accents that attracts a hip, Belltown crowd for drinks and conversation.... *Tel 206/284-0931. 100 Denny Way at 1st Ave. N.*
(see pp. 111, 112)

Tractor Tavern. One of the most successful small music clubs in town, eclectic mix of performers.... *Tel 206/789-3599. 5213 Ballard Ave. NW (take first exit off Ballard Bridge, left onto Leary Way, then left a block). Cover varies.*
(see p. 113)

Trolleyman Pub. Cozy brewpub selling those great Red Hook taps to a loyal crowd.... *Tel 206/548-8000. 3400 Phinney Ave. N.*
(see p. 111)

Vogue. Dance venue with DJs who cater to a young, pierced, Capitol Hill crowd.... *Tel 206/324-5778. 1516 11th Ave. Cover varies.*
(see p. 114)

Waterfront. Big singles scene meets new bar/restaurant, which overlooks Elliott Bay.... *Tel 206/956-9171. 2801 Alaskan Way at Pier 70.*
(see p. 112)

25
10
5
COIN RELEASE
PUSH
1
ABC 2
DEF 3
GHI 4
JKL 5
MNO 6
PRS 7
TUV 8
WXY 9
*
0
#
(401)555-1212
COIN RETURN
PULL

hotlines & other basics

Airports... The **Seattle-Tacoma International Airport** (tel 206/431-4444), universally known as **Sea-Tac**, is based in a municipality of the same name, 13 miles from downtown Seattle and slightly more from Tacoma. Sea-Tac is served by some 30 airlines that can whisk you nonstop to places as close as Portland and as far as Seoul, South Korea. New nonstop flights from international cities are added every year. Connections are made in Los Angeles (for Mexico, South America, and the Far East), Dallas-Ft. Worth (for American Airlines cities and the Caribbean), St. Louis (TWA connections), Minneapolis (Northwest), or Chicago and New York (Europe and the East Coast).

Airport transportation into the city... From Sea-Tac to downtown Seattle can be an expensive cab ride—$25–30. Pick up cabs on either end of the baggage claim area. The **Gray Line Airport Express** (tel 206/626-6088) is a bus that stops at several downtown hotels and costs about $8.50. **Shuttle Express** (tel 425/981-7000 or 800/487-RIDE) is a shared-ride van service; it costs $21 from the airport to downtown, with lower rates for additional riders going to the same stop. There are city buses to and from the airport, but their schedules are infrequent and it takes forever to get where you're going. Don't feel like you're going in circles, by the way, if 10 minutes after you leave the airport you pass another airfield and runway. That's Boeing Field, an airstrip for private planes and charters.

Baby-sitters... **Best Sitters** (tel 206/682-2556) will do the baby honors if your hotel doesn't already have arrangements with a service.

Buses and other public transit... Seattle bus service is handled by **Metro** (tel 206/553-3000), which has routes all over the city, a few of which are intelligible to nonfrequent riders. Transfers are free. There's a ride-free area downtown that goes roughly from Pioneer Square to Belltown, and Alaskan Way to 6th Avenue, but only up to 7pm. We hesitate to give bus information in this book because service is spotty, the routes are difficult to describe, and you don't want to spend your vacation time waiting for a bus, a transfer, and another transfer. To get from downtown to Seattle Center, there's a handy **monorail** that shoots nonstop from Westlake Center to the Seattle Centerhouse ($1.25). Along the waterfront there's a rather touristy **streetcar** ($1.10) that clangs along a track and provides an easy way to get from Pioneer Square to the Market, Aquarium, and all the way north to Pier 70.

Car rentals... You can save a lot of money and hassle by using public transportation if you're staying downtown, but once you venture out into the neighborhoods, you have to have wheels. You can't flag taxis on the street, and even if you call a cab service (see Taxis, below) you may wait forever for one to show up. Keep in mind that much of Seattle's topography involves steep hills that can be scary to drive if you're not used to them. The usual suspects for car rentals, all of which have outposts at the airport, are **Alamo** (tel 800/327-9633 or 292-9770, 1301 6th Ave.), **Avis** (tel 800/831-2847 or 448-1700, 1919 5th Ave.), **Budget** (tel 800/527-0700 or 682-2277, Westlake Ave. at Virginia St.), **Dollar** (tel 800/800-4000 or 682-1316, 1900 Boren Ave.), **Enterprise** (tel 800/325-8007 or 382-1051, 2116 Westlake Ave.), **Hertz** (tel 800/654-3131 or 682-5050, 722 Pike St.), **National** (tel 800/227-7368 or 448-7368, 2300 7th Ave.), and **Thrifty** (800/367-2277 or 625-1133, 801 Virginia St.).

Convention centers... Locals can't stand the **Washington State Convention & Trade Center** (tel 206/461–5840,

8th Ave. at Pike St.) because it extends over busy I-5 and creates enough of a visual distraction to slow down traffic even more than usual. It's nicely located, however, in the heart of downtown, and we have to grudgingly admit that it brings in a lot of business and tourism dollars.

Dentists, doctors, and emergencies... Call **911** for urgent care situations. Try to remember which part of the city you're in if you need emergency aid, as it can cost precious minutes to find you on E. Pine St. rather than Pine St. Doctor and dentist referrals may be had by calling **206/448-CARE.** Let's hope you won't need it, but if you do, **Harborview Medical Center** (tel 206/731-3000, 325 9th Ave.) is one of the best trauma centers in the country.

Events hotline... The ***Seattle Times*** (tel 206/464-2000) has an automated helpline with dozens of categories of information that you can access, from stock quotes and the winning lottery number to concert and movie times.

Ferries... One of the great chilling-out experiences on the West Coast is to board one of the big, comfortable passenger-and-car ferries in downtown Seattle and then cruise quietly to Vashon or Bainbridge islands or the town of Bremerton. The fare for passengers is about $4, it's only collected when you leave Seattle (free to return), and the rides are wonderfully scenic and pleasant when you take your hot latte to the heated outdoor deck. The ultimate cheap date: Do a round-trip at dusk to watch the downtown skyline light up. Call **Washington State Ferries** (tel 206/464-6400 or 800/84-FERRY) for schedules. For a straight shot from Seattle to Victoria that takes in lots of San Juan Islands views, the **Victoria Clipper** (tel 206/448-5000 or 800/888-2535) is a high-speed catamaran that makes the trip in two hours for foot passengers. Advance reservations are necessary because the thing is always packed.

Festivals and special events...

FEBRUARY: **Northwest Flower and Garden Show** (tel 800/229-6311, Washington State Convention & Trade Center) is an enormous show of houseplants, landscapes, nurseries, and gardens, with lots to see and buy.

MARCH: **Whirligig** (tel 206/684-7200, Seattle Centerhouse) presents a festival of indoor rides and games for young children, with incredible bouncy rooms and slides.

MAY: **Opening Day of Boating Season** (tel 206/325-1000, Montlake Cut between Lake Union and Lake Washington) is celebrated with a procession of yachts, sailboats, and rowing shells that bring home the point that Seattle is a great maritime city. May also sees the **Northwest Folklife Festival** [see Diversions].

JUNE: **Fremont Fair** (tel 206/632-1500, N. 34th St. in Fremont) kicks off with a wild parade celebrating the solstice, followed by a weekend fair of arts, crafts, and food.

JULY: **Bite of Seattle** is the headline event [see Diversions]. **Seafair** (tel 206/728-0123), held at various locations around town, is a festival dedicated to water, with hydroplane races, milk carton races, parades, and parties.

SEPTEMBER: The **Bumbershoot** music fest [see Diversions] is Seattle's biggest and best annual event.

Gay & lesbian hotlines & info... The ***Seattle Gay News*** (tel 206/324-4297) is a free community newspaper that you can find in most Capitol Hill bars and restaurants. The ***Pink Pages*** (tel 206/238-5850) is a directory of gay-friendly businesses. Find both at the **Beyond the Closet Bookstore** (tel 206/322-4609, 518 E. Pike St.),which also has good bulletin boards and resource literature. There is also a **Lesbian Resource Center** (tel 206/322-3965, 2214 S. Jackson St.) for all types of referrals.

Newspapers... Until recently, the ***Seattle Post-Intelligencer*** was the city's morning newspaper, while the larger ***Seattle Times*** snared the afternoon crowd. In 2000, however, the *Times* switched to morning distribution, which may drive the *Post-Intelligencer* out of business. The ***Seattle Weekly*** and ***The Stranger*** are entrenched alternative weeklies, with free distribution around town and equally good arts and entertainment listings.

Parking... Parking downtown can be a huge hassle if you're doing it on your own (rather than letting the hotel valet do it), but it's not impossible. The streets downtown are all metered and enforced until 6pm; spaces are precious but findable, particularly if you go away from heavy traffic areas like the Market and Belltown. There are several good lots on First Avenue between Lenora and Union streets ($12–15/day) and at Pacific Place (6th & Pine streets; $18/day). In the neighborhoods and at attractions, you can nearly always find free street parking or lots.

Restrooms... "Just go go go, I don't care how," to quote Dr. Seuss in *Marvin Mooney, Will You Please Go Now?* The trick is to walk into a hotel, bar, or restaurant like you own the place, pretend you're looking for a friend, and use your RRRadar (restroom radar) to find your way. There are few public bathrooms in Seattle, and the ones that are there (such as those in the Pike Place Market) are best left to the troops of homeless people who need them. But people here are nice: Ask most espresso shops or stores for The Room and they'll produce The Key.

Smoking... Puff away. Smoking is allowed in practically every bar, and usually at the bars of restaurants, but not in the dining rooms, although smoking may be permitted in outdoor areas. Public buildings like Safeco Field have designated smoking areas.

Taxes... In King County, Seattle's home, the sales tax is 8.8%. Hotel rooms and car rentals get hit with big surcharges (a whopping 28.3% for a car, which includes a 10% airport tax and an 18.3% special sales tax) that pay for things like our new ballpark.

Taxis & limos... Seattle is not a city where you can expect to flag a cab on the streets. The taxis are all found at the hotels or by phone call. Seattle taxi companies have taken some broadsides lately for being poorly regulated and shoddy in service and equipment. You take your chances, but try **Yellow Cab** (tel 206/622-6500) or **Far West Taxi** (tel 206/622-1717). Rates are $1.80 for the flag drop and $1.80 per mile. Another alternative is the towncar service provided by **Expresscar**, a division of Shuttle Express (tel 425/981-7000 or 800/487-RIDE), which uses Lincoln town cars ($45/hr.).

Time... Seattle is on **Pacific Standard Time**, which is three hours behind New York. Daylight Savings Time is observed in the summer, which can push the sunset as late as 9:45pm at the height of summer.

Tipping... The usual. Add at least 15% to a restaurant or bar tab, and yes, you should tip on the bar tab, too. When in doubt, lean towards the 20% side unless you basically hated the service. Cab drivers get 15%, too, and you should always take care of a doorman or bellman with a dollar per bag that they carry. Tip a valet car attendant a dollar when he brings your car back intact.

Travelers with disabilities... Seattle's city buses are equipped with wheelchair lifts, and drivers will help a wheelchair traveler get to a secure space on the bus. The city's hills can be awfully difficult to negotiate, but picking your spots and planning excursions carefully can flatten it out. The **Pike Place Market** has elevators that can lift you to or from Western Avenue and the waterfront.

Visitor information... The **Seattle-King County Convention and Visitors Bureau** (tel 206/461-5840, 520 Pike St., Ste. 1300, Seattle, WA, 98101-9927) maintains a visitor center inside the convention center, one at the airport in the baggage claim area, and one at the foot of the Space Needle. All provide free maps.

irreverent guide to Portland

introduction

I shall now attempt the rare feat of being the only guidebook author in history to characterize the city of Portland without making a single comparison to Seattle. Portland is... um...uh...well, you see...um....

Okay, I tried, but it can't be done. Ask anyone from, say, Nebraska, and they'll tell you that Seattle and Portland are inextricably bound together in the collective consciousness. They are the two cities that define the Pacific Northwest, that vague "up there" corner of the country, where they drink a lot of coffee and beer while sitting out another week of rain. To many people on the two-days-in-Portland-three-in-Seattle tour, the two cities are nearly interchangeable. Ask a first-time visitor for his impressions of either place, and the same descriptions pop up: such a beautiful city, gorgeous landscape, so progressive, such a vital downtown core, wonderful seafood, water and bridges everywhere, and boy, it rains a lot. All of which are perfectly valid. At a casual glance, the Rose City of Portland really is similar to the Emerald City that lies 180 miles north on the I-5 corridor. Portland, too, is bordered and split down the middle by water: in this case the Willamette River, which runs through town, and the awesome Columbia River, which provides the city's northern boundary. Peaks of the Cascade Range provide the majestic views on sunny days, in Portland's case—

Mount Hood to the east and flat-topped Mount St. Helens to the north. The downtown core of the city is vital and alive with new restaurants, shopping districts, and urban developments that keep businesses, visitors, and residents in the hub of the city—achieving a San Francisco paradigm that other big western cities like Phoenix and L.A. can only envy.

To those of us who live in the Northwest, the comparison with Seattle goes even further. There is a weird kind of déjà vu feeling when you go from Seattle to Portland and encounter many of the same names and features. Paul Allen, for example, the Microsoft billionaire who owns the Seattle Seahawks football team and has financed several new buildings in Seattle, also owns the Portland Trail Blazers basketball team and built the downtown arena, the Rose Garden. Caprial Pence made a name for herself as an outstanding chef in a Seattle restaurant before moving to Portland and opening Caprial's Bistro, one of the top eating spots in town. Each town has an Arboretum, a Fremont Bridge, a Fred Meyer department store, a Grand Central bakery, neighborhood brewpubs, and a Starbucks or independent coffee joint on nearly every corner. The cities are both cut into quadrants, designated NW, SW, NE, and SE, and you have to know your bridges and I-5 and 405 access points if you expect to get around quickly. A Seattleite moving to Portland can pick the neighborhood that most reminds him of home: The Pearl District in Portland resembles Seattle's Pioneer Square, Nob Hill equals Seattle's Queen Anne or Capitol Hill, and Hawthorne corresponds to Ballard or West Seattle. But there it stops—Portland puts on the brakes and the comparisons come grinding to a halt.

Look closer and you'll feel a distinctly different vibe in the Rose City. There's a peculiar kind of Oregon stubbornness, a we'll-do-it-our-way quality that you have to admire about Portland, even if you don't buy into it yourself. Portland may be less populated and less cutting-edge than Seattle, but that's entirely by choice. When Seattle was tearing up its old buildings downtown in the '70s to make way for modern skyscrapers, Portland was preserving its architectural heritage—and now can show off many gorgeous hotels and shopping centers set in wonderful old restored buildings. Instead of adding office space, Portland added public art in the form of delightful sculptures and fountains throughout downtown. Seattle sank its money into major-league sports teams and the facilities they require, while Portland built a light-rail system and began to clean up the polluted Willamette River. At every turn Portland has resisted sprawl (more or less successfully), and the quality of life to which Oregonians cling has been largely preserved. You see this independent attitude borne out in the joggers who hit the streets and parks in huge numbers, following a tradition of running that came out of the University of Oregon in the '70s and was marketed by local boy Phil Knight, who created Nike. You see it in the utterly casual dress of the locals, who make the Seattle-casual style look like Brooks Brothers. There are more ponytails and beards on Portland's men than you ever thought possible outside of a Grateful Dead reunion tour, more jeans than in Levi Strauss's wildest dreams. Teenage rebels still wear spiked, bright-orange hair here, and there's a large contingent of bewildered street people who look like they've just been bussed in from the Oregon boondocks and deposited on the downtown streets.

Portland has its own distinctive style, and stubbornly sticks to it. Yes, there are enclaves of big-city hipness in Portland. The Pearl District on art-walk night (the first Thursday of every month) brings out the sleekly dressed and the artfully coiffed, and restaurants like Oba! and Higgins are as chic as can be. But at times the place can remind you of *Pleasantville*, a kind of real-life *Donna Reed Show* or *Father Knows Best* stuck in time. The biggest event of the year is the wholesome Rose Festival, with the crowning of the Rose Queen making front-page news. It's downright strange, but you pull into a gas station here and attendants leap to your car, thanks to an Oregon law banning self-serve gas. The baseball field, called PGE Park, is in the heart of downtown, and people come out to cheer lustily for a minor-league team with the comforting knowledge that the players aren't multi-millionaires who threaten to leave every season. Portland prides itself on having one of the greatest independent bookstores in the country (Powell's), and there are water fountains, donated by a local businessman, continuously bubbling clean water on downtown street corners—how retro is that?

To Portlanders, Seattle is a confused city that wanted too much to be a big-time player, sacrificing its standards and cost-of-living for big-ticket development. Is there any comparison between the two cities? Not on your life, grins the Portlander as he makes his way down an uncrowded city street to a neighborhood brewpub, where everyone relaxes, rubs his beard, adjusts his ponytail, and orders another pitcher for the table.

Portland Neighborhoods

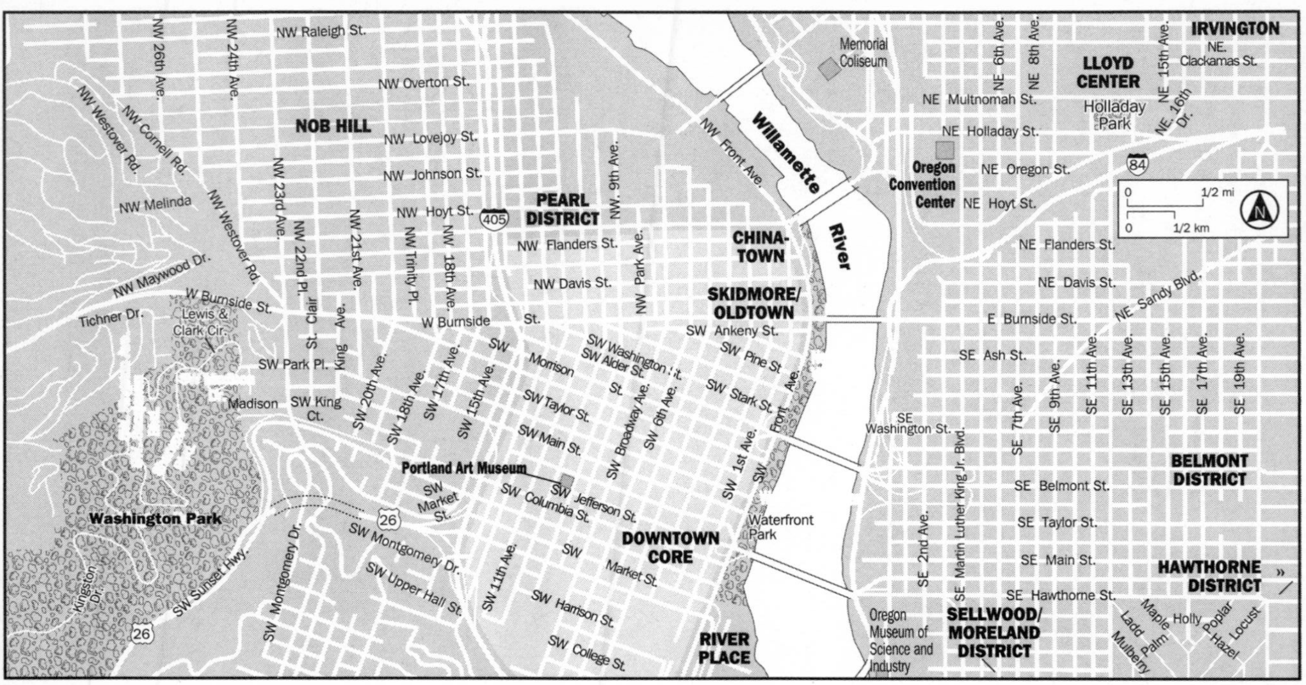

you probably didn't know

Why could Lewis and Clark never have worked for the tourism bureau?... "O! how horriable is the day," wrote William Clark in his journal of the horrid, rain-drenched winter that he and Meriwether Lewis spent on the Oregon coast in 1805–6. "The changes of the weather are exceedingly sudden," he wrote in another entry. "Sometimes tho' seldom the sun is visible for a few moments the next it hails & rains...." Their journals, published in 1814, touched off public perception of the Northwest as a rainy, soggy place.

What's the weather *really* like?... Okay, so Lewis and Clark weren't that far off the mark. Portland enjoys the same mild, wet weather as Seattle, with one significant difference. Although it's farther south, Portland is a good five to seven degrees cooler than Seattle throughout the year, thanks to the Columbia River gorge, which funnels colder air from the east and the Rockies directly into the city. In the winter, this means that Portland can get nasty ice storms that incapacitate the city for days at a time, and a summer day in July tops out at a cool 68 degrees on the average. The average rainfall is 37.2 inches a year (less than Atlanta and Houston, the tourist bureau proudly proclaims), but the relevant factor is that it falls over 154 days a year on the average, meaning lots of gray, cloudy days with light rainfall. July, August, and September are pretty much assured of being clear and dry.

What do Portlanders envy about Seattle?... They envy the Mariners and Seahawks pro sports franchises, because each year, when the Trail Blazers lose in the playoffs (a tradition that may be ending), for the rest of the year the local sports scene resembles that of Spokane. They envy Seattle's robust economy, spurred by national players like Microsoft and Amazon, which gives Seattle a more cosmopolitan atmosphere. In fact, Portland is home to some pretty big players, like Nike and Intel, but it can't quite shake the younger-sibling comparison.

What do Seattleites envy about Portland?... They envy the way traffic runs smoothly on the freeways, and the immense practicality of the MAX light-rail system connecting the downtown area to outlying suburbs west and east. They envy the ease of building bridges over the Willamette River (there are nine) compared with the difficulty of spanning immense Lake Washington, which only has two floating bridges, one of which sank a few years ago. They envy the delicious possibility of running into Tonya Harding, Portland's most notorious skater, at the mini mart. (Oh, come on, you *know* you do.)

Why are all these Washingtonians from across the border shopping in Oregon?... Because of those three magic words: no sales tax.

What's the Rose Festival's dirty little secret?... You should see the nearly rabid response of Portland's young, mostly single women when the big military ships roll into town during the Rose Festival in June. A fleet of destroyers, frigates, and patrol boats from the Navy and Coast Guard dock at the waterfront, and the 3,500-plus sailors are greeted in the most effusive ways by women who flock to the public tours and cruises on board the vessels. Cruising, indeed: When the sailors come to town, it's like last call at a Club Med disco.

Why are they called the Jail Blazers?... Portlanders love their Trail Blazers, the NBA team with a glorious history dating from the Bill Walton/Maurice Lucas era. The Blazers have been on the rise lately, thanks to a new arena, as well as shrewd dealings by GM Bob Whitsitt, but they still manage to have their fair share of scrapes with the law ("Officer, I swear that's not *my* marijuana!"), as well as fines and suspensions imposed by the league.

What does Bo know about Portland that we don't?... You speak of Bo Jackson, one of Nike's greatest pitchmen and a singular reason for the company's meteoric success in the '80s. Although it's well known that Nike is based in the suburb of Beaverton, it's not as well known that the advertising firm of Wieden & Kennedy—which conceived and produced all of those "Bo Knows" spots, as well as the "Just Do It" campaign—is headquartered in downtown Portland, not far from the original NIKETOWN store on SW 6th Avenue.

Do you know your bridges?... To master Portland driving, you need to know your way to and over the nine bridges that span the Willamette. In order from north to south, they are: the **Fremont Bridge,** which provides freeway access downtown on Routes 405 and 30; the **Broadway Bridge,** near the train station; the **Steel Bridge,** on which MAX travels on its way to the Rose Garden; the **Burnside Bridge,** which shelters the Portland Saturday Market; the **Morrison Bridge;** the **Hawthorne Bridge,** which will shoot you from downtown to the Hawthorne District; the **Marquam Bridge,** another highway thoroughfare that allows I-5 to continue on its north/south axis and connects to I-405; the **Ross Island Bridge,** which comes out near the Oregon Museum of Science and Industry; and the **Sellwood Bridge,** to the south of downtown, which provides quick access to Sellwood.

Where can I bum a free ride?... Downtown in MAX's ride-free area, which is basically from the west bank of the river in Old Town past Pioneer Courthouse Square to SW 13th Avenue on the west side of downtown (and extending to Lloyd Center in Fall 2001). Fares on the rest of the system depend on how far you travel and are issued on an honor basis: If a conductor asks to see your ticket, you'd better produce one or face a hefty fine. Each station has ticket machines that can make change, and don't forget to validate your purchased tickets in the machines on each platform before boarding the train.

What is the Portland equivalent of Starbucks?... Coffee People shops throughout the city look like Starbucks, smell like Starbucks, and have the same basic menu as Starbucks, but they're owned by a local firm and stubbornly resist the Starbucks-ization of Portland. Typically for Portland, they also have a better attitude: Their slogan is "Good Coffee, No Back Talk."

accomm

1

odations

Thank you, thank you, thank you, all you foresighted Portland city planners who never tore down the old lumber barons' turn-of-the-century wrought-iron buildings and Italianate masterpieces with terra-cotta ornamentation downtown. That kind of planning and civic awareness (well, okay, a sluggish local economy played a role, too) kept Portland from building skyscrapers, as Seattle did. In recent years, hotel companies have snapped up and restored the old dowager buildings, and the result is a collection of gorgeous hotels in historic buildings. This doesn't mean the hotel scene is dowdy or dated; the architecture and trim of classic buildings and spacious, high-ceilinged lobbies come equipped with state-of-the-art guest rooms and amenities like health clubs and pools. Many of them work equally well as classy business retreats and romantic getaways, and they're almost all located in the downtown core, close to shopping, the best restaurants and bars, and the MAX light-rail train.

Winning the Reservations Game

You'll understand why the burghers of Portland nicknamed the place "The Rose City" if you try to get a last-minute reservation during the Rose Festival month of June. Plan at least three months ahead if you want to attend the festival, and don't expect any discounts from the hotels. Summer is the high season, and although hotels don't generally raise rates, they don't offer many deals either. That doesn't mean that you can't test the waters for some specials to be thrown your way, such as trying to get the hefty parking fee ($16 a day at most downtown hotels) waived, or a few breakfast coupons added to the pot. But the real bargains kick in during the fall and spring, when hotels participate in the Visitors Association's Big Deal promotion, which lowers rates across the board. Expect savings of up to 50 percent. Call the **Portland Oregon Visitors Association** hotline at 87-PORTLAND (tel 877/678-5263) for a complete rundown of what's available. Some hotels come up with all sorts of special enticements for guests. The **Hotel Vintage Plaza**, for example, has packages for guests who bring their dogs or guests who want a romantic "Dream Escape," and the **Fifth Avenue Suites Hotel** magnanimously offered to sell out its entire property (including the restaurant) for the millennium for a mere $225,000. Such a deal! December is a favorite time to visit Portland, when the city is decorated, the stores are open for business with that fabulous no-sales-tax bargain that automatically knocks eight percent off of every purchase, and hotels woo visitors with free parking or special rates.

Is There a Right Address?

Portland's great hotels are located in the downtown core—roughly bordered by **West Burnside Street** to the north, **Southwest Market Street** to the south, **Southwest 13th Avenue** to the west, and the river to the east. The trick, then, is to decide precisely which flavor of downtown living suits you best. The really great news is that the whole downtown area is relatively flat and very easy to walk. Choose your lodging wisely and you might be able to park the car and leave it for your entire stay. Want to be near the river and the Tom McCall Waterfront Park for views and those all-important dawn jogs that keep you trim? You'll want to stay at the **RiverPlace** development or one of several hotels within a few blocks of the waterfront. Will you be going to concerts, visiting museums or doing business at **Portland State University**? You may choose to be within quick walking distance of the **Cultural District** and university on the south side of downtown. For shoppers, several excellent hotels are just off the SW 5th to 6th avenues' retail core, but if the chic **Pearl District** will be your hangout, you'll want to stay on the west side of downtown for quick forays at night to the galleries and trendy restaurants.

The **Convention Center** is across the river in the **Lloyd Center** neighborhood and near the **Rose Garden Arena**. You can stay near there in a hotel geared for conventioneers, or choose a downtown hotel with quick access to the MAX light-rail line, which puts you over the Steel Bridge and into the Convention Center in 10 minutes. This, of course, will make your name-tagged colleagues monstrously jealous. If it's neighborhood living that you crave, the **Concordia** neighborhood in **North Portland** is home to an outlandish converted grade school that now serves as a B&B, bar/restaurant, and neighborhood center, and there's a fancy Victorian home in **Irvington** that also does the B&B thang quite well.

The Lowdown

Your doorman awaits... It comes as a nice surprise in ultra-casual Portland to find uniformed doormen presiding over the entrances of several upscale downtown hotels (and no, the uniform *isn't* jeans and a T-shirt). Doormen have become a scarce commodity in many cities, but they're here in profusion to offer that unique feeling of being swept into exclusive urban digs. They also get your bags moving and keep an eye on the car until the valet comes to park it. Looking like he walked straight off the label of a gin bottle, the doorman at the **Heathman Hotel** is in full red Beefeater regalia as he greets you, giving instant notice that the hotel is going to be a visual treat. That sense is confirmed when you walk into a tasteful, woody lobby decorated with modern paintings, with another art gallery on the second floor. The rooms are on the small side, but comfortable and trimmed in teak. At the **Governor Hotel**, the dude at the door is done up in a long black coat with gold trim and a quasi-military officer's hat. Walk through his doors and you're in a stunning lobby with a wall-sized sepia painting of explorers Lewis and Clark on their continent-spanning expedition westward. Guest rooms are large and comfortable, and the baths have old-fashioned pedestal sinks and large tubs. An entrance to the fabulous walnut-paneled lobby of the **Benson Hotel** wouldn't be complete without Gary, the top-hatted doorman, ushering you in as if you're being announced at a debutante ball. While the guest rooms themselves aren't as magnificent, it's the best place in town for making deals and being seen. At the **Hotel Vintage Plaza**, the way is paved by an elegant gent in a dark blue trenchcoat, tie, and sweater-vest with the hotel logo; the first thing you may see inside are the complimentary bottles of Oregon wine available for afternoon tastings in the lobby. The guys at the door of the **Fifth Avenue Suites Hotel** preside over a busy sidewalk of shoppers and government workers, and can help you with all of those shopping bags you seem to acquire every time you walk down the street. Don't be surprised to run into celebs like Billy Joel or the other big-name acts who play the Rose Garden or Paramount and hang out at the Fifth Avenue. Be kind to your doorman: Use him, befriend him, give him a smile and a tip, and you will never wait long for a cab.

For quick convention access... The incredibly handy MAX light-rail train is especially useful to conventioneers, particularly if you want to escape the Convention Center crowds on the east side of the river at the end of the day and enjoy the food and nightlife downtown. A stay at the **Governor Hotel** (ask for a corner room with a fireplace) will put you within a few blocks' walk of the lively, artsy Pearl District and some good shopping while being only two blocks from the SW Yamhill Street MAX stop and a 10- to 15-minute ride over the river to the Convention Center. Returning to the Governor's deliciously comfortable lobby and rooms is ample reward for having done time on the convention floor. A couple of blocks closer, in the thick of downtown shopping, is the brand-new **Westin Portland Hotel,** which is going for a softer small-hotel look in a departure from the usual strictly business Westin approach. The buttercream-and-mustard-colored lobby has a library and a living room with a sandstone fireplace, but it's still pretty sedate and corporate. Its central location and proximity to the MAX, not to mention business-friendly features like in-room fax machines, will make it very attractive to the convention crowd. On the east side of downtown, the **Four Points Sheraton** has a bit of a motor-inn feel to it, but it's just across the street from Tom McCall Waterfront Park and less than a block from MAX's SW 1st Avenue stops—you can still get in a long run or walk in the park before heading to the convention center. Two blocks from MAX's Civic Stadium stop is the **Mallory Hotel**, a dowager with a faded ornate beauty, some of the best rates you're going to find downtown, and a fiercely loyal clientele who loves its homey restaurant and dark green lobby with crystal chandeliers. With its Old Town/Chinatown location, the **Embassy Suites Portland Downtown** is the closest of them all to the Convention Center—just a five-minute

Who Was Bubbly Benson?

Lumber baron, builder, water fountain guru—these all describe Simon Benson, who put his stamp on Portland in many ways at the turn of the century (the 20th century, that is). We remember him today not only for the Benson Hotel, which he built, still one of the most elegant lodgings in town, but for the Benson Bubbler water fountains that gurgle clean water night and day, rain or shine, around the city in distinctive four-fountain clovers rendered in wrought-iron. Benson installed 20 of them as a gift to the city in 1912 in hopes that it would slake his millworkers' thirst (fat chance; they continued to drink brew). The city installed another 40 over the years and they're a constant bubbling sight around town—remarkably free of gum and cigarette butts, too.

ride across the bridge on MAX. It urbanizes the usual Embassy Suites experience, with rooms trimmed in dark woods and terry-cloth robes in the bathroom. Pay the small premium for a mountain-view room and, if the sun is out, you'll be rewarded with vistas of Mount Hood. If you want to do it the opposite way, staying near the Convention Center and taking the train into the city for restaurants and entertainment, try **The Lion and the Rose**. This is a Victorian bed-and-breakfast in the Irvington neighborhood with splendid antique furniture and telephones and computer jacks in each room for taking care of business. Sitting down for breakfast at the gleaming mahogany table downstairs is a fine way to gear up for a day of deal making, and you can save a few bucks by making your own dinner in the kitchen. If business is going to keep you in town for upwards of a week or more, the **Residence Inn by Marriott** at Lloyd Center is a good bet. The 168 rooms boast that soothing, chain-hotel nonstyle and are more like apartments than guest rooms, with full kitchens and sitting areas, and there's a heated outdoor pool and three Jacuzzis. The Convention Center MAX stop is only a few minutes away for quick, surgical strikes into downtown for dinner and pub crawling.

Rooms with a view... There's no telling when the skies will clear up long enough to get good looks at Mount Hood or Mount St. Helens, but the Willamette River is always there, rain or shine. The **RiverPlace Hotel** is a modern lodging in the water's-edge development of the same name; its large rooms, done in bright blues and lavenders, look out over the river and a small marina. You'll pay quite a premium for that little strip of river view and the newness of it all. If it's any consolation, guests can work out at the gleaming new RiverPlace Health Club. The **Four Points Sheraton** isn't exactly at the side of the river, but across busy Naito Parkway from the Willamette. It does, however, have good views of the water and Tom McCall Waterfront Park, especially from the upper floors, and is right in the thick of things when the annual Rose Festival turns the park into a gigantic carnival. Don't expect much more than a standard double room with a cookie-cutter design; the location is the thing here. A view of a different kind is offered from the starlight rooms on the uppermost floor of the **Hotel Vintage Plaza**, which have clever angled skylights that are equally intriguing when it rains or shines—they give a loftlike feel to the small, comfortable hotel rooms. Be forewarned that the bar at the adjoining restaurant, Pazzo's, makes to-die-for Lemon Drops, those sweet concoctions of vodka and lemonade that can easily take command of an entire evening.

The best for business... You and I should have a nickel for every deal made in the lobby of the lavishly ornate **Benson Hotel**, which was built downtown in 1912 by lumber baron Simon Benson (he also gave the city its "Benson Bubbler" water fountains). It's paneled in an exquisitely textured Russian Circassian walnut that you simply can't find anymore, and guests have ranged from Madonna to Bill Clinton to the San Antonio Spurs (not at the same time, or the tabloids would be buzzing). The Benson has a rather brusque, corporate attitude that is reflected in efficient, if icy, service, and the smallish rooms, particularly in the older part of the hotel, are nothing to scream about. But that lobby is worth a million bucks. A much warmer refuge, also downtown, is the **Hotel Vintage Plaza**, which pays homage to Oregon wine by naming the rooms after area vineyards, patterning bedspreads and drapes with grapes and vines, and holding wine tastings for guests by the fireplace in the lobby every night. One suite is co-named after the celebrity who used it for all his Portland visits: Michael Jordan. Ever the thoughtful businessman, he chose a townhouse suite with a bedroom reached by staircase from a spacious living room with a glass dining table and wet bar (perfect for meetings with your local shoe company). Kimpton Hotels of San Francisco, which owns the Vintage Plaza, also gutted and completely rebuilt the **Fifth Avenue Suites Hotel**, a bright, cheerful downtown place with large oil paintings on the walls of the comfortable living rooms, suites decorated in yellow stripes with light carpets, and business amenities such as fax machines and two-line phones in every room. The living rooms are separated from the bedrooms by sliding doors. The **Embassy Suites Portland Downtown**, which occupies the 1912 space of the old Multnomah Hotel, completely overturns the usual Embassy Suites standard formula of an atrium and a basic breakfast buffet:

The hotel lobby is a great white wedding cake of decorative ornamentation on coved ceilings, the suites are done in dark woods and have marble bathrooms, and breakfast is a big, cooked-to-order spread in a spacious dining room. Indeed, the place is phenomenal, right down to a spacious health club with a large indoor pool. It's a quick shot to the Convention Center and centrally located to downtown office buildings. The granite high-rise a block from Nordstrom downtown is the new **Westin Portland Hotel,** which threw open its doors for business in the summer of 1999. It's a prototype for something called the "Westin2000" hotel concept, which boils down to combining business-friendly features like fax machines, speaker phones, and dataports in the rooms with a good health club, in-room CD players, and a friendly lobby with a fireplace. The newest star on the hotel horizon is the **Paramount Hotel,** a sister property to Seattle's digs of the same name, which has extra-spacious guest rooms and lots of business amenities in a terrific location just off Park Avenue (and a credit card's toss from Nordstrom). The lobby is a very cool place of marble and chandeliers.

Boutique hotels with big-hotel service... You can just about see the rheumy eyes of a weary business traveler light up when he walks into a lobby of a place like downtown's handsomely restored **Heathman Hotel**, with its emphasis on big, bold, modern art on the walls and quick, attentive service from the concierge and reception desk. There's an elegant little library upstairs, perfect for reading the paper at the end of a busy day, a wood-trimmed lounge with more great artwork (not to mention a jazz singer), and an excellent restaurant. The **Governor Hotel** gives you that comforting feeling, too, with a lobby full of leather wing chairs that practically call out your name, and soothing rooms with buttercream walls and light green accents. A corner room with a fireplace brings in lots of natural light and some downtown street atmosphere, and the attached Jake's Grill is a fine place for a late dinner or drink. The **Hotel Vintage Plaza** was one of the first to fulfill the dream of owner Bill Kimpton to provide businesspeople with a comfortable, nonchain-hotel experience. Its afternoon wine tastings of Oregon varietals in the lobby have been widely copied, and room service from the delightful Pazzo's restaurant off the lobby is a huge treat. Rooms are dark and quietly done in greens and maroons, with oversized Jacuzzi tubs in many. The **Fifth Avenue Suites Hotel**, which opened in 1996, updates the Kimpton experience with lighter, friendlier rooms and an excellent health club to go with the art and the living room–style lobby (and, lest we forget, the complimentary wine).

If you're bringing the kids... Want to play a delicious trick on your kids? Make them go to school, specifically the fabulous **McMenamins Kennedy School**. Those crazy McMenamin brothers [see Dining] bought a local schoolhouse a few years ago in North Portland's Concordia neighborhood and completely remade it into a neighborhood center, movie theater, bar/restaurant, and bed-and-breakfast. The 35 guest rooms used to be classrooms (many are still named after teachers); they now hold queen-sized beds, phones, and private baths to go with the original chalkboards and coat closets. It can be downright eerie, not to mention extremely entertaining, to walk the old halls (now decorated not with sixth-grade class projects but tile mosaics and original paintings), work out in the gym, eat a pizza in the cafeteria, or have a drink and a smoke in the Detention Bar. The **Embassy Suites Portland Downtown** gives you a two-room space to spread out the troops and adds Nintendo availability on the televisions and a large indoor pool that is more conducive to splashing and playing than swimming laps. Kids 18 and under stay free with parents, and you can save a fortune on the complimentary, cooked-to-order breakfasts served in the Arcadian Gardens room, which doubles as a bar with complimentary drinks for adults in the evening.

Make mine romance... You can just about imagine what a rainy weekend spent indoors at a romantic hotel can do for your love life (well, I hope you can imagine it). If it's lacy curtains, lavender print wallpaper, and a king-sized bed with a draped canopy that get the old juices flowing, then by all means book the Lavonna Room at **The Lion and the Rose**, a lovely remodeled Victorian B&B. It's located just a block away from the NE Broadway commercial strip and within walking distance of the Lloyd Center shopping mall, but the bed-and-breakfast itself, situated on a corner in a residential neighborhood, is peaceful and gracious, with overstuffed velvet furniture in the living room and an old-fashioned swing on the wrap-around porch. Movie buffs will love what the management has done with the in-room movie selection at the **Heathman Hotel** downtown. Instead of the usual four or five on-demand films, guests are offered an 18-page booklet that contains a selection of literally hundreds of classic movies that you can watch for free. Just call the hotel desk with your choice, and it will be piped into your hotel-room television. Believe me, you can watch an awful lot of classic old movies, and eat some fantastic room service food from the Heathman restaurant, in bed on a rainy weekend. The starlight rooms at the **Hotel Vintage Plaza** are utterly delightful, with a skylight that looks out onto neighboring buildings and the weeping Portland sky (yes, there are blinds on the skylight). Ask for a room that includes a Jacuzzi tub big enough for two, and you will find yourself getting very intimate and familiar. The Vintage Plaza also offers a "Dream Escape" package that includes chilled Dom Perignon champagne, fresh flowers, dinner, and even a pair of lovebirds in a gilded cage sent to your room. For a real throwback evening, take your inamorata back to school. **McMenamins Kennedy School** is the whimsically refurbished grade school that now doubles as a bed-and-breakfast, movie house, and bar/restaurant (will you be having a drink in the Honors Bar or the Detention Bar?). If you prefer to go for that noir-ish nostalgic feeling—and save a few bucks in the bargain—there's always the **Mallory Hotel**, which is perched on the edge of downtown and on the edge of dowdy. The lobby is all decorative plaster work, chandeliers, and carved wooden furniture; the dining room is darkened by heavy drapes and a gilded ceiling. The new **Paramount Hotel** is awfully comfortable and cozy, with its large rooms done in subtle stripes, and big, thick beige comforters on the bed that practically scream, "Snuggling begins here!" You can get your culture and shopping fixes quickly at the nearby museums and shops, then beat it back to your room for lively discussions about politics (or other euphemisms for getting romantic).

For fitness buffs... The **RiverPlace Hotel** has the edge for workout fanatics—it's not only located adjacent to the jogging paths at Tom McCall Waterfront Park, which you can run south along the river for miles if you want to pick your way through an industrial area [see Getting Outside], but it also allows you day memberships at the gleaming new RiverPlace Health Club. In a towering room supported by pillars, the smart **Embassy Suites Portland Downtown** offers a huge indoor pool in the basement as well as Jacuzzi tubs and a serviceable fitness center. At the Convention Center, the long-stay specialist **Residence Inn by Marriott**, whose guests are usually here for a week or more, offers an outdoor lap pool; a few bucks extra grants guests access to the full-service Lloyd Center Athletic Club, just a short jog away. The **Fifth Avenue Suites Hotel**, ever attentive to luxury touches, has an excellent in-house workout facility of Stairmasters, bicycle machines, and weight stations, but what really puts it over the top is the attached Aveda Spa for post-workout massages and aromatic treatments.

Moveable feasts... There's room service and there's dining, and usually you'll find a gaping difference between the two. For quality noshing while wearing little more than your complimentary bathrobe, head straight to one of the Kimpton properties, which have always understood that business travelers want great food in their rooms. At the **Hotel Vintage Plaza,** you can treat yourself to an Italian feed from Pazzo [see Dining]. Next time I go, I'm going to tell the waiter to just have the chef send up his personal favorites, and see what wonders of pasta and bruschetta and veal he dreams up. The **Fifth Avenue Suites Hotel** will send up an American feast from its Red Star Tavern & Roast House [see Dining], such as an expertly roasted chicken whose skin has been rubbed with sage, a pile of garlic mashed potatoes, and cornbread drizzled in honey that comes hot from a skillet. At moments like those you can forget every cold cup of room-service coffee or lifeless club sandwich you ever had. The **Heathman Hotel** also puts on a spectacular room-service feed, thanks to the efforts of French chef Philippe Boulot, who will send to your room anything from homemade pâté and bread to an elaborate five-course tasting menu.

Bang for the buck... Yes, there are cheap hotels near the airport and every kind of chain lodging in Portland's 'burbs, but you don't need us to help you find four plain white walls and a bathroom with a Sani-strip over the john. For value, the **Embassy Suites Portland Downtown** delivers a big-hotel feeling for considerably less than $150 a night, and you can comfortably pack the whole family into the two-room suites. The ornate old **Mallory Hotel** is a steal at $80 per night, especially now that the expanded MAX line puts it within quick reach of the whole downtown area. At the waterfront, the **Four Points Sheraton** isn't much for looks, but for around $100 a night it puts you right across the street from a great park and has views of the Willamette. If all of the above are still too dear, there's always the **Portland International Hostel**, across the river in the Hawthorne District, which is just what it promises: a youth hostel. It's mostly dormitories, with only one private room, but unlike some strict hostels, this one allows guests to come and go at any time throughout the day. If you have a special yearning to sleep in the bedroom of a kid who's off at college, try **Northwest Bed & Breakfast Travel Unlimited**, which can set you up as a guest in the home of a Portlander for a night or two.

The Index

$$$$	over $200
$$$	$150–$200
$$	$100–$150
$	under $100

Price applies to a standard double room for one night.

Benson Hotel. Portland's priciest and most pedigreed hotel, with turn-of-the-century elegance that starts with the splendid walnut-trimmed lobby.... *Tel 503/228-2000, fax 503/226-2709. www.bensonhotel.com. 309 SW Broadway Ave., 97205-3725. 287 rooms. $$$$*

(see pp. 144, 147)

Embassy Suites Portland Downtown. A smartly urbanized version of the standard Embassy Suites, set in the renovated Multnomah Hotel built in 1912. Breakfast room, health club with pool.... *Tel 503/279-9000 or 800/EMBASSY, fax 503/497-9051. www.embassyportland.com. 319 SW Pine St., 97204-2726. 276 rooms. $$*

(see pp. 145, 147, 149, 151, 152)

Fifth Avenue Suites Hotel. The one-bedroom all-suite rooms are bright and cheerful, with yellow-striped wallpaper and French posters for decoration. No kitchenettes, but room service is terrific. They also have in-room fax machines and a good health club, too.... *Tel 503/222-0001 or 800/711-2971, fax 503/222-0004. www.5thavenuesuites.com. 506 SW Washington St., 97204-1550. 221 rooms. $$$*

(see pp. 142, 144, 147, 149, 151)

Four Points Sheraton. Budget place with a great location on the east side of downtown, adjacent to the Tom McCall Waterfront Park.... *Tel 503/221-0711 or 800/899-0247, fax 503/274-0312. www.fourpointsportland.com. 50 SW*

Morrison St., 97204-3390. 140 rooms. $

(see pp. 145, 146, 152)

Governor Hotel. Large guest rooms in an elegant old building near the Pearl District.... *Tel 503/224-3400 or 800/554-3456, fax 503/241-2122. www.govhotel.com. 611 SW 10th Ave., 97205-2725. 100 rooms. $$$*

(see pp. 144, 148)

Heathman Hotel. Very elegant small hotel in the cultural district, with a well-deserved reputation for excellent, understated service. Close proximity to the Arlene Schnitzer Concert Hall.... *Tel 503/241-4100 or 800/551-0011, fax 503/790-7110. www.heathmanhotel.com. 1001 SW Broadway Ave., 97205-3096. 150 rooms. $$*

(see pp. 144, 148, 150, 151)

Hotel Vintage Plaza. Upscale Kimpton Hotels property downtown that draws its inspiration from Oregon wines.... *Tel 503/228-1212 or 800/243-0555, fax 503/228-3598. www.vintageplaza.com. 422 SW Broadway Ave., 97205-3595. 107 rooms. $$$*

(see pp. 142, 144, 147, 148, 150, 151)

The Lion and the Rose. Superbly appointed Victorian home, originally built in 1906 and beautifully restored as a B&B.... *Tel 503/287-9245 or 800/955-1647, fax 503/287-9247. www.lionrose.com. 1810 NE 15th Ave., 97212. 6 rooms. $$* **(see pp. 146, 149)**

Mallory Hotel. Fading dowager has smallish, clean rooms and a decor that's straight out of a swank urban hotel—from the '50s.... *Tel 503/223-6311 or 800/228-8657, fax 503/223-0522. www.malloryhotel.com. 729 SW 15th Ave., 97205-1994. 130 rooms. $*

(see pp. 145, 150, 152)

McMenamins Kennedy School. Fascinating restoration of a local grade school into a B&B with a restaurant, movie theater, bars, and a tiled Jacuzzi.... *Tel 503/249-3983 or 888/249-3983, fax 503/288-6559. www.mcmenamins.com. 5736 NE 33rd Ave., 97211. 35 rooms. $*

(see pp. 149, 150)

Northwest Bed & Breakfast Travel Unlimited. Service that arranges stays in private homes in the Portland area, at rates that vary from $65 to $150 per night.... *Tel 503/243-7616. $–$$.* **(see p. 152)**

Paramount Hotel. Snappy new digs in a nice location downtown offer some of the roomiest guest rooms in town, as well as big bathrooms done up in marble. Nice business amenities, too.... *Tel 503/223-9900 or 800/426-0670, fax 503/223-7900. www.portlandparamount.com. 808 SW Taylor St., 97205. 154 rooms. $$.* **(see pp. 148, 150)**

Portland International Hostel. The budget place to stay in town, right on the funky Hawthorne strip of bars and shops. There's 24-hour access to its single-sex dorms and one private room that sleeps four. Linens are available for an extra fee, and the kitchen is open to guests.... *Tel 503/236-3380, fax 503/236-7940. www.teleport.com/~hip. 3031 SE Hawthorne Blvd., 97214. 34 beds. $* **(see p. 152)**

Residence Inn by Marriott. Apartment-style lodgings near the Convention Center.... *Tel 503/288-1400 or 800/331-3131, fax 503/288-0241. www.residenceinnportland.com. 1710 NE Multnomah St., 97232-2138. 168 rooms. $$* **(see pp. 146, 151)**

RiverPlace Hotel. The only true waterfront property in town, cornerstone of the RiverPlace shopping development and marina.... *Tel 503/228-3233 or 800/227-1333, fax 503/295-6161. www.riverplacehotel.com. 1510 SW Harbor Way, 97201-5105. 84 rooms. $$$$* **(see pp. 146, 150)**

Westin Portland Hotel. Opened in summer 1999 with a concerted effort to lure business travelers. Standard Westin amenities, like a big health club and business-friendly guest rooms.... *Tel 503/294-9000 or 888/627-8401, fax 503/241-9565. www.westinportland.com. 750 SW Alder St., 97205. 205 rooms. $$$* **(see pp. 145, 148)**

Portland Accommodations

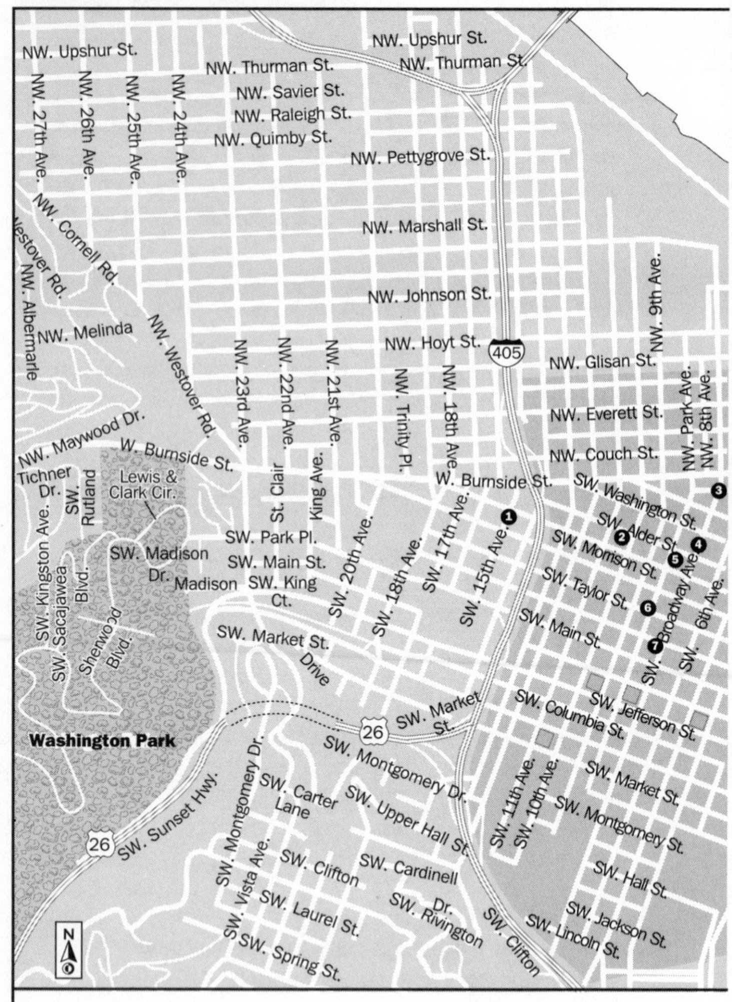

Benson Hotel **3**
Embassy Suites Portland Downtown **9**
Fifth Avenue Suites Hotel **8**
Four Points Sheraton **10**
Governor Hotel **2**
Heathman Hotel **7**
Hotel Vintage Plaza **4**
The Lion and the Rose **12**
Mallory Hotel **1**
Paramount Hotel **6**
Residence Inn by Marriott **13**
RiverPlace Hotel **11**
Westin Portland Hotel **5**

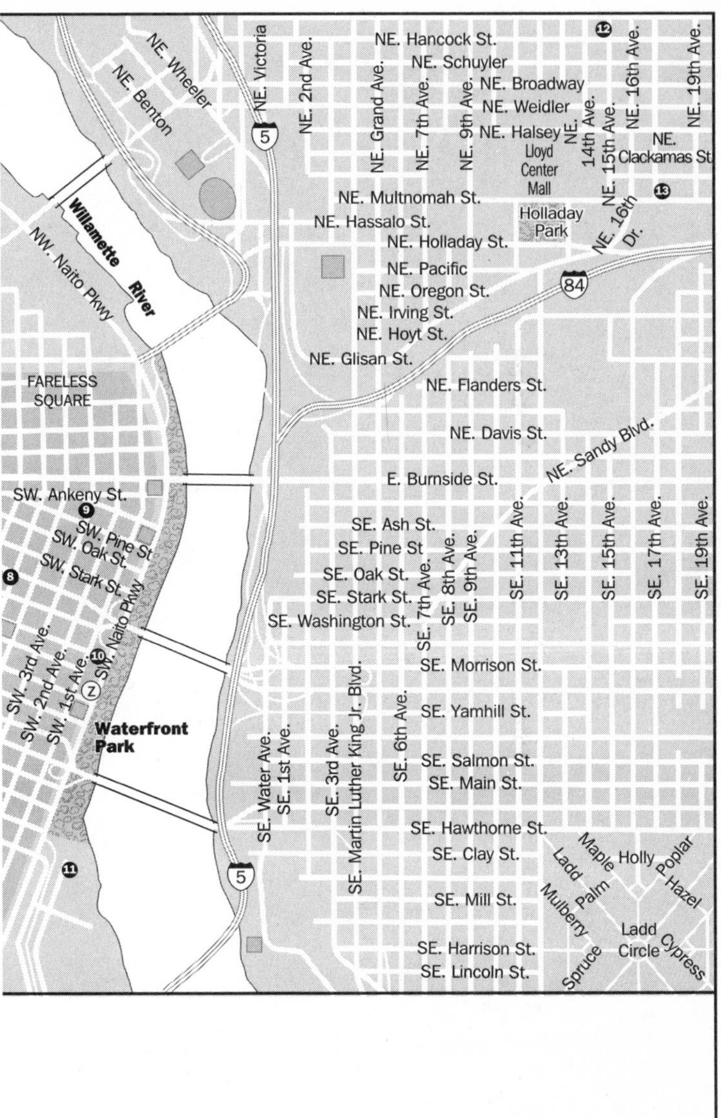

NE. Hancock St.
NE. Schuyler
NE. Broadway
NE. Weidler
NE. Halsey
NE. Clackamas St
Lloyd Center Mall
NE. Multnomah St.
NE. Hassalo St.
Holladay Park
NE. Holladay St.
NE. Pacific
NE. Oregon St.
NE. Irving St.
NE. Hoyt St.
NE. Glisan St.
NE. Flanders St.
NE. Davis St.
E. Burnside St.
NE. Sandy Blvd.
NE. Wheeler
NE. Benton
NE. Victoria
NE. 2nd Ave.
NE. Grand Ave.
NE. 7th Ave.
NE. 9th Ave.
NE. 14th Ave.
NE. 15th Ave.
NE. 16th Ave.
NE. 19th Ave.
NE. 16th Dr.
Willamette River
NW. Naito Pkwy
FARELESS SQUARE
SW. Ankeny St.
SW. Pine St
SW. Oak St.
SW. Stark St.
SW. Naito Pkwy
SW. 3rd Ave.
SW. 2nd Ave.
SW. 1st Ave.
Waterfront Park
SE. Ash St.
SE. Pine St
SE. Oak St.
SE. Stark St.
SE. Washington St.
SE. Morrison St.
SE. Yamhill St.
SE. Salmon St.
SE. Main St.
SE. Hawthorne St.
SE. Clay St.
SE. Mill St.
SE. Harrison St.
SE. Lincoln St.
SE. 7th Ave.
SE. 8th Ave.
SE. 9th Ave.
SE. 11th Ave.
SE. 13th Ave.
SE. 15th Ave.
SE. 17th Ave.
SE. 19th Ave.
SE. Water Ave.
SE. 1st Ave.
SE. 3rd Ave.
SE. Martin Luther King Jr. Blvd.
SE. 6th Ave.
Ladd
Maple
Holly
Poplar
Hazel
Palm
Mulberry
Ladd Circle
Spruce
Cypress
5
84
8
9
10
11
12
13
Z

din

ing 2

Simple, fresh, and good—those are the three central tenets of Portland's culinary philosophy. Bonus points are awarded, of course, for use of ingredients from Oregon producers. As Cory Schreiber of **Wildwood** put it, "People here like traditional things prepared well, and will order them over and over." Fine-dining places like **Higgins** and the **Heathman Restaurant** will offer the freshest local sturgeon, salmon, and crab, accompanied by crisp Pinot Gris and Pinot Noir wines from Oregon vintners. Bistros like **Wildwood** and **Caprial's Bistro** will build elegant dishes around freshly picked Oregon morels, asparagus, and herbs, and even the thick burgers and excellent small pizzas at brewpub-restaurants like the **Bridgeport Brew Pub** and the **Blue Moon Tavern & Grill,** with their fresh toppings and made-to-order service, are a cut above typical pub fare in most cities. The beer, of course, is locally made and first-rate, and no restaurant-bar worth its salt will have fewer than a half-dozen local brews on tap. The emphasis on fresh and local makes for a certain similarity in the menus around town, but you can count on a successful Portland restaurant to deliver the goods time and again.

Things Even Lewis and Clark Wouldn't Have Eaten

Those intrepid scouts from the east were mighty hungry the winter they camped out in Oregon, but one can't imagine even Lewis and Clark being hungry enough to wrap their lips around the greasy ***corndogs*** *sold from wagons at the Saturday market, the seemingly calcified day-old* ***cranberry-orange scones*** *at various coffee shops, or a* **Honkin' Huge Burrito,** *sold from lunch wagons around Pioneer Courthouse Square (they come in three sizes: small, medium, and* Honkin'*). Thanks anyway, but we seem to have lost our appetites.*

How to Dress

Portland is so utterly casual that if you really *want* to wear a coat and tie (gents) or your elegant Chanel suit (ladies), you'll feel like an overdressed dupe at all but a few classy eateries. The same goes for the chic black outfit, which will fairly scream, "I'm from New York and life is bleak!" In other words, wearing stylish clothes in most parts of town will draw the same startled looks you'd get if you spiked your hair and dyed it purple. Business wear will work at high-end restaurants like **Higgins**, **El Gaucho**, and the **Heathman Restaurant**, which attract their share of local lawyers and developers. The noir look will work in Pearl District trendsetters like **¡Oba!** or **Bluehour**. Everywhere else the dress code is strictly jeans and sportswear and even (insert shudder here) warm-up suits, if you're so inclined.

Getting the Right Table

In Portland, nobody knows or cares who is sitting at the number-one booth in the corner. Reservations can be made on the day of dining at most places, with the notable exceptions of **Bluehour** on any night, or **Higgins** and the **Heathman Restaurant** on nights when there is a show at the nearby Arlene Schnitzer Concert Hall (locally known as The Schnitz). You may also need to reserve further ahead for **¡Oba!** on first-Thursday art-walk nights in the Pearl District. It's worth calling a week ahead for any of these, or hope your concierge can pull a few strings. If the weather looks like it's going to shine (rather than rain), try to reserve an outdoor table at **Salty's on the Columbia, Harborside**, or the outdoor courtyard at **McMenamins Kennedy School**. Sidewalk and outdoor tables fill up fast on summer days at bar/restaurants like the **Blue Moon Tavern & Grill**; use your tourist status to your advantage by getting there before six to stake out a prime spot.

The Lowdown

Scene-makers where the food is as good as the look... Portland's independent restaurants have made huge strides in recent years, and are well on the way to proudly matching any city on the West Coast for atmosphere and creative cooking. You can't go wrong at any of these eateries, which is why they're generally packed with locals who will scramble to find a seat at the bar or the counter if a table's not available. **Wildwood** is a sleek, modern Nob Hill bistro with spare decoration and a no-nonsense approach to serving fresh, local cuisine. Its star chef, Corey Schreiber, is the only Portland chef to win a James Beard Foundation award for excellence; sit at the curving counter to watch him and his cohorts feed a massive wood-fired oven and produce exquisite dishes with big flavors, such as Trask River salmon nestled on a bed of sweet-pepper couscous, or a mushroom risotto that is finished in the oven. On the other side of town, in the Moreland neighborhood, **Caprial's Bistro**—home restaurant of chef and cooking personality Caprial Pence—does a similar turn. The cream-colored, light-filled room has piped banquettes on a parquet floor, with wines displayed handsomely on shelves along one wall as if it was a wine store. The selection process is more like a wine store too: you browse the displays and snag your favorite for the table. The open kitchen, fronted by a counter, produces delights like smoked-sturgeon chowder or a lamb sandwich with fennel jam for lunch; or for dinner, a hefty salmon encrusted with bread crumbs and stuffed with Gruyère. Menus change every month or so to keep on top of the local produce, and the desserts are terrific. For Mediterranean food that leans heavily toward French influences, head to **Castagna** in the Hawthorne district, where you can get a great bowl of bouillabaisse or interesting combinations like poached prawns in a tarragon mousseline or fettucine with roasted beets and arugula. The room is big and white and spare, with a cork floor, and next door there's an adjoining cafe with a bistro menu (try the mountain of crispy fries). **Pazzo,** at the Hotel Vintage Plaza, is a friendly (read: lighter and noisier) Italian bistro presided over by chefs who know their pasta. The rooms are arched red brick with thick smears of mortar on the walls; private parties love the bottle-lined wine cellar, which can be booked for parties of 10 or more; and the food is a sensational take on upscale Italian dishes. The paper-thin tuna carpaccio on a parsley sauce and the homemade ravioli with Taleggio cheese are utterly to die for. Portland's hippest dressers and trend-makers flock to two enormous restaurants in the Pearl District. **¡Oba!** is a jumping Latin eatery split in half by a long bar that's usually just as packed as the restaurant. While the bar crowd knocks back margaritas and Oba! Cocktails (hibiscus water, tequila, and Citronge liqueur), diners munch on tapas-sized *pinchos* of shrimp ceviche or chile-corn fritters, or big platters of roasted game hen, full-blooded prime rib, or Brazilian steak. The loft-sized space is all soaring sponge-painted walls, but good luck seeing the walls when it's packed with people. Also in the Pearl is **Bluehour**, which got the biggest buzz in town after opening in late 2000 with chef Kenny Giambolvo at the helm and restaurateur-extraordinaire Bruce Mackay running the front of the house. The cavernous space is decorated with flowing drapes and is packed with tables where diners chow down on pastas and risottos, roasted meats and fish. The menu is best described as Pacific Northwest meets and gets chummy with northern Italy. Desserts are sensational, too.

When you need to close the deal... Expense-account visitors to Portland will be sorry to hear that Atwater's lost its lease and went out of business, but there are still plenty of opportunities for business-style dining. The crown has been passed in large part to **El Gaucho**, the Seattle steak house that opened an outpost in Portland's ultra-elegant Benson Hotel. The fare is largely the same: huge, tender slabs of meat slathered in butter and sauces, with extra-large shrimp or crab cocktails to start with, scalloped potatoes on the side, and bananas Foster prepared tableside for dessert. Hello, cholesterol! The service is excellent and the prices will make your accountant's eyes roll around inside his head like a pair of marbles. Don't let the **Heathman Restaurant**, attached to the downtown hotel of the same name, fool you. Walk in, and you'll see that it's not a standard-issue hotel restaurant at all, but a classy French bistro with Andy Warhol's *Endangered Species* series on the walls. French chef Philippe Boulot's spectacular fare is more Paris than Portland—consider the Pacific halibut confit with a picholine olive relish, or a simple homemade pâté de campagne for an appetizer. Boulot occasionally brings in a colleague from France for special dinners that are nothing short of gastronomic events. The three-course prix-fixe menu for theatergoers is a steal at $19.99, and desserts by Boulot's wife, Susan, such as fresh berry napoleons, are a great reason to return after the show. Just up the street, **Higgins** is a suave, wood-paneled restaurant where the waiters wear long folded aprons and downtown suits congregate. Chef/owner Greg Higgins rarely fails to please, producing a Northwest cuisine with some distinctive accents, like clams steamed in white wine and red curry, with bits of spring onion for crunch and flavor. Those *not* on an expense account, take note: An adjoining bistro provides scaled-down versions of the food (and the prices).

Serious seafood... Dungeness crab and oysters come from the Oregon coast; enormous sturgeon swim in the Columbia River; and trout, shad, and salmon all come out of the lakes and rivers around Portland. All of which are a modest explanation as to why Portland has such a good selection of restaurants featuring seafood and freshwater fish. **Jake's Famous Crawfish** is the most historic; it started as a saloon and restaurant over a century ago, and although its section of downtown is on the decline (it shares a block with a methadone clinic), it's still a popular local draw. The dining rooms are all polished dark-wood tables and booths, and over the bar hang oil paintings that date back to the early days (the nude woman is said to be a portrait of Jake's lover, a painting commissioned by his irate wife). The fresh sheet printed atop each daily menu lists up to two dozen available fish, ranging from local stalwarts like Columbia River sturgeon to exotic imports like Hawaiian ahi tuna and California abalone. Sweet, nutmeggy crawfish are the house specialty. In the downtown cultural district, **Southpark**, (no, it has nothing to do with witty cartoon characters and everything to do with its location on the South Park blocks), which occupies a site that was long the home of the B. Moloch/Heathman Bakery and Pub, goes the opposite way of Jake's—it's elegant and modern, with parquet floors, burgundy upholstered booths, a stainless-steel wine bar, and an entire wall devoted to a mural of tippling connoisseurs. The seafood has a Mediterranean flavor as it emerges from a wood-fired oven: Delicious medallions of monkfish, for example, come wrapped in pancetta and drizzled with white truffle oil. Oenophiles haunt its wine bar to choose among

Where Hippie Meets Yuppie Over a Pitcher of Brew

Their green, oval signs have become something of a franchise in town, but that's only because brothers Brian and Mike McMenamin have hit upon the practically perfect casual dining and nightlife concept for Portland. Since 1974, they've been buying up and restoring faded old buildings and transforming them into wildly decorated bar/restaurants that feature their own microbrews (Terminator Stout and Hammerhead Ale are favorites). You have to see these places to believe them: a restored grade school whose cafeteria is now a great place for a burger or pizza and brew (every schoolboy's fantasy); two restored movie theaters where you can watch a second-run film while scarfing pizza and beer at your seat; and six brewpubs. The places are individually decorated with artwork commissioned for each property. Food service is casually excellent: Crispy-crust pizzas come with fresh toppings, and burgers are capped with Tillamook cheddar and/or grilled vegetables. There's always a beef stew, a salad dish, and a "high pasta" on the menu. So look for the green signs: You'll see a great cross section of Portlanders at any of these locations.

flights of varietals and some hard-to-find bottles you can sample by the glass. Overlooking the Willamette in the RiverPlace development, McCormick & Schmick's **Harborside** announces its intentions when you walk in and see stuffed, mounted fish on the hunter green walls. Harborside pairs a great view with a large selection of grilled and sautéed fish, as well as several seafood pastas and salads. If nothing short of a really big river will do, try **Salty's on the Columbia** in North Portland, where the white-draped tables have carafes of oyster crackers next to the salt-and-pepper shakers. Two decks look out over the Columbia River, and although the menu doesn't aim as high as other places in terms of selection and preparation, you can certainly get a decent piece of salmon or seafood brochettes to go with the view.

Satisfying your meat tooth... The **Red Star Tavern & Roast House**, the bar-restaurant at the Fifth Avenue Suites Hotel downtown, is making a go of preparing American regional cuisine—and to these ears, that means meat. Chef Rob Pando presides over a gorgeous modern room of burnished-copper chandeliers, golden-hued walls, floor-to-ceiling windows, and an open kitchen that instantly grabs you with its grills and rotisseries. A spit-roasted citrus-and-spice chicken is tender and bursting with flavor, and a wood-grilled steak comes with a big mound of smoked-cheddar-and-green-onion mashed potatoes and red wine butter. Don't miss the cornbread, cooked in an iron skillet and served with lavender honey. **Jake's Grill**, also downtown at the Governor Hotel, is the classic old urban chophouse, a room of dark woods and columns that stretch to high ceilings. The double-thick lamb chops are exquisite, the steaks are aged and tender, and the menu throws in family fare like meatloaf and macaroni and cheese for the kids. Hearty, traditional steak houses have come to Portland with a vengeance in the last year or two. At the top of the list for both price and quality is **El Gaucho**, at the Benson Hotel, which is mighty proud of its 28-day, dry-aged beef. Wrapping yourself around a 24-ounce porterhouse is the ultimate meat orgy. There are smaller cuts of filet mignon and New York strip, but your dog will be awfully disappointed. On a similar vein and with a similar purpose is **Morton's of Chicago**, the upscale steak house chain that recently staked out Portland (so to speak) with its tried-and-true offerings of thick slabs of steak and chops. Lobster, shrimp, and chicken dishes are also available for less carnivorous companions.

The view crew... RiverPlace is one of those urban developments designed to take advantage of a waterfront location, with shops and a marina and restaurants to go with the pricey condos. It's not in the same league as Baltimore's Inner Harbor (and as one writer pointed out, the Willamette River is no Chesapeake), but it does provide two of the better "view" restaurants in the city. **Esplanade**, in the RiverPlace Hotel, has walls sponged a light brown and blue-clothed tables, but all eyes turn to the picture windows fronting the river. The kitchen turns out upscale Continental cuisine, like a peppered rack of New Zealand lamb, or medallions of beef in a Pinot Noir sauce with the sweet tang of dried cherries. It's a good bet for the abundant Sunday brunch, too. On the opposite end of the esplanade, **Harborside** stacks diners on four levels so that everyone can enjoy the view, and the sidewalk promenade gets crowded quickly on warm days. Being a McCormick & Schmick property, the West Coast restaurant chain headquartered in Portland, practically assures a deft approach to seafood dishes, and the attached Pilsner Room does a good job with homemade Full Sail Ales, too. Up in north Portland, **Salty's on the Columbia** is a chain place (the other two Salty's are in Seattle) with a kind of ersatz sailing-ship decor that emphasizes the view, in this case, on the banks of the Columbia River. It aims to please everyone with a menu that includes salmon, steaks, and Maine lobster, which means you've got a fair chance that there'll be something on the menu that your kids are eating that week. Views of another sort are what you'll find at **Bluehour, ¡Oba!, Castagna,** and **El Gaucho.** The first two are where you'll get the best views of Portland's trendsetters and scenemakers as they quaff their cosmopolitans and martinis and delicately pick their way through their dinners. Castagna is where the hip, eastside people go to see and be seen these days, and El Gaucho is frequently a hangout for sports stars and visiting media types (especially when their agents are paying).

Where the pizza is as good as the beer... Laurel and Hardy, Sacco and Vanzetti, Penn and Teller, pizza and beer. Some things are just meant to go together, and it's not surprising that some of Portland's best brewpubs also serve up terrific pizza. The best might be the original **Bridgeport Brew Pub,** in the Pearl District, which stubbornly holds out in an old industrial building covered in hop vines (several other neighborhood brewpubs have moved or gone out of business). An upscale, yuppified, nonsmoking crowd (you know the type) comes here for Bridgeport's distinctive pizza, which uses wort, a by-product of the brewing process, to flavor the dough; it's served fresh and hot out of a wood oven. There's a second location on funky Hawthorne Boulevard. **McMenamins Kennedy School** is the zany renovated grade school in north Portland where pizzas come out of the oven in either individual or family-size pies. The "Principal's Special" has Canadian bacon, pepperoni, fennel sausage, olives, and onions. Take one outside with a pitcher of Hammerhead Ale and sit in the courtyard near the brick fireplace for the ultimate schoolyard dining experience.

Grand finales... Walk into one of the two **Papa Haydn** locations in town (the flagship restaurant on Nob Hill and a smaller store in Westmoreland), and your eyes are instantly riveted to the glass case at the counter where the goodies are kept. Though this is a handy stop for sandwiches and salads, the selection of desserts is the best in town, with more than a dozen items available—toothsome treats such as a brandy-and-espresso mousse wrapped in cake and glazed with dark chocolate, or a fallen chocolate soufflé brushed with raspberry brandy, decorated with whole berries, and rimmed with chocolate ganache. Good coffee is the perfect accompaniment. In your ramblings through the Sellwood antiques district, a sweet stop can be made at **Piece of Cake**, which primarily functions as a caterer (wedding cakes are a specialty) but also sells its gorgeous baked goods, whole or in slices, from its headquarters in the 1906 Otellia Jensen House. Take a piece of Black Forest cake or apple-rum cake packed with fruit and topped with cream cheese out to the rickety picnic tables on the patio. You'll feel like you've visited a favorite old aunt who happens to be a terrific baker. We're usually happy to find one or two things that strike a resonant chord on a dessert tray, but **Caprial's**

Bistro, also in Westmoreland, presents you with a selection that is worth pondering (I'm still thinking about the rhubarb crème brûlée and big chocolate profiteroles oozing chocolate cream), and cappuccinos come in tall soda-fountain glasses. A fine downtown stop after the theater or a classical concert is the **Heathman Restaurant**, where pastry chef Susan Boulot whips up amazing napoleons and a signature chocolate gourmandise cake that arrives at the table warm. "Somebody stop me!" I cry out in sugary ecstasy as I fly around the room like Jim Carrey in *The Mask*.

The Index

$$$$$	over $50
$$$$	$40–$50
$$$	$30–$40
$$	$20–$30
$	under $20

Price categories reflect the cost of a three-course meal, not including drinks, taxes, and tip. MAX stops are listed below only for restaurants located close to stations.

Bluehour. Hot new restaurant in the Pearl District where the northern Italian–influenced menu is as good as the dramatic setting.... *Tel 503/226-3394. 250 NW 13th Ave. Reservations suggested. $$$$* **(see pp. 160, 161, 162, 166)**

Blue Moon Tavern & Grill. Courtesy of the McMenamin brothers, a neighborhood bar with better-than-average pub grub.... *Tel 503/223-3184. 432 NW 21st Ave., Civic Stadium MAX stop. $* **(see pp. 160, 161)**

Bridgeport Brew Pub. One of the standard-bearers for the Portland brewpub experience, it makes a terrific and highly distinctive pizza.... *Tel 503/241-7179. 1313 NW Marshall St. Also at tel 503/233-6540, 3632 SE Hawthorne Blvd. $* **(see p. 167)**

Caprial's Bistro. Chef/owner Caprial Pence writes books, appears on TV, and produces wonderful bistro fare from this bright, airy cafe.... *Tel 503/236-6457. 7015 SE Milwaukie Ave. $$$* **(see pp. 160, 161, 167)**

Castagna. Cool, spare decor turns all of the attention onto the good, solid Mediterranean food. The cafe next door offers lighter fare.... *Tel 503/231-7373. 1752 SE Hawthorne Blvd. Reservations suggested. $$$* **(see pp. 162, 166)**

El Gaucho. Unabashedly high-cal steak house with huge portions, huge prices, and the best service in town from liveried waiters.... *Tel 503/227-8794. 319 SW Broadway Ave. at the Benson Hotel. Reservations advised. $$$$* **(see pp. 160, 163, 165, 166)**

Esplanade. A riverfront setting and the trappings of a big hotel dining room.... *Tel 503/295-6166. 1510 SW Harbor Way. Reservations advised. $$$* **(see p. 166)**

Harborside. A slick and refined seafood house with marvelous views of the Willamette River and a busy sidewalk scene.... *Tel 503/220-1865. 309 SW Montgomery St. Reservations advised. $$$* **(see pp. 161, 165, 166)**

Heathman Restaurant. Marvelous French-inspired food using fresh Northwest ingredients.... *Tel 503/241-4100. 1001 SW Broadway Ave., Pioneer Sq. S. MAX stop. Reservations advised. $$$* **(see pp. 160, 163, 168)**

Higgins. Fine-dining downtown restaurant for Northwest cuisine.... *Tel 503/222-9070. 1239 SW Broadway Ave. Reservations advised. $$$$* **(see pp. 160, 161, 163)**

Jake's Famous Crawfish. This Portland institution still delivers utterly fresh seafood from around the world in a comfortable old dining room.... *Tel 503/226-1419. 401 SW 12th Ave., Galleria/SW 10th Ave. MAX stop (but best to take a cab or drive). Reservations suggested. $$* **(see p. 162)**

Jake's Grill. Dark woods and hunter green accents give this the proper chophouse feel to go with a menu of delectable meats.... *Tel 503/241-2100. 611 SW 10th Ave., Galleria/SW 10th Ave. MAX stop. Reservations suggested. $$$* **(see p. 165)**

McMenamins Kennedy School. Dine in the former school cafeteria or take your pizza and burgers outside to a courtyard.... *Tel 503/249-3983. 5736 NE 33rd Ave. $* **(see pp. 161, 167)**

Morton's of Chicago. The Windy City blows into town with its classic steak-and-chophouse offerings.... *Tel 503/248-2100. 213 SW Clay St., at KOIN Tower. $$$$* **(see p. 165)**

¡Oba!. Hyper-popular Latin hangout in the Pearl District.... *Tel 503/228-6161. 555 NW 12th Ave. Reservations advised. $$* **(see pp. 160, 161, 162, 166)**

Papa Haydn. The luscious desserts are the main attraction at this cafe. Tables fill up in the late evening, so snag a spot early.... *Tel 503/228-7317. 701 NW 23rd Ave., long walk from Civic Stadium MAX stop. Also at tel 503/232-9440, 5829 SE Milwaukie Ave. $* **(see p. 167)**

Pazzo. A lively, atmospheric Italian restaurant that takes its food very seriously. Attached to the Hotel Vintage Plaza.... *Tel 503/228-1515. 627 SW Washington St., Mall/SW 5th Ave. MAX stop. Reservations suggested. $$$* **(see p. 162)**

Piece of Cake. Individual portions of delicious cakes, bars, and cookies sold in an old, historic Sellwood home.... *Tel 503/234-9445. 7858 SE 13th Ave. $* **(see p. 167)**

Red Star Tavern & Roast House. Big, bustling restaurant attached to the Fifth Avenue Suites Hotel celebrates regional American cuisine.... *Tel 503/222-0005. 503 SW Alder St., Mall/SW 5th Ave. MAX stop. $$* **(see p. 165)**

Salty's on the Columbia. Chain-restaurant approach to family dining, distinguished by an excellent location on the banks of the Columbia River.... *Tel 503/288-4444. 3839 NE Marine Dr. Reservations suggested. $$* **(see pp. 161, 165, 166)**

Southpark. Downtown restaurant with a menu of Mediterranean seafood and lots of visual punch.... *Tel 503/326-1300. 901 SW Salmon St., Library/SW 9th Ave. MAX stop. Reservations advised. $$$* **(see p. 164)**

Wildwood. Portland's favorite upscale bistro.... *Tel 503/248-9663. 1221 NW 21st Ave., long walk from Civic Stadium MAX stop. Reservations advised. $$$$* **(see pp. 160, 161)**

Portland Dining

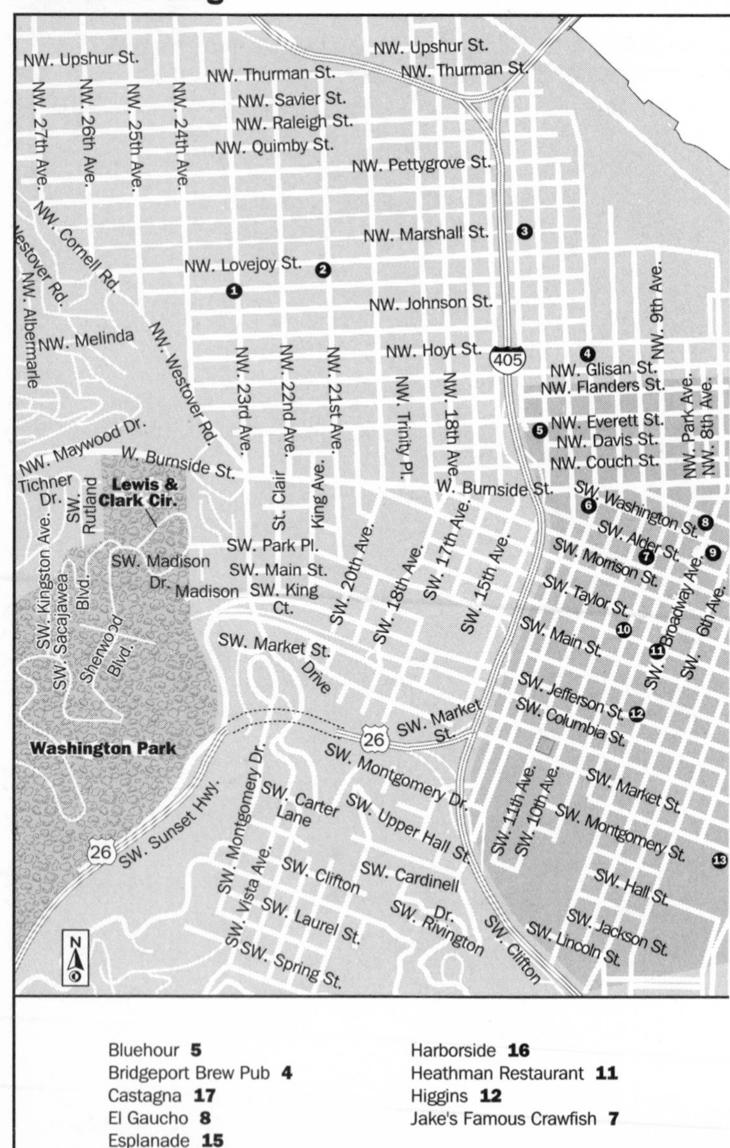

Jake's Grill **8**
Morton's of Chicago **13**
OBA! **6**
Papa Haydn **1**
Pazzo **9**
Red Star Tavern & Roast House **14**
Southpark **10**
Wildwood **2**

diver
THOMAS

3

sions

Okay, put down
the donuts long
enough for us to
count the ways
of exploring
Portland under
our own power.

Like the native Oregonians who so love to jog, we visiting bipeds can run like the wind (or in my case, like the glacier) through parks and forests and riverfront trails. We can stroll to our heart's content through the flat downtown and waterfront area to gaze upon lovely old buildings and public sculpture. We can wander across many bridges for a cool view of the **Willamette River** and **Mount Hood**. Finally, we can crawl back to our hotel on all fours after a night of pub-hopping (but that's a matter for the Nightlife & Entertainment chapter).

Oops, I almost went a whole page without comparing Portland with Seattle. There are good museums here, too, although not as many; outdoor public markets, though not as extensive; and awesome gardens that (dare I say it?) beat the dickens out of Seattle's for setting and scope. There is an annual civic celebration (**The Portland Rose Festival**) that names a queen, as a good festival should, and brings the locals out in droves; the **Oregon Zoo**, a fine zoo in a terrific city park; an artsy area (the **Pearl District**) of galleries and hipsters; and an amusement park (**Oaks Bottom**) that hearkens back to the old days of merry-go-rounds and roller rinks. In its diversions, Portland blends a classy urban exterior with the pace and atmosphere of a much smaller town. Point your toes in the right direction, and you'll quickly get caught up in it, too.

Getting Your Bearings

If your heart sinks when you enter a new city and see a quadrant street system of Southeasts and Northwests, try not to despair. Portland's grid system is relatively easy to master, and if you think of it in terms of neighborhoods, you can almost ignore the quadrants altogether. **Burnside Street** divides the city north and south, and the **Willamette River** divides it east and west. The downtown area is almost entirely centered in the **Southwest** quadrant, where every street begins with a SW designator. **SW 1st Avenue** is a block west of the river, and the north-south streets are then numbered all the way west to the hilly area just below **Washington Park** (except for **SW Broadway Avenue**, which is where 7th Avenue should be, and **SW Park Avenue**, which replaces 8th Avenue). When you're in a **Northwest** neighborhood, it means you've crossed north of **Burnside Street** but are still on the west side of the river, and essentially you're either in **Chinatown** (roughly **NW 3rd Avenue** to **NW Park Avenue**), the **Pearl District** (**NW Park Avenue** to **NW 15th Avenue**), or **Nob Hill** (**NW 16th Avenue** to **NW 23rd Avenue**).

On the other side of the river, **Lloyd Center** and **North Portland** are in the **Northeast** quadrant; the **Oregon Museum of Science and Industry** and the **Hawthorne District** are **Southeast** (the latter centered around **SE Hawthorne Street**); and *way* Southeast are **Westmoreland**, centered around **SE Milwaukie Avenue**, and **Sellwood**, centered around **SE 13th Avenue**. The free Portland Visitor's Maps at the **Portland Oregon Visitors Association (POVA)** [see Hotlines] are great for negotiating the downtown core, but are a bit like the famous Steinberg poster of Manhattan: Everything east of the Willamette is hazily rendered, with Sellwood and Moreland missing altogether.

The Portland Rose Festival

Portland's favorite celebration is dedicated to its favorite flower. Roses bloom in profusion all summer in the **International Rose Test Garden,** at **Washington Park**. For nearly the entire month of June every year, the city holds its much-ballyhooed **Rose Festival** (tel 503/227-2681), a series of celebrations to highlight the fact that another crappy winter is over and the sun may start to shine for a few days in a row. It all begins with the coronation of the Rose Festival Queen, some stellar high-school student whose ascension to the throne rates a front-page story in the morning newspaper. There is a big carnival with rides and food booths at the waterfront and a huge fireworks display fired off a barge in the middle of the Willamette River. Thousands of people pack Tom McCall Waterfront Park for that show, as they do the next night for the Starlight Parade downtown, with floats and marching bands. There is a rose show at the garden, of course, roses decorating parks like the Pioneer Courthouse Square, and a floral parade later in the month, and then everybody comes out to watch colorfully painted Dragon Boats race on the river. The whole thing winds up with car races, an air show, and an arts festival. The crowds are amazing, the flowers are gorgeous, most events are free, and it's a great way to get a big dose of local color very quickly.

The Lowdown

Best depiction of a kneeling giantess in bronze (and other civic art)... Thanks to a long-standing program that earmarks 10 percent of new-construction budgets for art, the downtown area is full of memorable sculptures and fountains. Statistics tell us that the second-largest hammered copper sculpture in the world is **Portlandia**, the gargantuan female who presides over the jarringly postmodern **Portland Building** (1120 SW 5th Avenue), but they're missing the point: She is easily the largest *bending* hammered copper sculpture (take that, Statue of Liberty), and her mammoth copper haunch alone is breathtaking. Also check out the **Salmon Street Springs** (where Salmon Street meets Tom McCall Waterfront Park), a computer-programmed fountain that shoots off 185 choreographed jets of water (and sends children shrieking and scattering). The city's oldest piece of public art is the **Skidmore Fountain** (SW First Avenue and Ankeny Street), a fusty old bronze that has four female figures holding a large bowl and another trough of circulating water meant for the dogs and horses, who once were part of the downtown street environment. And don't leave downtown without checking out the extraordinary trompe l'oeil painting on the outside of the **Oregon History Center**. At **Pioneer Courthouse Square** (between Broadway and SW 6th avenues, between Morrison and Yamhill streets) you'll find two landmarks: a bronze guy offering to share his umbrella (cloyingly titled ***Nice to Have Met You***) and the **Weather Station**, a tall pole that opens at noon and pops out a figure signifying what the climate has in store that day (pray you'll see the bronze sun). The Square itself is worth lingering in, with its coffee shop and rows of red brick steps for hanging out. There's nearly always something going on, whether it's a marketing sideshow from Las Vegas with Elvis impersonators performing on the hour, or the flowers that blanket the square during Rose Festival month and are offered for sale afterward. The place gets crowded at lunchtime in the summer, when free pop and jazz concerts are held at noon, and summer also brings a jazz series on Friday nights. They like to call it Portland's Living Room, and although the brick furniture is a bit hard, the company is pretty good.

Come Saturday morning (Sunday, too)... The area under the Burnside Bridge and Ankeny Square on the west side of the river is generally a hangout for homeless people and disaffected teens, but they grudgingly move over on weekends to make way for the artists, craftspeople, and late-model hippies who work the **Portland**

Saturday Market, one of the oldest and largest crafts markets in the country. Dozens of booths offer everything from batik dresses to leather sandals, wrought-iron fireplace tools to wooden yo-yos, and there are plenty of food carts offering highly debatable corn dogs, elephant ears, and Asian dishes. It's got kind of a groovy atmosphere, but never fear, most of the stands accept plastic. Don't forget to pop inside the **Skidmore Fountain Building** (SW Front Avenue opposite Ankeny Square), which has more shops and booths to check out [see Shopping]. Yes, the Saturday market is open on Sundays, too, but then it disappears during the week like a Bedouin encampment.

Gawking and walking downtown... Portland's gracious downtown buildings from the days of the lumber barons are decorated in cast-iron and terra-cotta ornaments, columns, friezes, and gargoyles. As you stroll around, look for plaques on many of the buildings explaining their histories and architectural styles. The more organized among you may want to pick up maps of self-guided walking tours from the **POVA** counter (SW Naito Parkway at SW Salmon Street) or from the bright, Lego-like lobby of the **Portland Building** (1120 SW 5th Avenue), itself a startling exception to downtown's turn-of-the-century look. (It was architect Michael Graves's postmodern debut, and its weird diagonals and ivory and sandstone columns are still controversial among locals.) Better yet, take a lively guided tour of downtown architecture with historian Gary Ripley of **Personalized Tours & Travel**, who's full of great stories about how Portland works (such as how statues get moved and why the trees nearly obscure the Portlandia statue in summer).

Gardens so grand you'll throw in the trowel... The **International Rose Test Garden,** in Washington Park, is the real deal, a scrupulously tended 4.5-acre plot of exotic roses that include those glamour girls Elizabeth Taylor, Climbing Ophelia, and Sweet Juliet. Begun in 1917, it's the oldest test garden in the country, which may incline it toward something of a rigid, political air that smacks of gardening committees and rosy ruling bodies. But spread out grandly on its ridge, the garden offers breathtaking views of the city on a reasonably clear day, not to mention the heady sight of 8,000 roses in 550 varieties. Even more inspiring, for the nonrose fanatic at least, is the **Japanese**

Garden, on a hillside across the street. Whereas the rose garden looks its best in sunshine, for maximum effect you've got to see this place on a misty, damp, cool morning (more common in Portland anyway), when the artful little piles of smooth black rocks lie slick and glistening. Muse over big pebble gardens raked in concentric circles, bamboo channels spilling water with a delicate sound, a waterfall that backdrops a marvelous koi pond, and a large teahouse and pavilion. The whole thing is surrounded by tall pine, maple, and fir trees, with another killer view of the city, and there are so many quiet little dips and valleys dotted with solitary benches that it's easy to leave behind the tour groups and enjoy a peaceful moment. Which is pretty much the point of a Japanese garden, isn't it? The newest cool garden in town is the **Classical Chinese Garden**, which was brought over, volcanic rock by volcanic rock, from China and assembled by Chinese artisans on a city block in Chinatown (do you get that it's authentically Chinese?). Pagoda-roofed buildings are intricately carved and utterly peaceful, and a waterfall and pond provide good *feng shui* as you stroll among the plants on wooden walkways. A delicate, dark-wooded teahouse looks like it was hand-delivered from a Mongolian mountainside, and is a great place to linger over a cup of oolong.

Come see-um museums... It's fitting in a town that's home to one of the great ad agencies of the past 20 years (Wieden & Kennedy, which did all of Nike's big campaigns) that Portland hosts the **American Advertising Museum**, a collection of original prints, neon signs, and recordings of radio and TV spots. Removed from their usual context, they make a fascinating mirror of the culture. Nostalgia buffs will love the place, with its rare original Burma Shave roadside signs and vintage clips (where were you when you first heard, "I can't believe I ate the whole thing"?). But here's the downer: It's only open to the public on Saturday afternoons, so be sure to schedule ahead. In its peaceful setting on the South Park Blocks, the **Portland Art Museum**, a compact gray building by local architect Pietro Belluschi, may remind New Yorkers of a miniature version of the Metropolitan Museum of Art. The permanent collection here spans 35 centuries, from Northwest Coast tribal artifacts right up to originals by Monet and Picasso, but the real attractions are the big shows that it regularly hosts, such as the great modern art collection of the Sara Lee Corporation that toured the country before being sold. Across the street, the **Oregon History Center** documents the pioneer experience with exhibits. It does a better job of providing research and archives to historians than of mounting public exhibits, but there are some nice oddities on display, such as the actual coin used in a toss to decide if the new settlement on the banks of the Willamette would be called Portland or Boston. For interactive fun, **OMSI (Oregon Museum of Science and Industry)**, on the east bank of the river just south of the Hawthorne Bridge, is all hands-on exhibits on the natural sciences, computer science, and technology. See if you can figure out which bone had osteoporosis, what the difference is between a resistor and transistor, and how a computer translates input into binary pulses (and yes, you will be tested).

Elvis has left the building, and other cheesy attractions... The 24-hour **Church of Elvis**, one of those kitschy attractions that always seem to make it into guidebooks, might prove a trifle disappointing on closer inspection. First of all, it's only open a few hours a day ("usually between noon and five," reads a hand-painted sign at the door), and it's in a second-floor walk-up in a rundown neighborhood around the corner from a strip club. Resident artist Stephanie G. Pierce presides over her collection of camp, which is not exclusively Elvis-oriented; you're welcome to confess, get sermonized, get married, play with coin-op machines, or have your photo taken with the King. We gracefully pass on this one, with a heartfelt, "Thank you...thank you very much." If you really need to see the smallest park in the world, go to the corner of SW Naito Parkway and Taylor Street to view tiny 24-inch-wide **Mill Ends Park**—basically a hole left over from a power pole that was filled in and covered with grass. How adorable. Now follow it up with a contest to see who can punch the lightest (you go first).

Where kids get their kicks... The sprawling **Oregon Museum of Science and Industry (OMSI)** is easily one of the best science museums in the country. All soaring glass and steel girders, it looks like the Pompidou Centre on its perch alongside the east bank of the Willamette. You can turn your kids loose in it for hours and find plenty of fascinating things to do yourself, such as sit in a simulated earthquake room, view samples of brain tissue, encode a message to be transmitted into outer space, or learn the inner workings of computers. A real submarine is docked there, too, and is open for tours.

Second-run movies, first-rate setting... The McMenamin brothers [see the sidebar in Dining] hit upon a great idea when they began to restore classic old Portland movie houses in the '80s. Instead of competing with the multiplexes to turn a profit on first-run films, they took a different tack, screening second-run films and transforming the theaters into "theater pubs," with tables between each row of seats, and pizza and pitchers of beer available alongside the popcorn in the snack bar. The results are utterly comfortable and enjoyable moviegoing experiences (great for those rainy winter evenings) at the **Kennedy School**, **Bagdad,** and **Mission theaters.** One small caveat: Minors aren't allowed into every show, because of the beer.

Paddlewheel or jetboat? The Willamette cruise... Ever ride in a jetboat? The open-air speedboats can do some amazing turns and circles in tight quarters. The craft's maneuvering skills aren't really put to the test on **Willamette Jetboat Excursions'** tours of the Willamette River, but the boat can get into some tight spaces to get great looks of Willamette Falls, houseboat communities, and drydocks. You pass fishermen hauling in shad and salmon and the mansions of Portland's elite along the way, and if you ask the driver nicely, he'll turn a couple of doughnut spins on the way back to the dock at OMSI. **Sternwheeler Riverboat Tours** offers a sedate ride on a stately, two-story paddlewheel boat that plies the river for tours three seasons of the year and then heads up to the Columbia Gorge in the summer. The **Portland Spirit** is a 75-foot yacht that does brisk business on lunch, brunch, and dinner cruises on the river, and then turns into a lively dancing cruise ship on Saturday nights.

And they're off... If racing of the four-wheeled and four-legged variety is your game, you have three options for whiling away some time (and money) at the track in Portland. Greyhound racing is on its way out in many parts of the country that don't cotton to raising dogs to run fast and then destroying them when they slow down, but it's still going strong at **Multnomah Greyhound Park** through the summer months. The pooches light out after a fake rabbit on a rail (and boy, are they disappointed when it disappears before they can catch it). Racers of the thoroughbred variety are found thundering down the backstretch at **Portland Meadows** in the winter and spring. The Northwest has a lively tradition of horse racing that is kept alive here and at Seattle's Emerald Downs [see Getting Outside in Seattle], and the action is vigorous. Satellite wagering on other tracks is conducted here, too, if you really have a nose for the ponies. Motorheads should go directly to the **Portland International Raceway** to immerse themselves in quite a lively car culture. It has a busy schedule of everything from drag races and go-karts to motocross and motorcycle events, and the big boys come to town to compete in a CART race every year during the Rose Festival.

The Index

American Advertising Museum. It offers a pretty irresistible combination of the attractive powers of master advertising plus a mirror of the society and the marketing techniques that created our consumer culture.... *Tel 503/226-0000. 5035 SE 24th Ave. at Raymond St. Open noon–5pm Sat; available to tour groups other days. Admission charged.*

(see p. 180)

Bagdad Theater. Your Arabian Nights in this restored movie house might include one of 20 beers on tap at the snack bar and slices of pizza at your seat while you watch second-run films for a mere $2.... *Tel 503/669-8754. 3702 SE Hawthorne St.* **(see p. 182)**

Church of Elvis. A funny, arty monument to kitsch and the King (not necessarily in that order), where you're welcome to confess, get sermonized, get married, or play with coin-op machines.... *Tel 503/226-3671. 720 SW Ankeny St. at Broadway Ave. Generally open daily noon–5pm, and sporadically at night (call ahead). Admission charged.* **(see p. 181)**

Classical Chinese Garden. Lovely garden assembled by Chinese artisans and buffered from city noise by a high white wall. Inside, you'll find pagodas and plants, including many varieties of orchids.... *Tel 503/228-8131. NW 3rd Ave. & NW Everett St. Open 9am–6pm, April–Oct, 10am–5pm Nov–March. Admission charged.* **(see p. 180)**

International Rose Test Garden. The numbers say it all: 8,000 rosebushes from 550 varieties planted in a 4.5-acre garden perched on a hillside overlooking the city. The blossoms in spring and summer are dazzling.... *Tel 503/823-3636. 400 SW Kingston Ave., Washington Park. Washington Park MAX stop, board shuttle to gardens. Open daily dawn to dusk. Free.* **(see pp. 177, 179)**

Japanese Garden. It carries a reputation as one of the most authentic Japanese gardens outside of Japan for good reason: The grounds are immaculate, the gardens exquisite. See it on a rainy day for maximum effect.... *Tel 503/223-0913. 611 SW Kingston Ave., Washington Park. Washington Park MAX stop, board shuttle to gardens. Open 9am–8pm summer, 10am–6pm spring and fall, 10am–4pm winter. Admission charged.* **(see p. 179)**

Kennedy School Theater. Cozy little movie house in a converted grade school that now serves as a B&B, restaurant, pub, and meeting place for the Concordia neighborhood, and you can bring beer and pizza to your seat.... *Tel 503/288-2180. 5736 NE 33rd Ave.* **(see p. 182)**

Mission Theater. The first of the McMenamin brothers' restored movie houses that show second-run movies for two bucks and make their money on pizza and beer sales....*Tel 503/223-4031. 1624 NW Glisan St. in Nob Hill.* **(see p. 182)**

Multnomah Greyhound Park. Razor-thin greyhounds race their hearts out at this throwback old dog track. The action is fast and lively, with 4 races an hour and active wagering.... *Tel 503/669-2283. NE 223rd Ave. in Wood Village. Open daily May–Sept. Admission charged.* **(see p. 183)**

Oregon History Center. The Oregon Territory remembered, from the early settlers who came looking for good farmland to recent developments like the building of Portland's light-rail system in an attractive, downtown setting.... *Tel 503/306-5221. 1200 SW Park Ave. 10am–5pm Tues–Sat, noon–5pm Sun. Admission charged.* **(see pp. 178, 181)**

Oregon Museum of Science and Industry (OMSI). You'll go here to amuse the kids and end up wanting to stay longer than they will to play with the interesting, interactive displays on science and technology.... *Tel 503/797-4537. 1945 SE Water Ave. (east bank of Willamette between Ross Island and Hawthorne bridges). Open 9:30am–5:30pm Tues–Sat, till 7pm in summer. Admission charged.* **(see pp. 177, 181)**

Oregon Zoo. It's fun just to get there, as you take MAX from downtown to Washington Park and emerge from a deep, underground station onto the front steps of the zoo, which has terrific elephant and chimpanzee environments, among many others.... *Tel 503/226-1561. 4001 SW Canyon Rd. in Washington Park. Washington Park MAX stop. Open daily 9:30am–4pm, till 6pm in summer. Admission charged.* **(see p. 176)**

Personalized Tours & Travel. Gary Ripley leads a lively tour around the downtown area that is complete with historical info and great stories about how Portland works (such as how statues get moved and why the trees nearly obscure the Portlandia statue in summer).... *Tel 503/248-0414. 800 NW 6th St. Tours customized to each group; he'll meet at your hotel. Admission charged.* **(see p. 179)**

Pioneer Courthouse Square. Portlanders are proud of their civic "living room," a red-brick central square of sculptures and frequent free concerts and events, particularly during the summer.... *No phone. Bordered by SW Broadway Ave., 6th, Morrison, and Yamhill streets, Pioneer Courthouse Sq. MAX stop. Free.* **(see p. 178)**

Portland Art Museum. Keep an eye out for the excellent special exhibitions it brings in on a regular basis that include the top touring art shows in the country. Permanent collection includes everything from Northwest Indian masks and artifacts to French Impressionist paintings.... *Tel 503/226-2811. 1219 SW Park Ave., Library Station MAX stop. 10am–5pm till 9pm first Thur of every month). Admission charged.* **(see p. 180)**

Portland Building. Stroll by to see the beneficent Portlandia kneeling down from her mezzanine perch to lend a hand, and to see what you make of Michael Graves's postmodern design..... *No phone. 1120 SW 5th Ave., Pioneer Sq. S MAX stop. Inside open 9am–5pm Mon–Fri. Free.* **(see pp. 178, 179)**

Portland International Raceway. The Jeff Gordons of the Northwest come here to fulfill their speed dreams on a busy, active racing track that hosts both motorcycle and car events throughout the year.... *Tel 503/823-RACE. 1940 N. Victory Blvd. in West Delta Park (3 mi. north of downtown). Admission charged.* **(see p. 183)**

Portland Meadows. Live racing of Northwest thoroughbreds throughout the winter; satellite wagering year-round.... *Tel 503/285-9144. 1001 N. Schmeer Rd. Racing Oct–April; post time 6:30pm Fri; 12:30pm Sat–Sun. Admission charged.* **(see p. 183)**

Portland Rose Festival. It takes place around the whole city during the month of June. Don't miss the fireworks show and Starlight Parade that kick off the opening weekend, the lovely Floral Parade of floats, and the Dragon Boat races on the river contested by local crews.... *Tel 503/227-2681. Venues around the city throughout the month of June. Most events free.* **(see pp. 176, 177)**

Portland Saturday Market. A long-standing tradition of craftsmanship and street-fair quality goods from local and

Northwest vendors, it goes up every Saturday morning and comes down Sunday afternoons near the waterfront on the west side of the Burnside Bridge; kind of a groovy atmosphere, but most of the stands accept plastic.... *Tel 503/222-6072. Bordered by SW Ankeny St., First Ave., Burnside St., and Front Ave. March–Christmas Eve; 10am–5pm Sat, 11am–4:30pm Sun. Free.* **(see p. 179)**

Portland Spirit. The tables are set with white tablecloths and china for leisurely lunch and dinner cruises on a 75-foot yacht with two decks, and a dance party with live music on weekends....*Tel 503/224-3900 or 800/224-3901. Berth at Tom McCall Waterfront Park. Daily departures.* **(see p. 182)**

Sternwheeler Riverboat Tours. The Sternwheeler Columbia Gorge is a big, old-fashioned paddlewheel cruiser with three decks (two of them inside and dry) that plies the Willamette for tours most of the year, but moves to the Columbia River Gorge in the summer.... *Tel 503/223-3928. Meets at Tom McCall Waterfront Park, just north of the Morrison Bridge. MAX to Yamhill District station. Daily tours. Admission charged.* **(see p. 182)**

Willamette Jetboat Excursions. A fast, open-air tour boat, it plies the Willamette from the northern drydocks all the way down to an up-close-and-personal view of Willamette Falls to the south; be prepared to get splashed, especially in the front row.... *Tel 503/231-1532 or 888-JETBOAT. Meets at 1945 SE Water Ave. near OMSI. Daily departures. Admission charged.* **(see p. 182)**

Portland Diversions

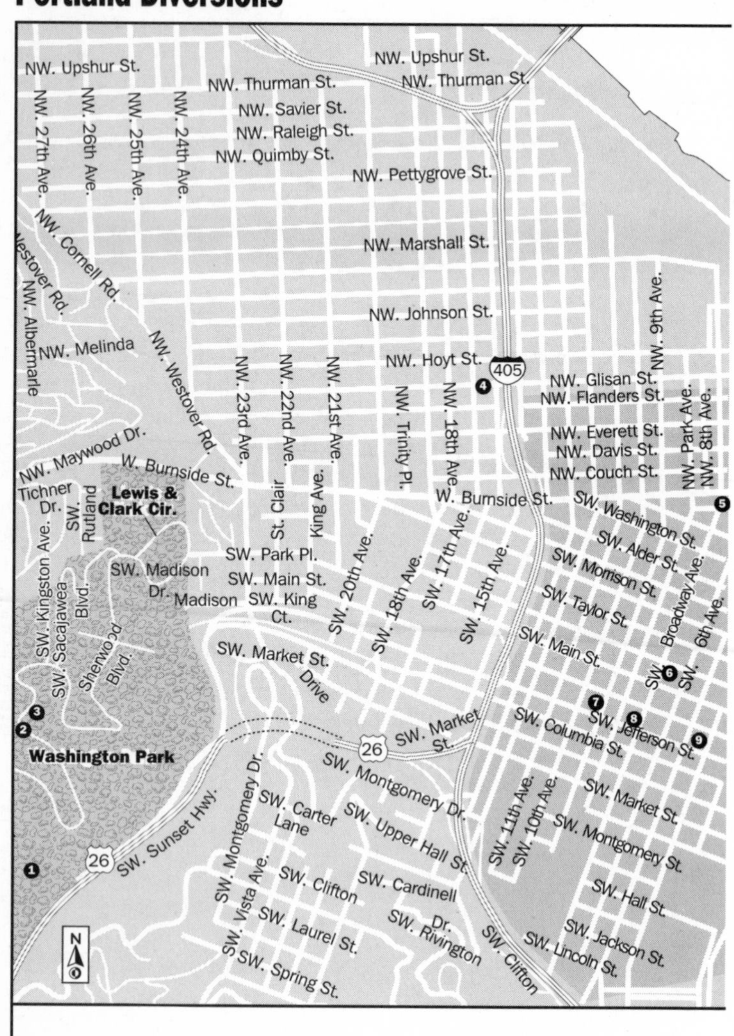

Church of Elvis **5**
Classical Chinese Garden **10**
Int'l Rose Test Garden **3**
Japanese Garden **2**
Mission Theater **4**
OMSI **15**
Oregon History Center **8**
Oregon Zoo **1**

Pioneer Courthouse Square **6**
Portland Art Museum **7**
Portland Building **9**
Portland Saturday Market **11**
Portland Spirit **13**
Sternwheeler Riverboat Tours **12**
Willamette Jetboat Excursions **14**

getting

4 outside

Despite the rainy climate, Oregonians are as passionate about getting outdoors as if they lived in the middle of the Sun

Belt. Hey, rain is simply a state of mind. Weather that would bench an Angeleno or cause a Phoenician to mope inside his stucco house all day is viewed by a Portlander simply as an opportunity to stay cool. Getting outdoors is the reason most folks fall in love with Portland, and locals cherish the natural environment as something to be enjoyed—with great care and stewardship, of course—as often as possible, rain or shine, adding or shedding layers of clothing as needed. It's a city of runners who pound the trails along the river all hours of the day and night, hikers who head for vast parks (and even an active volcano) within city limits, and paddlers who enjoy some of the best kayaking and white-water rafting in the country. Even the golfers play year-round; they wouldn't dream of letting a little moisture prevent them from getting in a fast 18 holes. Despite the proximity to water, it's not a great town for swimming, maybe because it rarely gets hot enough to make you die for a dip. The Willamette is too funky from city pollution, despite a huge 1970s cleanup that saved its fish life, and although there are modest beaches on the Columbia River, it's a little too muddy and rugged for good swimming. The fishing on both rivers, however, is spectacular; there are days when you can practically walk across the Willamette on the decks of the boats lined up to haul in big runs of salmon and shad. The best ski areas are in central Oregon near the boomtown of Bend, and the ocean is 90 miles away over rugged coastal mountains, making both a bit too far for a day trip. Instead, if you want to get out of the city altogether, the mountains of the Cascade Range beckon on clear days. If you find you have even the tiniest bit of Portlander in you, you'll heed the call.

The Lowdown

Climb every mountain... The likeliest culprit for an alpine getaway is snow-capped **Mount Hood**, an hour's drive east from downtown Portland. For the record, Mount Hood tops out at 11,235 feet, making it a modest peak within the whole Cascade Range (hey, what's a few thousand feet between friends?), but plenty big for exploring. Call the **Mount Hood Information Center** (tel 503/622-3360) for tips on what's blooming or which trails are open. A good base of operations is the **Timberline Lodge**, a huge stone-and-timber shelter at

6,000 feet that was built in the '30s; from here you can catch chair-lift rides year-round to see the awesome **Palmer Snowfield.** Trails lead from the lodge, too, and **Paradise Park** lies a fairly easy 4 ½-mile trek from the lodge on the **Timberline Trail**, which continues some 40 miles around the peak of the mountain. The path around **Trillium Lake**, just east of the town of **Government Camp**, makes for a gentle, peaceful hike that is great for kids; look for splendid fields of the namesake flowers. There are also five ski areas on the mountain that provide decent, if unspectacular, downhill and Nordic skiing into the spring. **Mount St. Helens**, or what's left of it since it blew its top in 1980, is also a quick trip just over the Washington border from Portland. Stop first at the visitor center at **Silver Lake** (tel 360/274-2100) to buy the necessary admission tickets that allow you to visit any part of the mountain. Going close to the summit to see the new **Johnston Ridge Observatory** is fairly mind-blowing; you can peer into the still-fuming crater. It's fun to grab flashlights and explore the exotically named **Ape Caves**, which are centuries-old lava tubes, the uppermost one being the longest lava tube in the continental United States at 2 (dark) miles long. Hiking on the mountain is like going to geology school; the views of the blast zone are unbelievable.

Happy trails to you... It's nice to know that all of those hiking boots and running shoes on the feet of restaurant diners and bar patrons in Portland aren't just fashion statements. There really is marvelous hiking within the city, beginning northwest of downtown at **Forest Park**, which is the largest forested city park in the country, with more than 50 miles of wooded trails to explore. To commune with everyone from serious walkers to ultra-marathoners in practice, head to the **Wildwood Trail**, beginning near the zoo in **Washington Park**. The last third of its 24-mile course runs through undisturbed woodlands in Forest Park. Look for the trailhead at the end of NW Cornell Street or the Leif Erickson gate to the Forest Park, at NW Thurman Street. Branching off onto one of the old logging roads and fire lanes that shoot off into the wilderness will give you a truly solitary backwoods experience. Many of the fire lanes are available to mountain bikers, too (trail maps are available from **Portland Parks & Recreation**, tel

503/823-5132, 1120 SW 5th Avenue). **Leif Erickson Drive** in **Forest Park** is a killer 11-mile gravel path that leads in and out of ravines and offers great views of the faraway Willamette. **Fat Tire Farm Mountain Bike Company** (tel 503/222-3276, 2714 NW Thurman Street), handily located near the Leif Erickson gate, can set you up with gear. Across the river, the **Oaks Bottom Wildlife Refuge** is a haven for birdwatchers, who tramp its 160 acres of woods to spot any of 140 species of birds that inhabit the park. It's an instant oasis of calm and tranquility, giving you an idea of what the riverbank might have looked like a hundred years ago. Park your car at the trailhead on SE Milwaukie Boulevard (at Mitchell Street); another trailhead can be found in **Sellwood Park** at SE 7th Avenue. Joggers hit the paved path at **Tom McCall Waterfront Park** for flat, scenic runs along the river. At lunchtime and right after work it looks like the New York Marathon is being staged out there. The park trail itself goes 1.75 miles, but if you follow the crowds, they'll lead you through some little-used industrial areas south of RiverPlace and hook up with another trail in **Willamette Park** south of Tom McCall, which can give you a round-trip run of 6.5 miles. Skaters hit the same trails armed with rental skates and protective gear from **Sportworks** (tel 503/227-5323, 421 SW 2nd Avenue). For cyclists, the city publishes a map of bike trails called *Bike There* ($3.95 at any bike shop or **Powell's Travel Store** at Pioneer Courthouse Square) that outlines an elaborate array of urban biking opportunities, including the **Springwater Corridor** (access at SE Johnson Creek Boulevard), a refinished 20-mile former railbed that cuts across the city from the neighborhoods of Westmoreland to Gresham. Also on the east side of the river, locals hike or peddle to the reservoir atop **Mount Tabor Park** (SE 60th Avenue and Salmon Street), named for its dormant volcano that's well within the city limits and could blow its top any day, but hopefully not when you're running the various dirt trails, from 1 to 5 miles in length, which wind up on top with great views of the west side of the city.

Up the river (preferably with a paddle)... Except for the crewed Dragon Boat races every year during the Rose Festival, Portland has surprisingly little paddling culture (most of the kayaking is done on the whitewater rivers outside the city). It's a pity, because the **Willamette River** has a gentle flow that's easy to navigate, and the **Columbia River** offers some dramatic wildlife viewing on little islands within the **Lewis and Clark National Wildlife Refuge**. The **Portland River Company** (tel 503/229-0551, 315 SW Montgomery Street) is ready, willing, and able to get you on the water in stable, rented kayaks. They'll point you south on the Willamette from their RiverPlace launch for an easy paddle to **Ross Island**, which has a resident bald eagle and several great blue heron. They also offer guided tours of the Willamette ($35 for a two-and-a-half-hour trip) or an all-day paddle on the Columbia ($80), where you may see everything from tundra swans to the endangered Columbian white-tailed deer.

Serious paddlers head off to the nearby **Deschutes**, **White Salmon**, and **Clackamas** rivers to shoot rapids that go all the way up to Class IV at times; the rapids can get particularly hairy when the Cascade snowpack begins to melt in the spring and fills the rivers with fast, cold water. **River Drifters Whitewater Tours** in Beaverton (tel 503/224-9625 or 800/972-0430; they'll send you a map to the site where you'll begin the tour) leads day paddles or multi-day excursions. Ask at **Andy & Bax Sporting Goods**, another good paddling and rafting source (tel 503/234-7538, 324 SE Grand Avenue), about the **Bob's Hole Rodeo**, an event usually held in May at a heralded rapid in the Clackamas.

Great public golf... Portland has one of the great municipal golf courses in the country, the **Heron Lakes Golf Course** complex (tel 503/289-1818, 3500 N. Victory Boulevard). It consists of two 18-hole courses designed by the artistic hand of Robert Trent Jones, Jr. The Great Blue is the one you want to play if you have game, but be prepared to watch a few of your Titleists splash down into the numerous ponds, creeks, and sloughs that break up the lovely green fairways. The Green Back course is slightly shorter and easier, but still worth playing. Head pro Byron Ricks has presided over the courses for many years, and they run as smoothly and are as well-maintained as any munis you've ever played. Students of the game and the truly golf-obsessed will want to make the pilgrimage from

Portland to the **Pumpkin Ridge Golf Club** (tel 503/647-4747, 12930 Old Pumpkin Ridge Road, Cornelius), about a 45-minute drive west from Portland, to play the Ghost Creek course. Designed by Robert Cupp, who has built some beauties throughout the Northwest in the '90s, it has been listed among the top-100 public courses ever since it opened in 1992; Tiger Woods won his last U.S. Amateur Championship here in a memorable match. It's also one of the few privately owned courses that don't serve as centerpieces for real estate developments. Ghost Creek, with its sister course, the private Witch Hollow, is a beautifully maintained, tough layout.

Hooking the big one... Fishing has become a hot political issue in recent years in the Northwest, and when you read that the Federal government has stepped in to protect dwindling salmon habitats, you might assume that fishing is all but extinct in urban areas like Portland. But then you float down the **Willamette** and see dozens of anglers hauling in fat, shiny shad, bass, and crappie, and you realize that you're not grasping the whole picture. Recreational fishing is, in fact, thriving around here, and although the salmon season has been drastically shortened, anglers are still hauling out their share of 30-pound beauties every year during a brief spring season. Silvery shad run thick in the spring through the Willamette, and anglers pull them up from the shore or from boats by the dozen. They go after different game the rest of the year, and there's plenty of it. The **Columbia** yields sturgeon, those practically prehistoric, bottom-feeding behemoths that can go as big as 12 feet long. Landing one of these babies is like pulling up a fighting log from the depths. Find out what you need to know about seasons and licenses from the **Oregon Department of Fish and Wildlife** (tel 503/229-5403, PO Box 59, Portland, 97207). For guided tours with the people who know where the fish are, contact **Page's Northwest Guide Services** (tel 503/761-9750).

Skating with the ice queen... We'd be remiss if we didn't mention the favorite sport of local tragic heroine Tonya Harding, Portland's unofficial trailer-park-culture queen who rose near to Olympic glory, only to go down in flames over charges of a plot to break her rival's legs with a crowbar. In simpler times, Tonya learned her axels and spins at the **Ice Chalet Clackamas** (tel 503/786-6000, Clackamas Town Center), one of several public skating rinks built in the middle of area shopping malls. The other good rink is at the **Lloyd Center** shopping mall (tel 503/288-6073, MAX stop at Lloyd Center), where the ice is in a sunken area beside the food court (handy for skating off those Cinnabon calories).

shop

5

ping

"What is it about Portland's retail landscape that's so different?" you wonder as you wander the city streets, your eye constantly caught by interesting little specialty shops and storefronts in restored historic buildings. The answer may take a while in coming (so we'll save you the trouble): This town is almost 100 percent chain-free, as if by civic ordinance. The Gaps and Pottery Barns and FAO Schwarzes of the world are entirely absent from the streets. Instead, they're trundled away to malls in the 'burbs or at least tucked inside the mall **Pioneer Place**, which itself resembles an old downtown department store. It's an odd feeling to walk the streets of a big, thriving American downtown and not find any of those tried-and-true retail touchpoints—it's like going off to Europe and discovering a new culture altogether. You have to work a little bit harder and do more exploring, but the locally owned boutiques have tons of interesting things. Enjoy the hunt.

Target Zones

The **downtown** retail core is centered around **SW Broadway** and **SW Fifth avenues**, a few blocks in either direction from **Pioneer Courthouse Square**. In between the hotels on Broadway, you'll find Native American art galleries and home furnishings, **Nordstrom** and sportswear stores. Fifth Avenue is home to department store **Meier & Frank** as well as **Pioneer Place**, the most upscale mall in town, which is appropriately anchored by Portland's first **Saks Fifth Avenue**. The pickings get slimmer and more downscale as you head toward the river and north to the Skidmore part of Old Town, where the **Portland Saturday Market** holds forth as the reigning urban crafts fair. The **Pearl District,** just northwest of the downtown core, is where most of the art galleries and artsy stores are located. **Sellwood**, across the river and far southeast, has an enviable strip of antiques stores housed in restored homes that proudly display their heritage on plaques. **Nob Hill**, the strip between NW 21st and NW 23rd avenues, is where the moneyed sort congregate to pick through designer clothes and household decor items in fancy boutiques, in between slugging down gallons of coffee at the espresso shops on every corner. Across the river near the convention center, **Lloyd Center** is the same shopping mall that you'll find in practically every city in the country, with middle-of-the-road chain stores to go with its **Nordstrom** anchor. The one thing that distinguishes it from every other shopping mall is the big ice-skating rink in its center atrium. It received a big boost in business when the MAX lightrail opened a stop a block away. You'll also find a lively new strip of retail on **NE Broadway**, just north of Lloyd Center.

Bargain-Hunting

Prices aren't negotiable at Portland's many antiques stores, but they're certainly cheap, especially at the big bargain-basement places like the **Portland Antique Company** and **Stars Antiques Mall**, which are basically huge garage sales crammed under one roof. The crafts vendors at the **Portland Saturday Market** may be in the mood to dicker, although their prices are usually fixed, too. It's worth a try, though, especially toward the end of Sunday when they're faced with packing everything back up into the Volkswagen van and carting it back to the commune for another week.

Trading with the Natives

Outside of the department stores, which will practically accept an IOU written on a cocktail napkin for payment (we said practically), you'll have a much easier time paying with an out-of-state check at most of the independent stores if you flash your VISA check-cashing card. The policies change from place to place, so ask first and hope they haven't been burned by bounced checks shortly before you walked into their lives.

Hours of Business

Stores are generally open from 9 or 10am to 5 or 6pm, Monday through Saturday. The malls generally stay open until 9 on Friday and 10 on Saturday, and go 11 to 6 on Sunday. Most of the Sellwood antiques shops are closed on Mondays, and Pearl District art galleries generally go from 11–5, extending their hours until 9 on the first Thursday of every month.

Sales Tax

Zip, zero, zilch, nada, nothing, bupkus. No sales tax, 24 hours a day, 365 days a year. Zippo, rien, nadissima. It's one of Oregon's most redeeming features.

The Lowdown

How many books fit into an acre?... The answer is a lot, at **Powell's City of Books**, which occupies a full city block on W. Burnside Street, a short walk from downtown hotels and shops. There are some 750,000 volumes on the shelves at a time; the store has even printed a map to show you how to get around—and it's not a cute gimmick, but an absolute necessity. Browsing is the thing here that brings people back time and again, as well as the readings by national authors in the Purple Room. Used books are parked right next to new ones, and a new computer system allows the staff to have a fair idea whether a certain title is in stock at any of their stores. But generally you can walk up to nearly any employee, say an author's name or a book title, and hear him or her shoot back, "Oh, that's in the Rose Room under Metaphysics." Take your treasures to the bare-bones coffee shop, which also has an enormous magazine collection. The main store of Powell's is like a lightning rod of the community; people treasure it, and those who have moved away make a point to return here every time they're in Portland. But it's not the only Powell's in town. Powell's is so inventory-happy that whole categories of books have been shifted to other locations, which can be more than a little annoying if you've trekked to the mecca only to find that your book on raising daffodils is across town. **Powell's Technical Bookstore,** a few blocks from the mothership, has a complete selection of titles on computers, electronics, and engineering. At Pioneer Courthouse Square, which is a bit of a hike but is in the center of downtown, you'll find the underground location of **Powell's Travel Store**, with guidebooks like this one (buy a dozen for your friends!), travel essays, and maps. There is a small shop at the airport, another in the suburb of Beaverton, and a few doors apart from each other on Hawthorne Boulevard are **Powell's Books on Hawthorne**, with a healthy collection of general titles in its own right, and **Powell's Books for Cooks and Gardeners**, which adds kitchen stuff like linens, refrigerator magnets, and gardening pots and tools to the thousands of volumes on how to grow it, cook it, and eat it.

For that rugged, active person lurking inside you... God knows why, given the weather here three-quarters of the year, but Portlanders love to play outside. The secret lies in acquiring the right gear, and there are plenty of stores to outfit you with the proper layers. The flagship store of **Columbia Sportswear** is a sprawling space on Broadway, decorated with lots of natural woods and the bright colors of its lightweight, breathable parkas, jackets, and shells that shed rain while keeping you warm. The stuff is not cheap, and you can save some cash by heading across the river to the **Columbia Sportswear Factory Outlet**, where you can save 30 to 50 percent on an irregular piece or odd size. Likewise for the shoes at **NIKETOWN**, which is practically a shrine to the little local shoemaker that made good, and was one of the first high-concept retail outlets in the country (what hath they wrought? See REI in Seattle). NIKETOWN displays all the Air shoes that you need for your game, with breathtaking prices, but you can get them at considerable savings at the **Nike Factory Store** across the river. The outlet does best with closeouts and discontinued lines, so if your teenager absolutely has to have the newest pair of Nikes, you'll have to bite the bullet and buy them downtown. For traditional sporting goods, we like **Caplan Sportsworld** and **Andy & Bax Sporting Goods**, two local stores with lines of balls, sticks, rods, reels, and the kind of warm and cozy gear that you used to find only at army-navy stores. Portland also has several stores devoted to serious outdoor exploration. For mountain-climbing necessities like crampons and ice axes, or full lines of tough clothing and gear for skiing and snowboarding, check out **The Mountain Shop,** near Lloyd Center.

All the tunes all the time... In the blocks near Powell's are two music stores that can solve most of those what-are-we-gonna-listen-to-tonight-honey? dilemmas. **Django's,** near downtown, is an old-time rock-and-roll headquarters, with racks of used CDs and albums. It's here that you can find a complete Doors or Springsteen compilation and, overcome by the zeitgeist of the place, actually be willing to spring for them. But I need something a little more *funky*, you whine. Go down the street, young one, to **Ozone**; hear the blast of superheated rap when you walk in, and browse the considerable collection of rap, hip-hop, and metal therein. Pick yourself up a nice little studded leather collar and a bong from their adorable merchandise counter while you're at it. **Crossroads,** on southeast Hawthorne, is a neat idea, a collective of music vendors under one roof who stock thousands of records, including some hard-to-find LPs. **Music Millennium,** with two locations (northwest Portland and east Portland), is simply a megastore with a vast selection of all things rock, as well as jazz, folk, and an annex devoted to classical music.

For that uniquely Portland look... Just because you don't *have* to wear fashionable clothes to get along in Portland society doesn't mean that you *can't*. If you can stand the stares on the bus from people who think you're a fashion model, check out these places for clothes that are a considerable cut above the standard jeans and flannels. The fashions in **Aubergine**, in the Pearl District, might look familiar to other urbanites; the owners regularly shop in New York to pick up their elegantly casual styles for professional women. **Dakota,** in Nob Hill, is very modern and very Melrose, with sophisticated looks for serious nightclubbing and dancing, including some of Portland's slinkiest dresses. Downtown, **Poker Face** takes it back even further, with antique clothes from the '40s, '50s, and '60s, including some very cool rockabilly wear that will practically force you to slick your hair back and put on a Carl Perkins tape. Want to really fit in with Portland's earthy look? Stop by **CP Shades,** in Nob Hill, for long, flowing dresses and skirts in batik and prints for that gracefully aging hippie look. Downtown, **Nordstrom, Saks Fifth Avenue,** and **Meier & Frank** all have plenty of fashions to rifle through on a rainy day, of course, and don't forget the **Nordstrom Rack**, a crowded—make that crammed—basement downtown with astonishing prices on the fashions that aren't quite making it in the big store. You can occasionally even find items that never appeared in the big store. Their loss is your gain, and when you add in the amount you're saving on the sales tax it can feel like you're shopping in Mexico.

Artful and interesting... The crafts scene in Portland is booming, beginning with the **Portland Saturday Market**, held on weekends under the Burnside Bridge downtown, where you can find all sorts of interesting things cooked up by artists and craftsmen in the country and brought to market in the city. The clothes run towards things you'd wear to a Grateful Dead concert, but if you're into beads and jewelry and batik, you'll find plenty of those. Odd housewares pop up, too, like forged-iron dinner triangles for calling Hoss and Little Joe to the supper table. Don't forget to peek at the shops inside the Skidmore Fountain Building, too. For serious crafts by craftspersons with national reputations, **The Real**

Mother Goose, downtown, has all kinds of handmade treasures, including rocking chairs made of polished woods, inlaid boxes, and a selection of handmade clothing. It's the jewelry case, though, that invariably makes people stop in their tracks for long, longing gazes. Designers are on hand to create custom pieces, too. Nob Hill's **Twist** is another spot (two, actually, counting a small store in Pioneer Place) that works with excellent craftspeople who design exquisite jewelry, glassware, and decorative items, again with the biggest emphasis being on the jewelry. In the heart of downtown, the **Quintana Gallery** has the best collection of Native American arts in town, including masks, pottery, and totem poles from coastal tribes.

Where shopping equals noshing... My late Uncle Paul, a butcher by trade, spent his lengthy dotage going into stores and browsing the selection of meats. I thought it was odd when I was a child, but I understand it completely now. To feel that electric thrill of discovering a new deli with its enticing foods and gourmet products, waltz into the family-owned **Martinotti's Cafe & Delicatessen** downtown, where you'll find an excellent selection of Italian cheeses and several varieties of Dolcetto wine. Waltz out with a thick salami sandwich as your reward. Across town on Hawthorne Boulevard, **Pastaworks** is a specialty grocery store and deli with the ambitious agenda of educating its customers about cheeses, wines, pastas, and sauces; the staff conduct cooking classes and publish a newsletter, in case the locals ever want to wean themselves away from the great takeout Pastaworks sells and try to cook the stuff themselves. In upscale Nob Hill, **City Market** announces its intention of being serious about food with 10 kinds of sausage, a whole roasted pig resting fatly on a platter at the meat counter, and a good selection of produce, wines, and prepared foods. For fresh food and produce, a small **Farmer's Market** takes place every Saturday morning on the South Park Blocks, near the Portland Art Museum and the campus of Portland State University. Look for anything from early-season asparagus and ripe cherries to goat cheeses and honeys made by local producers. It's a modest scene, especially in spring, but it grows lively when the big produce harvests hit in midsummer. Get there before 10am for the best pickings.

Zones of antiquities... It's awfully cool that Portland has its own street, SE 13th Avenue, that's devoted to antiques. It's even cooler that the strip of shops is in quiet residential Sellwood, and that the stores are practically all set in restored homes that are antiques in their own right. Driving into Sellwood is like finding a totally happening small town, rising like a mirage on the edge of the city. There are some 40 businesses on the strip and its side streets, and you can spend whole days and weekends browsing their wares. **Southern Accents**, for example, has cane and slat-backed rockers that would look just perfect on your antebellum porch. **Satin and Old Lace Shades** is there to meet, as the staff put it, "all your Victorian needs" (to which I mutter, Sherlock Holmes–like, "You don't know the half of my Victorian needs, Madam."). Any of the Sellwood shops can give you a walking map to all the antiques stores in the neighborhood. For more of a garage-sale antiques atmosphere, check out the two **Stars Antiques Mall** shops across the street from each other on SE Milwaukie in West Moreland. The enormous spaces (some 17,500 square feet in all) are crammed with knickknacks, old appliances, games, toys, clothes, and practically everything else that man has ever coveted, tossed away, and then coveted again. What you won't find, however, is the snappy little cowhide-and-leather purse that I snatched up for my wife. You'll have to find your own. The **Portland Antique Company,** in the Pearl District, goes after the goods from Asia and Europe, with a nice selection of furniture and cabinets from both places that can make a bold statement in your house (or just give you a place to hide the TV...you decide).

Home decor... For those times when you wished your home resembled a cozy bed-and-breakfast instead of, say, a penal institution, you need a makeover from **The Compleat Bed & Breakfast,** in Nob Hill. It sells all of those big, soft pillows, extra-thick comforters, and accessories that you find at great B&Bs. Now if they could just throw in some muffins and croissants and fresh-squeezed orange juice for the breakfast part. If your mind keeps returning to that restoration job you're planning when you get home, get yourself to **Rejuvenation House Parts** on the east side. It's an incredible source of info and fixtures, and a visit here will have you cheerfully ripping out whole walls and moldings the minute you get home. They can even match or restore antique fixtures.

The Index

Andy & Bax Sporting Goods. A sporting goods store focusing on camping gear and supplies for whitewater rafting.... *Tel 503/234-7538. 324 SE Grand Ave.* **(see p. 203)**

Aubergine. A clothes store for grown-up women, with casual and corporate looks.... *Tel 503/228-7313. 1100 NW Glisan St.* **(see p. 204)**

Caplan Sportsworld. Old-time sporting-goods store.... *Tel 503/226-6467. 625 SW 4th Ave., Morrison/SW 3rd Ave. MAX stop.* **(see p. 203)**

City Market. Gorgeous food store with excellent specialty products.... *Tel 503/221-3004. 735 NW 21st Ave.* **(see p. 205)**

Columbia Sportswear. Flagship store for the maker of outdoor activewear.... *Tel 503/226-6800. 911 SW Broadway Ave.* **(see p. 202)**

Columbia Sportswear Factory Outlet. Mostly the same gear as above, but at substantial savings.... *Tel 503/238-0118. 1323 SE Tacoma St.* **(see p. 203)**

The Compleat Bed & Breakfast. Home accessories for that B&B look.... *Tel 503/221-0193. 615 NW 23rd Ave.* **(see p. 206)**

CP Shades. Groovy styles in natural fibers.... *Tel 503/241-7838. 513 NW 23rd Ave.* **(see p. 204)**

Crossroads. A cooperative of record dealers that specialize in classic rock albums... *Tel 503/232-1767. 3130-B SE Hawthorne Blvd.* **(see p. 203)**

Dakota. Fashionable duds from international designers.... *Tel 503/243-4468. 2285 NW Johnson St.* **(see p. 204)**

Django's. Cool, atmospheric used-record and disc shop.... *Tel 503/227-4381. 1111 SW Stark St.* **(see p. 203)**

Farmer's Market. Produce and other farm-fresh foods from open-air stalls.... *No phone. South Park Blocks (SW Park Ave. between SW Jackson and SW Market sts.). Sat mornings.* **(see p. 205)**

Martinotti's Cafe & Delicatessen. Wonderful Italian deli downtown.... *Tel 503/224-9028. 404 SW 10th Ave.* **(see p. 205)**

Meier & Frank. Downtown department store and Portland institution. Four locations... *Downtown: Tel 503/223-0512. 621 SW 5th Ave. .* **(see pp. 200, 204)**

The Mountain Shop. Rugged outdoor gear for the mountain climber who lurks within.... *Tel 503/288-6768. 628 NE Broadway.* **(see p. 203)**

Music Millennium. A local music store with huge stock, emphasis on popular music of the last 40 years.... *Tel 503/231-8926. 3158 E. Burnside St.; also tel 503/248-0163. 801 NW 23rd Ave.* **(see p. 203)**

Nike Factory Store. Great deals on discontinued lines from the local shoemaker. So why were the originals so expensive in the first place?.... *Tel 503/281-5901. 3044 NE Martin Luther King Jr. Blvd.* **(see p. 203)**

NIKETOWN. The original shrine to Nike, advertising, Michael Jordan, and everything else that made Nike the huge success it is. Breathtaking shoe prices.... *Tel 503/221-6453.*

930 SW 6th Ave., Pioneer Square S. MAX stop. **(see p. 203)**

Nordstrom. Finally, something Seattle and Portland can agree on: Nordy's is a local treasure and the best department store in town.... *Tel 503/224-6666. 701 SW Broadway Ave.* **(see pp. 200, 204)**

Nordstrom Rack. The basement location isn't much for looks, but the prices are phenomenal.... *Tel 503/299-1815. 401 SW Morrison St.* **(see p. 204)**

Ozone. Music with an attitude, the attitude being young, aggressive, loud, and alternative.... *Tel 503/227-1975. 1036 W. Burnside St.* **(see p. 203)**

Pastaworks. Italian specialties in a big, open supermarket space.... *Tel 503/232-1010. 3731 SE Hawthorne Blvd.* **(see p. 205)**

Poker Face. Great vintage clothes and cool designs for night-clubbing.... *Tel 503/294-0445. 128 SW 3rd Ave.* **(see p. 204)**

Portland Antique Company. Huge collection of furniture and decorative items.... *Tel 503/223-0999. 1314 and 1211 NE Glisan St.* **(see pp. 201, 206)**

Portland Saturday Market. The biggest crafts fair in town, every weekend in the Skidmore district of downtown.... *Tel 503/222-6072. Bordered by SW Ankeny St., First Ave., Burnside St., and Front Ave. March–Christmas Eve.* **(see pp. 200, 201, 204)**

Powell's Books for Cooks and Gardeners. Specialty bookstore, which also has kitchen and garden items.... *Tel 503/235-3802. 3747 SE Hawthorne Blvd.* **(see p. 202)**

Powell's Books on Hawthorne. A Powell's general-bookstore outpost on Hawthorne.... *Tel 503/238-1668. 3723 SE Hawthorne Blvd.* **(see p. 202)**

Powell's City of Books. One of the greatest (and largest) bookstores in the country, a must-see for any book enthusiast.... *Tel 503/228-4651 or 800/878-7323. 1005 W Burnside St.* **(see p. 201)**

Powell's Technical Bookstore. Powell's clever way of shunting all of the engineers and computer geeks off to a separate location for their books.... *Tel 503/228-3906. NW Park & Couch Sts.* **(see p. 202)**

Powell's Travel Store. Below street level storefront in Pioneer Courthouse Square, a great repository for guidebooks, maps, and travel literature.... *Tel 503/228-1108. SW 6th & Yamhill sts., Pioneer Square S. MAX stop.* **(see p. 202)**

Quintana Gallery. Best place in town to see and purchase authentic Native American arts and crafts.... *Tel 503/223-1729. 501 SW Broadway Ave.* **(see p. 205)**

The Real Mother Goose. Top-notch crafts store gathers the work of artists from around the country (two more locations in Washington Sq. and the airport).... *Tel 503/223-9510. 901 SW Yamhill St., Library/SW 9th Ave. MAX stop.* **(see p. 204)**

Rejuvenation House Parts. Awesome selection of stuff and tips to fix up The Money Pit.... *Tel 503/238-1900. 1100 SE Grand Ave.* **(see p. 206)**

Saks Fifth Avenue. A little bit of the other Fifth Avenue in Portland, it anchors the ritzy Pioneer Place downtown shopping mall.... *Tel 503/226-3200. 850 SW 5th Ave., Mall/SW 4th Ave. MAX stop.* **(see pp. 200, 204)**

Satin and Old Lace Shades. Sellwood antiques store that specializes in lacy, hand-sewn shades.... *Tel 503/234-2650. 8079 SE 13th Ave.* **(see p. 206)**

Southern Accents. Classic rockers and handcrafted furniture on the Sellwood Antique Row.... *Tel 503/231-5508. 7718 SE 13th Ave.* **(see p. 206)**

Stars Antiques Mall. Billed as Portland's largest antiques malls, with two across-the-street locations.... *Tel 503/239-0346 and 235-5990. 7027 SE Milwaukie Ave.* **(see pp. 201, 206)**

Twist. Lovely pottery, jewelry, and crafts in an upscale store in posh Nob Hill.... *Tel 503/224-0334. 30 NW 23rd Place. Also in Pioneer Place, tel 222-3137.* **(see p. 205)**

night
enterta

6

life & inment

If life imitated *Cheers*, Portland would be Norm: It just wants to go out for a beer. Nearly everywhere you go in the city, there's a warm, inviting place where locals gather to share a pitcher, read the paper, munch on a pizza, or begin a night on the town. If it's not a bar or brewpub, then it's a cafe or wine bar with casual seating, friendly service, and an atmosphere that tempts you to linger. In the heart of **downtown** it's the elegant hotel bars and historic restaurants that provide the venue, with polished wood interiors and upholstered booths. The **Pearl District** is for scene-makers who crowd into a few hip bars or an elegant old brewpub in between gallery hopping and shopping. It becomes a kind of cafe society on **Nob Hill** and in **Westmoreland**, with bistros and restaurants that have lively bars or outdoor seating. **Hawthorne** and the **Belmont** district remain steadfastly funky and irreverent; here you'll find bars where people bring their dogs and meet their neighbors before heading off to a music club or a movie. The unifying element is the beer—damned good beer, I might add—that runs through the city's nightlife like the river that cuts through town.

Sources

The ***Willamette Weekly*** is the local arts and entertainment paper, distributed free all around town. Its club listings are the best, and it publishes fun inserts like the McKenzie Brothers–esque "Beervana and Vinotopia: A Guide to the Culture of Drinking." On Fridays, ***The Oregonian***, Portland's daily paper, publishes a big arts and entertainment guide that covers everything playing in town and offers reviews and feature stories. Online, go to **portland.citysearch.com.**

Liquor Laws and Drinking Hours

Oregon state law puts the drinking age at 21. With so many college students in town, this limit is closely watched, so you might as well have your ID out when you order a beer if you're anywhere close to that age. Bars can serve until 2am—depending on business, they'll stay open until then or shut down around 11pm Some of the dance clubs will go much later. Hard liquor is only sold in state stores around town, but beer and wine are available at nearly every supermarket and convenience store.

Getting Tickets

Ticket Central, a POVA kiosk located at Pioneer Courthouse Square, is a one-stop clearinghouse that consolidates **Ticketmaster** (tel 503/224-4400), **Fastixx** (tel

503/922-8499), and **Artistix** (tel 503/275-8352) services into one location. You can buy your way into virtually any show, sporting event, or concert in town. They offer half-price tickets on the day of a show, too (tel 503/275-8358).

The Lowdown

Where beer is king... In this supreme beer-drinking city, microbrews develop fierce loyalties and nobody would dream of drinking those lowest-common-denominator national brews. Brewpubs are still a vital part of the neighborhood and drinking scene here, thanks in large part to the efforts of the McMenamin brothers, who have made quite a successful business out of turning old buildings into friendly bar-restaurants. I love their **McMenamins Kennedy School** in Northeast Portland, a converted schoolhouse whose cafeteria has been transformed into a pleasant bar-restaurant, with an outdoor patio warmed by a tall wood-burning fireplace. You've gotta love the drinking areas known as the Honors Bar and the Detention Bar (they're nearly identical, but you can smoke in the Detention Bar). On Nob Hill, the McMenamin brothers' **Blue Moon Tavern & Grill** remains stubbornly resistant to the yuppiefication of the neighborhood, providing pool tables, wooden booths, and an old-time drinking atmosphere that's an antidote to the increasingly upscale restaurants on NW 21st and 23rd avenues. Whole generations of beer drinkers have now grown up on McMenamins Hammerhead Ale and Terminator Stout. An older, professional crowd still heads to the **Bridgeport Brew Pub** on the very edge of the Pearl District's warehouse row. The place is cavernous and atmospheric, with hop vines clinging to the outer brick walls and smooth ales and lagers being poured inside. In an industrial fringe before the retail shops start in Hawthorne, the **Lucky Labrador Brewing Co.** is a true neighborhood hangout, where pet dogs sprawl at their owners' feet at the outdoor picnic tables; the humans drink the house brew and argue the local political scene while the dogs bark at each other. It's decorated with paintings of dogs playing pool, and I wouldn't be surprised to see one of the canine customers follow suit someday. The **Tug Boat Brewing Co.** is certainly one of Portland's tiniest brewpubs—not shown on most tourist maps, it's on a narrow side street off of Broadway. The pub area is a living room–sized space decorated incongruously with muskets and old books on shelves, with a small stage in the corner for folky musicians. The house brew is Tugboat Bitter, one of the hoppiest, bitterest ales you'll ever taste. For a collegiate and jock scene, the **Rock Bottom Brew Pub** downtown is a perfectly preppy place offering just-passable house brews with silly names like Cryin' Coyote Western Ale or Falcon Red. On game nights the TV sets mounted on the walls garner all the attention.

Watering holes with style... Want to dress up and do some sophisticated bar-hopping? Start downtown in the walnut-trimmed lobby of the **Benson Hotel**, one of the ritziest and snootiest places in town, where the cocktail waitresses will practically throw you out on the marble entrance if you linger too long. Don't linger, therefore—down your cosmopolitans and then head across the street to **Pazzo**, the cheerful brick-walled bar at the Hotel Vintage Plaza, where you might spot an out-of-town slab (my term for a celebrity) while working your way through one of the huge drinks served. Then make your way to **¡Oba!**, the Pearl District's trendiest retreat, where a long bar is packed with the local art-going crowd and everyone acts like they're a slab. Scarf a couple of tapas snacks from ¡Oba!'s Latin menu, then peel off to the middle of Nob Hill for an atmospheric hour in the **Gypsy**, with its purple walls, sparkly gold and silver chairs, and pinball-table decor. Order a couple of Party Bowls (potent 60-ounce cocktails with names like Gypsy Juice) to make the night take on a whole new giggling aspect. Stagger out of there and head for Chinatown to enjoy the cocktail lounge at the sublimely named **Hung Far Low**, a dark, dingy place with some of the strongest (and cheapest) cocktails in town. Finish off with last call nearby at the long wooden antique bar of **Jake's Grill**, as the waitresses count their tip money and your barfly colleagues begin to nod off. What a night.

For vintage sipping... And then there are the times when we want to chill out, calm down, and discuss world affairs over a nice flight of French varietals in a hushed, atmospheric little wine bar. The **Blue Tango Bistro & Wine Bar** on Nob Hill is just the ticket. Inviting blue overstuffed chairs face a fireplace in the center of the small room, but you may prefer to head for the dark bar across the back wall, where you can sip 2-ounce samples or full glasses of dozens of different bottles. A good place to get acquainted with our Oregon Pinot Noirs, a local specialty. A little brighter and more upscale is the long, gleaming stainless-steel wine bar at **Southpark,** in the cultural district downtown. Ask for a sampler of Washington, French, and California varietals, or try the tasting menu—neat pairings like a plate of three Spanish cheeses with a glass of Spanish port. If it's Italian wine you're after, check out the **Enoteca at Assiggio** at Sellwood's Assaggio restaurant, a small, dark space with a staff that knows its way around Barolos, Barbarescos, and Dolcettos. Grab a space when you can, because they quickly get scarce.

Where to go to rock 'n' roll... I'd be the first to stand before a live microphone, thrust a fist into the air, and shout, "Portland rocks!" There are several big, well-supported clubs in town that bring in national touring acts, not to mention arenas that turn into huge festival facilities when the really big kids come to town. Both Portland and Seattle benefit from the tour-scheduling logic that figures: "If we're going to go all the way up there to perform, we might as well play both cities"—which means an act that you see one week in Seattle will probably be in Portland the next. First stop in Portland is at the magnificent **Crystal Ballroom**, a McMenamins project that rehabbed an about-to-be-demolished downtown dance hall. It's an eerie sensation to step onto its warehouse-sized dance floor and feel it move and bounce underfoot—the whole thing is supported on ball bearings, one of the few remaining "floating dance floors" in the country. The Ballroom brings in cover bands like Super Diamond, as well as second-tier touring acts like Link Wray or Merl Saunders, and Sunday nights feature bands for ballroom dancing or swing. For the kind of nostalgic acts that many baby boomers adore, check out the **Aladdin Theater**, a former porno house in Westmoreland that is now a smoke-free, comfortable nightclub where the likes of Echo & The Bunnymen and folky Chris Smither still bring out the locals. More cutting-edge—meaning younger and hipper—is the **Roseland Theater & Grill**, a former church downtown that now preaches the gospel of hip-hop and heavy metal with the likes of Coolio and the antisocial, apocalyptic Rammstein playing their version of a little light dinner music. Big-time acts fill plenty of different venues around town. On any given week during the summer, you might see Jewel downtown at the **Rose Garden Arena**, Dave Matthews or Lyle Lovett at the **Portland Meadows** horse track (it becomes an open-air concert hall all summer long), or Lilith Fair at the **PGE Stadium** on the west side of downtown. Check arts and entertainment listings well ahead of time in the local newspapers, and buy your tickets in advance.

Just for dancing... If enslaving yourself to the recorded sound is what you have in mind for the evening's entertainment, hustle on down to **The Embers** downtown, a mostly gay disco with flashing lights, a tiered dance floor, pounding disco music, and as much Spice Girls as you can handle in one night. The drag shows are fabulous, too. Also downtown, the **Lotus Card Room & Cafe** brings in a very dressy, very good-looking crowd who make their way into the farthest of three rooms to get very sweaty over New Wave, disco, and '80s covers (the club should post a sign that says, Caution: Slippery When Wet).

Cool and jazzy... Portland's best jazz club is **Jazz de Opus**, which looks a bit more like the downtown steak house that it is than a darkly atmospheric place for those syncopated rhythms. Touring acts play here, as well as some of the better local jazz musicians. The **Crystal Ballroom** occasionally hosts jazzy chestnuts like Chick Corea, as does the tony **Arlene Schnitzer Concert Hall** (aka The Schnitz), and **Jimmy Mak's** is an atmospheric little *boite* with a dozen tables that brings in local and national acts for cool sessions. Catch a set by local drumming legend Alan Jones for some jumping jazz. The classy **Heathman Hotel** and **Benson Hotel** downtown each bring combos and singers into their lobby lounges for a little cool entertainment over cocktails. None of it will make you want to quit your day job and take up the saxophone, but you can sure impress a date with your savoir faire if you start to sing along with "Lush Life."

Gay gatherings... The drag shows at **The Embers** downtown are a thing of local legend, and the dancing just may be the hottest in town, as a mostly gay crowd cuts loose under pulsing lights to throbbing disco music. You go, boy! The most notorious drag show, however, is conducted by the multitalented Darcelle at his club, **Darcelle XV**, in a slightly funky part of Old Town. On weekends, there's a late-night Chippendales-style show that drives the boys mad. Lady lesbians (as if there were any other kind) get down to DJ music at the **Egyptian Club** in the Hawthorne District, with pool tables, dancing, and the occasional wet T-shirt contest that gets out of hand.

The pro sports scene... Recent years have been good to the **Portland Trail Blazers**, the much-adored local NBA franchise that is Portland's only major-league sports team. The team came together in a way that hasn't been seen since the Bill Walton era of many decades past and makes annual runs at the Western Conference title. But hometown fans have high hopes that the team is about to shed its "Jail Blazers" (thanks to the occasional drug arrest or DWI charge) image and become a real force in the NBA. You can catch Blazers games at the **Rose Garden Arena** downtown, but it's a tough ticket, especially if they're playing one of the good Western Conference teams. For a Bull Durham moment, Portland brings you the **Portland Beavers**, a minor-league team that plays in PGE Stadium. The Beavers recently moved up from class A to AAA in the minor-league system, which puts their players one tantalizing step away from the big-league San Diego Padres and raises the competition and athleticism several notches, too. Ice hockey is also popular through the winter, when people come out to cheer the minor-league **Portland Winter Hawks**, also at the Rose Garden. Tickets are cheap, and it's a great way to learn the game and watch some monster hits (and fights) from the scrappy players.

The play's the thing... Oregon is known for its Shakespearean theater, especially the summer festival held down the road in the town of Ashland. A lot of that talent filters into Portland, making for quite a lively and competent theater scene. **Portland Center Stage** is a large, professional company with big productions at the Portland Center for the Performing Arts downtown. They grew out of the Shakespeare Festival in Ashland, know their way around the Bard's work quite well, and have taken over as the leading theater company after the closing of the Portland Repertory Theater. **Artists Repertory Theatre**, a wonderful small company that works out of the marvelous Reiersgaard Theatre downtown, stages mostly American plays with intriguing additions—witness one of its 1999 hits, a reworking of Molière's *The Misanthrope* in a modern grunge setting (the lead actor was a dead ringer for the late Kurt Cobain). Most of the Broadway-style musicals performed by touring companies take place downtown at the **Kelle Auditorium.**

Culture nights at the Civic and the Schnitz... The Schnitz is Arlene Schnitzer Concert Hall, a restored gem on Broadway that still has its Portland marquee outside from earlier days when it was a big concert hall. It's now the home of the **Oregon Symphony Orchestra**, which hosts a spirited season under conductor James DePreist. The musical bill of fare leans towards big orchestral works by the likes of Rachmaninoff and Tchaikovsky, but also throws in pops stuff like nights with Ray Charles or a salute to Glenn Miller and the big bands. The **Portland Opera**, another nationally known company, is not so wedded to the classics that it can't throw in an occasional musical, which yields surprising pleasures—when's the last time you heard *Show Boat* performed by the really big voices? The opera company mounts five productions a year downtown at the Kelle Auditorium, which also hosts the lively **Oregon Ballet Theatre**. Under the direction of James Canfield, this dance group stages a beloved *Nutcracker* every December as well as modern American works and even some world premieres.

Second-run movies, first-rate setting... The McMenamin brothers—they of the brewpubs all over town—hit upon a great idea when they began to restore classic old Portland movie houses in the '80s. Instead of competing with the multiplexes to turn a profit on first-run films, they took a different tack, screening second-run films and transforming the theaters into "theater pubs." They installed tables at each row of seats and sell pizza and pitchers of beer (some 20 brews on tap) alongside the popcorn in the snack bar. The result is an utterly delightful movie-going experience (great for those rainy winter evenings) at the **McMenamins Kennedy School** in northeast Portland, **Bagdad Theater** in Hawthorne, and **Mission Theater** in Nob Hill. And dig those ticket prices—only $2 (don't worry, they make it up on beer and pizza sales).

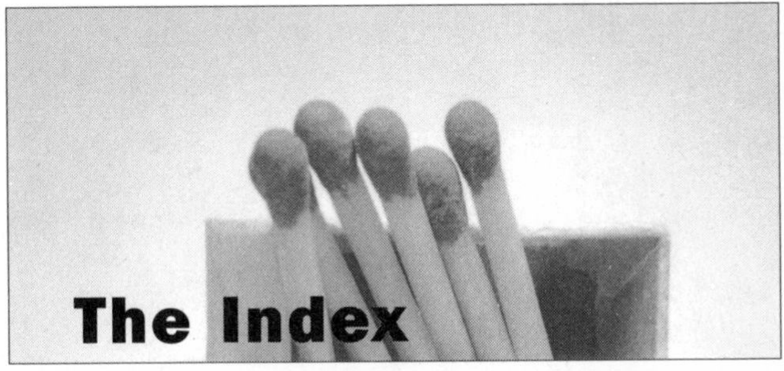

The Index

Aladdin Theater. A favorite folk and rock club.... *Tel 503/233-1994. 3017 SE Milwaukie Ave.* **(see p. 217)**

Arlene Schnitzer Concert Hall. Locally known as "The Schnitz," this classy joint showcases classy jazz.... *Tel 503/228-1353 or 800/228-7343. 1111 SW Broadway Ave., Pioneer Square MAX stop. Sept–June.* **(see p. 218)**

Artists Repertory Theatre. Great, small theater company with an excellent, versatile space for productions.... *Tel 503/241-1278. 1516 SW Alder St., Civic Stadium MAX stop. Shows held throughout the year.* **(see p. 220)**

Bagdad Theater. Arabian Nights in the McMenamins' restored movie house, with draft beers and pizza.... *Tel 503/669-8754. 3702 SE Hawthorne St.* **(see p. 221)**

Benson Hotel. Elegant lobby bar of the downtown hotel.... *Tel 503/228-2000. 309 SW Broadway Ave.* **(see pp. 216, 218)**

Blue Moon Tavern & Grill. Brings a neighborhood pub feel to trendy NW 21st.... *Tel 503/223-3184. 432 NW 21st Ave. Civic Stadium MAX stop.* **(see p. 215)**

Blue Tango Bistro & Wine Bar. Classy little wine bar and bistro; fabulous wine selection.... *Tel 503/221-1466. 930 NW 23rd Ave.* **(see p. 216)**

Bridgeport Brew Pub. One of the last remaining Pearl District brewpubs, in a corner of the warehouse district.... *Tel 503/241-7179. 1313 NW Marshall St. Also at tel 503/233-6540. 3632 SE Hawthorne Blvd.* **(see p. 215)**

Crystal Ballroom. Wonderfully restored ballroom still draws rock, swing, and ballroom dance crowds.... *Tel 503/778-5625. 1332 Burnside St. Cover varies.* **(see pp. 217, 218)**

Darcelle XV. Every drag queen should have her own club; this one is Darcelle's.... *Tel 503/222-5338. 208 NW 3rd Ave. Cover varies.* **(see p. 219)**

Egyptian Club. Much-beloved lesbian dance club and bar.... *Tel 503/236-8689. 3701 SE Division St. Cover varies.* **(see p. 219)**

The Embers. Hot, mostly gay disco.... *Tel 503/222-3082. 110 NW Broadway Ave. Cover varies.* **(see pp. 218)**

Enoteca at Assaggio. Snug wine bar attached to swell Italian restaurant.... *Tel 503/232-6151. 7742 SE 13th Ave.* **(see p. 217)**

Gypsy. Dark, fun cocktail lounge attached to a diner-style restaurant.... *Tel 503/796-1859. 625 NW 21st Ave.* **(see p. 216)**

Heathman Hotel Lounge. Coolly tasteful hotel bar.... *Tel 503/241-4100. 1001 SW Broadway Ave., Pioneer Sq. S. MAX stop.* **(see p. 218)**

Hung Far Low. Strong drinks, barking waitresses, funky lounge off a Chinese restaurant.... *Tel 503/223-8686. 112 NW 4th Ave., Skidmore Fountain MAX stop.* **(see p. 216)**

Jake's Grill. Atmospheric old saloon attached to the Governor Hotel.... *Tel 503/241-2100. 611 SW 10th Ave., Galleria/SW 10th Ave. MAX stop.* **(see p. 216)**

Jazz de Opus. Steak house restaurant also features some of the best touring jazz acts that come to town.... *Tel 503/222-6077. 33 NW 2nd Ave. Cover varies.* **(see p. 218)**

Jimmy Mak's. Cool, atmospheric little jazz club.... *Tel 503/295-6542. 300 NW 10th Ave. Cover varies.* **(see p. 218)**

Kelle Auditorium. Home of the Oregon Ballet Theatre, the Portland Opera, and numerous touring artists.... *Tel 503/796-9293 for recorded show info. SW 3rd Ave. at SW Clay St.* **(see p. 220)**

Lotus Card Room & Cafe. Three-room bar and dance club, a favorite of the young and fashionable.... *Tel 503/227-6185. 932 SW 3rd Ave. Cover varies.* **(see p. 218)**

Lucky Labrador Brewing Co. Friendly, down-home brewpub where you can bring your dog.... *Tel 503/236-3555. 915 SE Hawthorne Blvd.* **(see p. 215)**

McMenamins Kennedy School. Converted grade school, now a neighborhood hot spot: movie house, bar, restaurant, even a B&B.... *Tel 503/228-2192 (movie theater 503/288-2180). 5736 NE 33rd Ave.* **(see pp. 215, 220)**

Mission Theater. The first of the McMenamin brothers' restored movie houses.... *Tel 503/223-4031. 1624 NW Glisan St.* **(see p. 221)**

¡Oba!. Scene-maker bar in the hip Pearl District.... *Tel 503/228-6161. 555 NW 12th Ave.* **(see p. 216)**

Oregon Ballet Theatre. Top local classical dance troupe.... *Tel 503/222-5538. Performances at Kelle Auditorium, 1120 SW 10th Ave. Oct–June.* **(see p. 220)**

Oregon Symphony Orchestra. Treating Portlanders to classical music for over a century. The restored Arlene Schnitzer Concert Hall is a gem.... *Tel 503/228-1353 or 800/228-7343. 1111 SW Broadway Ave., Pioneer Square MAX stop. Sept–June.* **(see p. 220)**

Pazzo. Friendly bar/restaurant attached to the Hotel Vintage Plaza.... *Tel 503/228-1515. 627 SW Washington St., Mall/SW 5th Ave. MAX stop.* **(see p. 216)**

PGE Stadium. Home of the Portland Beavers baseball club and a venue for concerts and sports events.... *Tel 503/223-*

2837. SW 20th Ave. & SW Morrison St., Civic Stadium MAX stop. **(see p. 218)**

Portland Beavers. Class AAA minor-league baseball team.... *Tel 503/223-2837. SW 20th Ave. & SW Morrison St., Civic Stadium MAX stop.* **(see p. 219)**

Portland Center Stage. Polished professional theater company, an offshoot from the Oregon Shakespeare Festival.... *Tel 503/248-4496. 1111 SW Broadway Ave., Pioneer Sq. MAX stop. Oct–April.* **(see p. 219)**

Portland Meadows. Horse-racing track becomes a concert venue, festival-style, in summer.... *Tel 503/285-9144. 1001 N. Schmeer Rd.* **(see p. 218)**

Portland Opera. All of the divas and less of the attitude, they're not above crooning Broadway musicals along with the Mozart.... *Tel 503/241-1802. Performs at Kelle Auditorium, SW 3rd Ave. at SW Clay St. Sept–May.* **(see p. 220)**

Portland Trail Blazers. The biggest and best game in town, one of the NBA's small-market success stories.... *Tel 503/231-8000. Rose Garden Arena, One Center Court Sq., Rose Quarter TC MAX stop.* **(see p. 219)**

Portland Winter Hawks. Minor-league hockey team.... *Tel 503/238-6366. Games at the Rose Garden Arena, One Center Court Sq., Rose Quarter TC Max stop.* **(see p. 219)**

Rock Bottom Brew Pub. Chain brewpub that attracts a collegiate and fraternity crowd with homemade brew.... *Tel 503/796-2739. 206 SW Morrison St., Yamhill District MAX stop.* **(see p. 216)**

Rose Garden Arena. The centerpiece of the Rose Quarter complex, where the high-flying Trail Blazers and the hard-hitting Winter Hawks play. Also a venue for big rock concerts and big-name touring acts.... *Tel 503/235-8771. One Center Court Sq., Rose Quarter TC MAX stop.* **(see pp. 218, 219)**

Roseland Theater & Grill. Hip-hop, rap, and metal club for Portland's hungry young headbangers.... *Tel 503/219-9929. 8 NW 6th Ave.* **(see p. 217)**

Southpark. Upscale wine bar is great paired with food from the Mediterranean kitchen.... *Tel 503/326-1300. 901 SW Salmon St., Library/SW 9th Ave. MAX stop.* **(see p. 217)**

Tug Boat Brewing Co. Funky little hole-in-the-wall that makes distinctive brews in the back.... *Tel 503/226-2508. 711 SW Ankeny St.* **(see p. 215)**

25
10
5
1
ABC 2
DEF 3
GHI 4
JKL 5
MNO 6
PRS 7
TUV 8
WXY 9
*
0
#
COIN
PUSH
(401)555-1212
COIN RETURN PULL

hotlines & other basics

Airports... The **Portland International Airport (PDX)** (tel 503/335-1234 or 877/POX-INFO) is a scant 10 miles northeast of the city, located alongside the Columbia River. Connections are made in Los Angeles (for Mexico, South America, and the Far East), Dallas-Ft. Worth (for American Airlines cities and the Caribbean), St. Louis (TWA connections), Minneapolis (Northwest), or Chicago and New York (Europe and the east coast).

Airport transportation into the city... Cabs from the airport to downtown run about $25. **Gray Line Airport Shuttle** (tel 503/285-9845 or 800/422-7042) is a bus that stops at downtown hotels for about $15 per passenger. **Tri-Met's public Bus 12** (fare $1.15) runs continuously from the airport to the SW 6th Ave. transportation mall. If you're headed to a suburb like Beaverton or Tigard, look in the terminal for information on direct **Airporter** shuttles to those places.

Baby-sitters... Check with your hotel or call **Wee-Ba-Bee Child Care** (tel 503/786-3837).

Buses... Tri-Met (tel 503/238-RIDE) is the public transportation authority that runs buses throughout the metropolitan Portland area. Most buses use the transit mall on SW 5th and 6th avenues, and the 300-block downtown area is a ride-free zone. Other parts of the city are identified by symbols (a beaver, a fish, or a rose, for example) on the bus stops for quick reference. The fare is $1.15 for most bus trips, and the service goes until about 12:30am for most runs. The jewel of Portland's transportation system, especially for visitors, is the **Metropolitan Area Express,** known by all as **MAX**, a light-rail train that runs on the streets for 33 miles between the suburban towns of Gresham and Hillsboro, including several stops through the heart of downtown on SW Yamhill and SW Morrison streets, and then along SW 1st Avenue and across the river to the Oregon Convention Center. You should buy and validate tickets from the automated booths at each MAX stop; rides are on an honor basis, but if a conductor catches you without a ticket, the fine can be pretty steep.

Car rentals... The aforementioned public transportation is great if you're staying downtown, but considering the spotty nature of local cab service, for roaming out into the neighborhoods you'll need to get yourself a car. Arm yourself with a street map and stay alert: Portland has plenty of one-way streets and confusing freeway entrances and exits. The usual suspects for car rentals, all of which have rental counters at Portland International Airport, are **Avis** (tel 800/831-2847 or 503/227-0220, 330 SW Washington St.), **Budget** (tel 800/527-0700 or 503/249-6500, 2033 SW 4th Ave.), **Dollar** (tel 800/800-4000 or 503/228-3540, 132 NW Broadway), **Hertz** (tel 800/654-3131 or 503/249-5727, 1009 SW 6th Ave.), **National** (tel 800/227-7368; no downtown location), and **Thrifty** (800/367-2277 or 503/227-6587, 632 SW Pine St.).

Convention centers... The **Oregon Convention Center** (tel 503/235-7575; NE Martin Luther King Jr. Blvd. and Holladay St.) is the odd-looking thing on the east side of the Willamette River with the two green-paneled spires rising up for no apparent reason. There's a handy MAX light-rail stop right at its front door, and you can clear convention cobwebs with a walk over the nearby Steel Bridge.

Dentists, doctors, and emergencies... When the tooth starts aching, contact the **Multnomah Dental Society** (tel 503/223-4738) for a referral. Doctors can be found through the **Medical Society Doctor Referral Service** (tel 503/222-0156). For all emergencies, dial **911** and, as with Seattle, try to remember which quadrant of the city you're in if you need help.

Festivals and special events...

FEBRUARY: The **Portland International Film Festival** (tel 503/221-1156; Northwest Film Center, 1219 SW Park Ave.) imports three weeks' worth of artful films from around the world to Portland, shown in several different downtown venues.

APRIL: The **Trillium Festival** (tel 503/636-4398, Tryon Creek State Park) is a weekend celebration with guided walks to see beautiful bursts of wildflowers.

JUNE: The **Portland Rose Festival** [see Diversions] is the city's major blowout, with special events and celebrations throughout the entire month. If you're planning a visit at this time, try to book hotel reservations at least three months in advance.

JULY: The **Oregon Microbrewery Festival** (tel 503/778-5917, Tom McCall Waterfront Park) gives you an opportunity to get to know your local microbrews before you hit the bars, all for the price of a $2 mug. Food, games, and shopping, as well.

AUGUST: **The Bite: A Taste of Portland** (tel 503/248-0600, Tom McCall Waterfront Park) is an outdoor eating extravaganza, with dozens of booths selling some of the best dishes from local restaurants.

SEPTEMBER: **Art in the Pearl** (tel 503/690-7900, North Park Blocks) means booths of handmade art from painters, potters, sculptors, and craftspeople lining the grassy park blocks. There's good ethnic food, as well.

Gay & lesbian hotlines & info... ***Just Out*** (tel 503/236-1252) is a monthly newspaper for and about the gay community. You can usually find it at Powell's bookstores; call for other locations.

Newspapers... ***The Oregonian*** is the only daily game in town, and it does a pretty good job of covering the community. For arts listings and alternative features and news, pick up the ***Willamette Weekly*** at most coffee shops and bars.

Parking... Finding spaces to park on the street downtown can be tough going. If you're determined to keep your vehicle out of a parking garage, head past the busiest downtown streets like Broadway and SW 5th Avenue to fringe areas like Old Town or the Cultural District. Be sure to check the limits on your parking meter and feed it accordingly. Smart Park garages are the best deals in the city, with rates generally below $1/hour; look for them at 815 SW 4th Avenue at Yamhill, or 620 SW 3rd Avenue at Alder.

Restrooms... There are public facilities in **Tom McCall Waterfront Park**, but not particularly ones you'd care to use. Best bet: Avail yourself of the restrooms before leaving your hotel, restaurant, or museum.

Smoking... Portland is much stricter about smoking than Seattle. Many restaurants and bars are smoke-free, as are all public buildings and public transportation; some grudgingly provide a smoking area. Be sure to check first before you light up, or else incur the wrath of the clean-lunged locals.

Taxes... The good news is, the state of Oregon has no sales tax. The bad news is, hotel rooms in Portland get dinged for 9 percent.

Taxis & limos... While it's not a good city for curbside hailing, Portland does have taxi services that are a little more reliable than Seattle's. Try **Broadway Cab** (tel 503/227-1234) or **Radio Cab** (tel 503/227-1212) for pickups; you'll pay $2.50 for the first mile and $1.50 for each additional mile. Some hotels have deals worked out with cab companies where the fare can go straight to your hotel charges. Contact your hotel's front desk for more information.

Time... Portland is on **Pacific Standard Time,** which is three hours behind New York. Daylight Savings Time is observed in the summer, which can push the sunset as late as 9:45 at the height of summer.

Tipping... Portlanders are nice folks, but they expect a tip for services rendered, just like everyone else. Plan on tipping 15 percent of a restaurant or bar tab, more if warranted; cab rides, 15 percent; $1 per bag for a doorman or bellman; $1 for a valet parking attendant.

Travelers with disabilities... All **MAX trains** have wheelchair lifts and dedicated wheelchair spaces, as do many **Tri-Met buses**. Tri-Met may also be able to offer special door-to-door bus service to travelers with disabilities; contact 503/238-4952 to find out the qualification criteria.

Visitor information... The **Portland/Oregon Visitors Association** (tel 503/222-2223, 26 SW Salmon St.) has a central visitor's center on the ground floor of the World Trade Center (26 SW Salmon St.), where you can pick up basic maps of Portland's downtown area and all the brochure information you can carry away in two hands. If you'd like to have a copy of the visitor's guide sent to you before you come to Portland, call 800/962-3700.

Ace Hotel, 15, 20
A Contemporary Theater (ACT), 116, 118
Aladdin Theater, 217, 221
Alexis Hotel, 15, 18, 20
Alki Beach, 81
American Advertising Museum, 180, 183
American Backpackers Hostel, 19, 20-21
American Youth Hostel (AYH), 19, 21
Andaluca, 44, 45
Andy & Bax Sporting Goods, 195, 203, 207
Anthony's Pier 66 & Bell Street Diner, 37, 45-46
Ape Caves, 193
Archie McPhee, 95, 97, 98
Argosy Cruises, 68, 69, 70
Arlene Schnitzer Concert Hall, 218, 221
ARO.space, 114, 118
Artistix, 215
Artists Repertory Theatre, 220, 221
Assaggio, 44, 46
AT&T Summer Nights at the Pier, 117-118
Aubergine, 204, 207

B&O Espresso, 44, 46
Bagdad Theater, 182, 183-184, 221
Bainbridge Island Ferry, 60, 69, 74, 79
Ballard, 59, 67, 87, 108
Ballard Firehouse, 113, 118
Ballard Pool, 82
Baltic Room, 114, 118
Barnes and Noble, 92, 98
Belltown, 11, 59, 87, 108
Belmont, 214
Benson Hotel, 144, 147, 153, 216, 218, 221
Best of All Worlds, The, 97, 98
Betsey Johnson, 91, 98
Biringer Farms, 36, 46
Bite of Seattle, 59, 70
Blazing Saddles Bike Rentals, 78-79
Bluehour, 160, 161, 162, 166, 168
Blue Moon Tavern & Grill, 160, 161, 168, 215, 221
Blue Tango Bistro & Wine Bar, 216-217, 221
Bob's Hole Rodeo, 195
Boeing Tour, 62-63, 70
Bon Marché, The, 92, 98
Bop Street Records & Tapes, 96, 98
Borders, 92, 98
Brasa, 35, 39, 42, 46
Bridgeport Brew Pub, 160, 167, 168-169, 215, 222
Broadway Bridge, 139
Buckaroo, The, 113, 119
Bud's Jazz Records, 96, 98
Bumbershoot, 60, 70
Burke-Gilman Trail, 78
Burke Museum of Natural History and Culture, 63, 71
Burnside Bridge, 139
Burnside Street, 176

C.C. Filson Co., 93, 98
Café Bambino, 44, 46
Café Campagne, 36, 46
Café Juanita, 40-41, 43-44, 46
Caffe Ladro, 44, 46
Camlin Hotel, 16, 21
Campagne, 35, 36, 42, 46
Canlis, 34, 39, 46
Capitol Hill, 58, 67, 87, 108
Caplan Sportsworld, 203, 207
Caprial's Bistro, 160, 161-162, 167-168, 169
Carkeek Park, 61, 71
Cascadia, 33, 39-40, 42, 46-47
Cascadia Marine Trail, 79-80
Cassis, 40, 47
Castagna, 162, 166, 169
Center for Wooden Boats, 79
Century Ballroom, 114, 119
Chez Shea, 36, 47
Children's Museum, The, 63, 66, 71
Chinatown, 176
Chinook's at Salmon Bay, 38, 47
Church of Elvis, 181, 184
Cinerama Theater, 62, 71
City Market, 205, 207

Clackamas River, 195
Classical Chinese Garden, 180, 184
Cloud Room, 112, 119
College Inn, 17, 21
Colman Pool, 82
Columbia River, 195, 196
Columbia Sportswear, 202-203, 207
Columbia Sportswear Factory Outlet, 203, 207
Commodore Motor Hotel, 16, 21
Compleat Bed & Breakfast, The, 206, 207
Concordia, 143
Convention Center, 143
CP Shades, 204, 208
Crocodile Cafe, 113, 119
Crossroads, 203, 208
Crystal Ballroom, 217, 218, 222
Crystal Mountain Resort, 81
Cucina Fresca, 35, 47
Cultural District, 143

Dahlia Lounge, 34, 41, 47
Dakota, 204, 208
Darcelle XV, 219, 222
DeLaurenti Specialty Food Market, 90, 94, 99
Deluxe Junk, 90, 95, 99
Department of Fish & Wildlife, 80
Deschutes River, 195
Dick's Drive-In, 43, 47
Dimitriou's Jazz Alley, 114, 119
Discovery Park, 62, 71
Django's, 203, 208
Doc Maynard's Public House, 110, 119
Downtown (Portland), 200, 214
Downtown (Seattle), 10, 58
Dusty Strings, 96, 99

Eddie Bauer, 91, 93, 99
Egyptian Club, 219, 222
El Gaucho (Portland), 160, 163, 165, 166, 169
El Gaucho (Seattle), 33, 34, 41, 47
Elliott Bay Book Company, 92, 99
Embassy Suites Portland Downtown, 145-146, 147-148, 149, 151, 152, 153
Embers, The, 218-219, 222
Emerald Downs, 83
Empty Space Theatre, 116, 119
Enoteca at Assiggio, 217, 222
Esplanade, 166, 169
Etta's Seafood, 34, 38, 41, 47
Experience Music Project, 62, 63, 66, 71
Fandango, 35, 40, 48
Farmer's Market, 205, 208
Fast Forward, 91, 99
Fastixx, 214-215
Fat Tire Farm Mountain Bike Company, 194
Fenix/Fenix Underground, 110, 113-114, 119
ferries, 60, 69, 74, 79
Fifth Avenue Suites Hotel, 142, 144, 147, 149, 151, 153
5th Avenue Theatre, 117, 119
Five Spot, The, 43, 48
Flying Fish, 35, 38, 41, 48
Forest Park, 193, 194
Four Points Sheraton, 145, 146, 152, 153-154
Four Seasons Olympic, 12, 17, 19, 21
Fremont, 59, 67, 87, 108
Fremont Antique Mall, 91, 99
Fremont Bridge, 139
Fremont Sunday Market, 88
Fritzi Ritz, 90, 99
Frye Art Museum, 64, 71
Fullers, 39, 42, 48

GameWorks, 63, 66, 72
Garden Court, 111, 119
Georgian Room, The, 34, 35, 40, 42, 48
GlamOrama, 91, 95, 99
Golden Gardens, 62, 72, 81
Golf Club at Newcastle, 82
Gordon Biersch Brewery Restaurant, 111-112, 119
Government Camp, 193
Governor Hotel, 144-145, 148, 154
Great Jones Home, 97, 99
Great Wind-up, The, 90, 97, 99
Green Lake, 78, 79, 82

Green Lake Boat Rentals, 79
Green Lake Community Center, 83
Green Tortoise Backpackers Hostel, 19-20, 21
Gregg's Green Lake Cycle, 78
Gypsy, 216, 222

Hale's Brewery and Pub, 111, 120
Half-Price Books Records Magazines, 92, 99
Hampton Inn and Suites, 18-19, 21-22
Harborside, 161, 165, 166, 169
Hawthorne Bridge, 139
Hawthorne District, 177, 214
Heathman Hotel, 144, 148, 150, 151, 154, 168, 218, 222
Heathman Restaurant, 160, 161, 163, 168, 169
Heron Lakes Golf Course, 195
Higgins, 160, 161, 163, 169
Hiram M. Chittenden Locks, 64-65, 72
Hotel Edgewater, 10, 14, 22
Hotel Monaco, 10, 13, 18, 22
Hotel Vintage Park, 13, 18, 22
Hotel Vintage Plaza, 142, 144, 147, 148-149, 150, 151, 154
Hung Far Low, 216, 222
Hunt Club, The, 34, 42, 48

Ice Chalet Clackamas, 197
iCon Grill, 41, 43, 48
Inn at Harbor Steps, 15, 22
Inn at Queen Anne, 16, 19, 22-23
Inn at the Market, 14-15, 23
International Rose Test Garden, 177, 179, 184
Intiman Theatre, 66, 116, 120
Irvington, 143
Isadora's Antique Clothing, 91, 100
Ivar's Salmon House, 37-38, 43, 48

J&M Cafe and Cardroom, 110, 120
Jack's Fish Spot, 35, 48-49, 89, 90, 100
Jackson Park Golf Course, 82
Jake's Famous Crawfish, 162-164, 169
Jake's Grill, 165, 170, 216, 222
James Cook Cheese Co., 94-95, 100
Japanese Garden, 179-180, 184
Jazz de Opus, 218, 222
Jefferson Park Golf Course, 82
Jillian's Billiard Club, 112-113, 120
Jimmy Mak's, 218, 223
John Fluevog Shoes, 91, 100
John Hay elementary school, 83
Johnston Ridge Observatory, 193

Kelle Auditorium, 220, 223
Kells Irish Restaurant and Pub, 36, 49, 112, 120
Kennedy School theater, 182, 184, 220-221, 223
Kerry Park, 60, 72
Key Arena, 116, 118, 120

Lake Union, 59, 79
Lake Washington, 59, 68, 79, 80, 82
Leif Erickson Drive, 194
Le Pichet, 36, 40, 49
Lewis and Clark National Wildlife Refuge, 195
Lincoln Park, 80
Linda's Tavern, 115, 120
Lion and the Rose, The, 146, 149-150, 154
Lloyd Center, 143, 177, 197, 200
Lotus Card Room & Cafe, 218, 223
Lowell's Restaurant, 35, 36, 49
Lucky Labrador Brewing Co., 215, 223

Madison Park, 67
Magic Mouse, 97, 100
Magnolia, 59
Mallory Hotel, 145, 150, 152, 154
Mariners Clubhouse, 94, 100
Market Magic, 95, 100
Marquam Bridge, 139
MarQueen Hotel, 16, 19, 23
Martinotti's Cafe & Delicatessen, 205, 208

Matthews Beach, 82
Mayflower Park Hotel, 17, 23
McMenamins Kennedy School, 149, 150, 154, 161, 166, 170, 215, 223
McMenamins Kennedy School theater, 182, 184, 220-221, 223
McMenamins Pub & Brewery, 112, 120
Meier & Frank, 200, 204, 208
Merchants Cafe, 110, 120
Mill Ends Park, 181
Mint, 97, 100
Mission Theater, 182, 184-185, 221, 223
Moore Theatre, 117, 120
Morrison Bridge, 139
Morton's of Chicago, 165-166, 170
Mountain Shop, The, 203, 208
Mount Hood, 176, 192
Mount Hood Information Center, 192
Mount Rainier, 60
Mount Rainier National Park, 80
Mount St. Helens, 193
Mount Tabor Park, 194
Multnomah Greyhound Park, 183, 185
Museum of Flight, 62, 72
Music Millennium, 203, 208

NE Broadway, 200
Neighbours, 114, 120
New Orleans Restaurant, 110, 114, 121
Nice to Have Met You, 178
Nike Factory Store, 203, 208
NIKETOWN, 203, 208-209
Nob Hill, 176, 200, 214
Nordstrom (Portland), 200, 204, 209
Nordstrom Rack, 204, 209
Nordstrom (Seattle), 91-92, 100
North Cascades National Park, 80-81
Northeast Portland, 177
Northgate, 87
North Portland, 143, 177
Northwest Bed & Breakfast Travel Unlimited, 152, 155
Northwest Folklife Festival, 59, 72
Northwest Outdoor Center, 79
Northwest Portland, 176
NW 3rd Avenue, 176
NW 15th Avenue, 176
NW 16th Avenue, 176
NW 23rd Avenue, 176
NW Park Avenue, 176

Oaks Bottom, 176
Oaks Bottom Wildlife Refuge, 194
Oba!, 160, 161, 162, 166, 170, 216, 223
OK Hotel and Cafe, 110, 121
Old Navy, 91, 100
Oliver's, 110-111, 121
Olsen's Scandinavian Foods, 95, 100
Olsen Violins, 96, 100
Olympic National Park, 81
Oregon Ballet Theatre, 220, 223
Oregon Department of Fish and Wildlife, 196
Oregon History Center, 178, 181, 185
Oregonian, The, 214
Oregon Museum of Science and Industry (OMSI), 177, 181-182, 185
Oregon Symphony Orchestra, 220, 223
Oregon Zoo, 176, 185
Ozone, 203, 209

Pacific Northwest Ballet, 66, 117, 121
Pacific Place, 87
Pacific Science Center, 63, 66, 72-73
Page's Northwest Guide Services, 196
Painted Table, The, 35, 42, 49
Palace Kitchen, 34, 41, 49
Palisade, 37, 49
Palmer Snowfield, 193
Pampas Club, 112, 114, 121
Papa Haydn, 167, 170
Paradise Park, 193
Paramount Hotel (Portland), 148, 150, 155
Paramount Hotel (Seattle), 15-16, 17, 23

Paramount Theatre, 117, 121
Pastaworks, 205, 209
Patagonia, 93, 100
Pazzo, 162, 170, 216, 223
Pearl District, 143, 176, 200, 214
Personalized Tours & Travel, 179, 185
PGE Stadium, 218, 223-224
Philadelphia's Deli, 35, 49
Piece of Cake, 167, 170
Pike Place Fish, 89, 90, 101
Pike Place Market, 11, 32, 58, 86-87, 88, 89-90, 101
Pioneer Courthouse Square, 178, 185-186, 200
Pioneer Place, 200
Pioneer Square, 11, 58, 87, 108, 109-110
Pioneer Square Hotel, 16, 23
Piroshky, Piroshky, 36, 49
Play It Again, Sports, 93-94, 101
Poker Face, 204, 209
Portland Antique Company, 201, 206, 209
Portland Art Museum, 180-181, 186
Portland Beavers, 219, 224
Portland Building, 178, 179, 186
Portland Center Stage, 219-220, 224
portland.citysearch.com, 214
Portlandia, 178
Portland International Hotel, 152, 155
Portland International Raceway, 183, 186
Portland Meadows, 183, 186, 218, 224
Portland Opera, 220, 224
Portland Oregon Visitors Association (POVA), 142, 177, 179
Portland Parks & Recreation, 193-194
Portland River Company, 195
Portland Rose Festival, The, 176, 177, 186
Portland Saturday Market, 178-179, 186-187, 200, 201, 204, 209
Portland Spirit, 182, 187
Portland State University, 143
Portland Trail Blazers, 219, 224
Portland Winter Hawks, 219, 224
Port Ludlow Golf Course, 82
Powell's Books for Cooks and Gardeners, 202, 209
Powell's Books on Hawthorne, 202, 209
Powell's City of Books, 201-202, 210
Powell's Technical Bookstore, 202, 210
Powell's Travel Store, 194, 202, 210
Puget Sound, 81
Pumpkin Ridge Golf Club, 196
Pyramid Alehouse & Brewery, 111, 121

Queen Anne, 11, 59, 67-68
Queen Anne Pool, 82
Quintana Gallery, 205, 210

Rasa Malaysia, 35, 49-50
Ray's Boathouse, 37, 50
Real Mother Goose, The, 204-205, 210
Red Star Tavern & Roast House, 165, 170
REI, 93, 101
Rejuvenation House Parts, 206-207, 210
Residence Inn by Marriott (Portland), 146, 151, 155
Residence Inn by Marriott (Seattle), 19, 24
Ride the Ducks, 68-69, 73
River Drifters Whitewater Tours, 195
RiverPlace development, 143
RiverPlace Hotel, 146, 150-151, 155
rivers that drain into Puget Sound, 80
Rock Bottom Brew Pub, 216, 224
Rose Garden Arena, 143, 218, 219, 224
Roseland Theater & Grill, 217-218, 225
Ross Island, 195
Ross Island Bridge, 139

Rover's, 35, 38, 40, 50

Saks Fifth Avenue, 200, 204, 210
Salmon Day Tackle, Guides & Outfitters, 80
Salmon Street Springs, 178
Salty's on Alki Beach, 38, 50
Salty's on the Columbia, 161, 165, 166, 170
Satin and Old Lace Shades, 206, 210
Sazerac, 41-42, 42-43, 50
SE 13th Avenue, 177
SE Hawthorne Street, 177
SE Milwaukie Avenue, 177
Seattle Aquarium, 64, 73
Seattle Art Museum, 63-64, 73
Seattle Asian Art Museum, 64, 73
Seattle Center, 59, 66, 73
Seattle Centerhouse, 114, 121
Seattle Children's Theater, 66, 116, 121-122
seattle.citysearch.com, 108
Seattle Convention & Visitors Bureau, 10
Seattle Gay News, 108
Seattle Mariners, 115, 122
Seattle Opera, 66, 117, 122
Seattle Parks and Recreation, 83
Seattle Post-Intelligencer, 108
Seattle Repertory Theatre, 116, 122
Seattle's Best Coffee, 36, 50
Seattle Seahawks, 115, 122
Seattle Sheraton Hotel & Towers, 13, 18, 24
Seattle Sonics Team Shop, 94, 101
Seattle Super Saver, 10
Seattle SuperSonics, 115, 122
Seattle Symphony, 117, 122
Seattle Thunderbirds, 115-116, 122
Seattle Times, 108
Seattle Underground Tour, 65, 69, 73-74
Seattle Weekly, 108
Sellwood, 177, 200
Sellwood Bridge, 139
Sellwood Park, 194
Seward Park, 82
Shea's Lounge, 47
Shopping District, 10-11, 59, 87
Shorey's Bookstore, 92-93, 101
Showbox, 113, 122
Silver Cloud Inn - Lake Union, 14, 17, 19, 24
Silver Lake, 193
Skidmore Fountain, 178
Skidmore Fountain Building, 179
sledding hill, 81
Snoqualmie Pass, 81
SoDo, 58
Sorrento Hotel, 10, 13-14, 18, 24
Southcenter, 87
Southeast Portland, 177
Southern Accents, 206, 210
Southpark, 164-165, 171, 217, 225
Southwest 13th Avenue, 143
Southwest Market Street, 143
Southwest Portland, 176
Space Needle, 65-66, 75
Spirit of Washington Dinner Train, 69, 74
Sport Fishing of Seattle, 80
Sportworks, 194
Springwater Corridor, 194
Stars Antiques Mall, 201, 206, 211
Steel Bridge, 139
Sternwheeler Riverboat Tours, 182, 187
Stevens Pass, 81
Still Life in Fremont, 45, 50
Stranger, The, 108
Sur La Table, 90, 97, 101
SW 1st Avenue, 176
SW Broadway Avenue, 176, 200
SW Fifth Avenue, 200
SW Park Avenue, 176

Thumpers, 115, 123
Ticket Central, 214
Ticketmaster, 214
Ticketmaster Northwest, 109
Ticket/Ticket, 109
Timberline Lodge, 192-193
Timberline Trail, 193
Tini Bigs Lounge, 111, 112, 123
Tom McCall Waterfront Park, 194
Top Ten Toys, 97, 101
Tower Records, 96, 101